This Compulsion in Us

ALSO BY TINA MAKERETI

Once Upon a Time in Aotearoa
Where the Rēkohu Bone Sings
The Imaginary Lives of James Pōneke
The Mires

As editor
Black Marks on the White Page (with Witi Ihimaera)

This Compulsion in Us

Tina Makereti

TE HERENGA WAKA
UNIVERSITY PRESS

Te Herenga Waka University Press
Victoria University of Wellington
PO Box 600, Wellington
New Zealand
teherengawakapress.co.nz

ISBN 9781776562299

A catalogue record is available from the
National Library of New Zealand.

Published with the assistance of a grant from

Printed in Singapore by Markono Print Media Pte Ltd

Author's Note

As indicated, many of these essays have been published or presented elsewhere. For their publication in this collection, each piece has been edited afresh, and many have been revised. Interspersed with these are moments of memoir written between 2018 and 2024. These are dated according to the approximate time period they encompass.

Contents

He Whare Taonga ~ Make Way for Them

Postscript

He Whare Tūpuna

~

By Your Place in the World

Meeting the Ancestor on the Road

When I began to write, that was the place I had to go, that's where the information was, where the images were, that's where the language, the color came; in these tales, folk tales, attitudes, the normal, easy acceptance of signs. And then things began to happen that were really quite startling.

Toni Morrison, when asked about meeting her ancestors[1]

I have come away for the weekend to write to you from Taranaki. I didn't originally plan to come here, on this weekend, to write this piece—I had, in fact, planned to go to Waitangi with a group of other Indigenous writers from Aotearoa and the Pacific. Our hui was suppressed by a COVID-19 lockdown in the north, so in order not to waste the space in my schedule, I decided to go somewhere closer to where I live. And I'm sorry to labour the details here, which will all become relevant to the story I wish to tell, but I also received a sudden, unexpected gift of some money to use only for a writing retreat.

From the room in which I write and sleep, I can see Mount Taranaki, if he is showing himself, for he often wears a hat of clouds, and sometimes cloaks himself entirely so that you wouldn't know he was there if you didn't already know he's there. Taranaki's stunning volcanic form undeniably dominates the skyline when he allows it: cone-shaped, snowy at the peak, surrounded by fertile volcanic soils in a wide circle that extends to the ocean. Looking at a topographical map, you can imagine the eruption, just as we do as we climb over metres of large black boulders to get to the sea. Last night we ate in his company, taking our chairs outside since he was showing his face so clearly, and it was a friendly, peaceful time with him. It was the 5th of November, a date which is significant to Taranaki and his people, of whom I am one. Much of the time, I am a distant, estranged daughter of the mountain, but we have a saying: 'E kore au e ngaro, he kākano i ruia mai i Rangiātea', meaning 'I shall never be lost, for I am a seed sown from Rangiātea', Rangiātea being one of the names for the place of all Māori ancestral origins. The proverb has many metaphorical applications, but in this case, I hope it is a way of expressing to you, a stranger possibly from another country in another hemisphere, that to be Māori means never to lose one's connection to homeplaces, no matter how far away you are. Another saying, 'Ko au te mounga, ko te mounga ko au'—'I am the mountain and the mountain is me'—offers a different way of understanding this belonging. There is no separation between us and our lands, waters, and mountains, but this is not just a metaphor, not just an intellectual exercise. As Māori philosopher Carl Mika explains:

Landscapes have the capacity to shape how we think. Tau (2001) argues here, in line with Māori epistemology, that Māori knowledge reflected the self onto the landscape. In that act, place and self are inseparable, being immediately formed by each other. Calderon continues that 'truth' is contextual and concretely formed by our embeddedness within the landscape.[2]

In some real, visceral, embodied way, I am that mountain. The fact that I am not always *with* the mountain is a story about colonisation, loss of land, systemic violence and oppression, family fracture and whakamā, which is a word most commonly translated as shame or embarrassment, but which also denotes a deep, consuming anguish that in this context is associated with the loss of identity and culture resulting from the colonial process. But this is also a story about survival, migration, intermarriage, love, enormous strength and courage.

We have not the many hours, days, words and pages it would take to tell that tale, but perhaps I can give you a little piece of it. The 5th of November is known in this area as Te Rā o te Pāhua, or the Day of Plunder, in remembrance of the day in 1881 on which Parihaka was invaded. Parihaka is a peaceful village at the foot of the mounga, Taranaki, established in the 1860s and led by the prophets Tohu Kākahi and Te Whiti o Rongomai, who guided their people under a doctrine of peace. Violence was outlawed, and instead the community thrived under values of unity, faith, discipline and resistance to land alienation and cultural assimilation. But Parihaka was on valuable land, and within 15 years had become the largest Māori settlement in the country. This made the village a target despite its peaceful principles, and while the inhabitants of Parihaka chose non-violence, they weren't without strength of conviction and the will to fight in other ways. Their resistance to the imposition of colonial settlement on their land was met with fury by the government. On that spring day exactly 140 years ago, the Native Affairs Minister ordered the invasion of Parihaka by 1500 armed forces, who prepared themselves for violent battle. When the troops arrived, they did not encounter the bloody revolt they had expected. Instead, they were greeted by women and children singing and offering them loaves of bread. But this did not halt the attack, in which 1600 Māori were evicted from their homes, women and men were assaulted, men were arrested and imprisoned without trial, and buildings and crops were plundered and destroyed by troops. Tohu and Te Whiti, as well as many others, were exiled, though they returned many years later and preached pacifist resistance until the end.

Parihaka still stands on its original site, well-loved and cared for by its people, and reconciliation with the present-day government has begun, but the size and great economic and political independence of the original village is gone. Physically and emotionally, the damage of what happened on Te Rā o te Pāhua is still with us, as is the damage of successive assaults on our wellbeing.

My great-great-grandparents were followers of Te Whiti and Tohu and deeply involved with the pacifist community at Parihaka. That movement was so significant to our family that my great-grandfather (their son) and other family who migrated to Waikawa at the top of the South Island, over 443 kilometres away, took the teachings of Te Whiti and Tohu with them to their southern home, and when their descendants built a new marae in the 1980s, they adorned the meeting house with carvings of the Taranaki leaders, prominent among other ancestors.

I booked accommodation in Taranaki belatedly, looking only for somewhere nice to write where our dog could stay with us. Again, I thought I was going elsewhere: hoping to find a place in New Plymouth, half an hour away, rather than in the rural area where we are now, so I only noted how close we'd be to the mounga in a vague way, and to Parihaka not at all—the personal and professional stresses of the last few weeks having been too overwhelming for me to be more aware of exactly where we were going, or exactly when. So being in this place in this particular moment, with Taranaki actually in sight (or in implied sight) every time I look up, feels like a small miracle, like something that wasn't engineered by me, considering I had planned to be elsewhere entirely. Sometimes we sleepwalk through life, not out of laziness or ignorance, but out of the sheer fortitude needed to get through the next week of work, or the loved one's illness, or the bills or the shopping or the appointments, and I have been hanging on for a moment to write, and breathe, though I didn't know that this is where I needed to be to take that breath. But they knew. The tūpuna and the mounga.

Which brings me to Toni Morrison, and the 'normal, easy acceptance of signs'. We call these signs tohu (yes, the word is also the name of the Parihaka leader). A tohu can tell us when something is right, or wrong, whether to trust and move forward, or maybe to wait and listen for the next tohu. A mountain appearing on your horizon when you weren't intentionally moving towards it is a pretty big tohu. And without this tohu, I wouldn't have been able to tell you the story of Parihaka, or the story of my mounga. And I realise, as I write this, that without this guidance I wouldn't have known how to get to the next bit, which is harder, but these stories have offered me a way in.

Mika demonstrates in philosophical terms the world view which forms the basis of the experiences I'm relating here, but he does so while emphasising that, according to Indigenous thought, 'all things, including ourselves, are participants in a thoroughly fluid and unlimited event, in which the self is never quite definite'.[3] That is to say, Indigenous thought is based on a profound state of uncertainty, because all things in the world are interconnected and relational and therefore able to shift and be reshaped without end. This uncertainty can also be described as unknowability: at all times, for Māori, the unknown underlies all that is known. In Māori conceptualisations of the universe—most eloquently expressed in our creation whakapapa, a word that is usually translated as 'genealogies', but also demonstrates our fundamental underlying connection with each other and all other things, taking us back, quite literally, to the inception of the universe—'there [is] a real emphasis on the dual phenomenon of essence/nothingness. Thinking for indigenous peoples hence calls for a tentative approach to a topic or concern that takes into account the interconnectedness, obscurity and imprecision of the world.'[4] This might go some way towards explaining our openness to tohu, for if our personal experiences and thoughts are not the main things that form our understanding of the world and our relationship with it, if we are, as Mika describes, embedded within a whole and constantly shaped and influenced by all things that occur within this whole (world), would it not be wise to pay attention to the ways in which things, and our relationships with them, constantly shimmer in and out of focus (like a mountain on the horizon), or even shift with great physical force? When we don't pay attention, what is the cost?

As well as writing to you from a very specific time and place, I am also writing to you from an apocalypse. You are experiencing this apocalypse too, and we are hurting, but like the other apocalypses my people have suffered, like the apocalypse of colonisation, of influenza, of invasion and confiscation, one of the things that the apocalypse is forcing us to do is think and behave differently. The imposition of end times is painful and violent, and the innocent are not saved from it any more than the less innocent. We are all being forced to change, and most of us are resisting that change, but there is no doubt that many of us also hear a small voice telling us that *in this case*, change is necessary. We are on the precipice of a much greater apocalypse, and so it feels like this one has something to tell us, and if we can just be quiet and listen, we might avoid that steeper cliff ahead of us.

It's easy for me to sound philosophical about this. Our people, Māori people, Taranaki people, Moriori people, Indigenous peoples, Black peoples, migrant peoples, refugee peoples, we've seen the end of the world before. We may have seen it many times. The end times occur for me as a Māori person in slow motion—because it is happening in the past and in the present and in the future all at once, and much of that time it has been invisible, in a larger sense, because no one is paying attention, or specific people are wilfully diverting attention elsewhere so that our slow apocalypse can continue without interference. This is what happened with Parihaka: for the longest time it was a story that was ignored, or mistold.

But make no mistake, it was an ending. Sometimes I imagine what kinds of lives we might have had if Parihaka, or any of the other ancestral communities I descend from, had been left to continue flourishing. The quickest answer: my whānau, my family, would be landowners. In fact, we would hold vast tracts of land, and given the industry that marked the success of Māori communities prior to the colonial land wars and confiscations, we would likely be highly educated (though in a more culturally appropriate way), healthier, bilingual and wealthy. In a wider sense, fewer of us would be in prisons. There would be less whakamā and grief and depression. Less addiction. Fewer suicides. Less family dysfunction. And while capitalism is no answer to anything, and wealth has its own pitfalls, imagine what impact communities like Parihaka, with a bit more power, could have had on the world.

The truth is, even those of us who come from places like Parihaka have to spend lifetimes finding out about them, lifetimes getting back to them. The truth is—even a Māori child from an extremely fractured background can get quite far into the story that is her life without being touched by the apocalypse as directly and catastrophically as her ancestors were. She will experience the apocalypse only through history books that explain how it came to be, Indigenous scholars who explain things in gracious but unrelenting terms, and family stories of how bad things were for her grandparents and all the great-greats, or her cousins, and news stories of others who weren't quite so lucky as her. These will be painful things to face, and she will feel the indignities of prejudice and ignorance both in the society around her and within her family, but she won't touch death, she won't really feel like she is in the midst of an ending.

Not until later.

Every so often there is a quickening. This is one of those times. In the last few years, I have come to know intimately how our people are dying faster than other people, and I have seen how many of my people face untimely and avoidable mortality, or simply deep existential pain of the kind that can kill, and how we have walked through the darkness together, over and over.

And I have been forced to see, also, that while I have always counted myself fortunate, as far as these things go— that colonisation manifested itself in my life only as family dysfunction, abandonment, stolen children, poverty, casual racism and emotional abuse rather than more physically harmful acts—I have been forced to see how deeply embedded I was and always have been in a system that rests on the eradication of my people and our way of seeing the world, and how that system has harmed and continues to harm me and my children, in ways that clearly and horrifically create potentially mortal wounds.

And yet, again, mine is a slower, softer, gentler apocalypse than others are experiencing. The privilege of a backyard, a summer trip, all my children still living, and my parents. The privilege of a roof, and food, so much food. The sweet privilege of writing these words, even while other work calls me. None of this is lost on me. I am alive. You are here, reading these words. There are people who love us.

This is an essay about genre. I have taken a circuitous route because it is impossible to tell you anything about genre from a Māori perspective without giving some sense of what it is like to inhabit a Māori perspective. Note I have used the non-specific 'a', for there is no single monolithic Māori point of view, but perhaps there are identifiable themes. And perhaps I need to share with you one more mountain story before I can explain what any of this has to do with genre. From the mounga's own website:

It is said Taranaki Mounga was formerly known as Pukeonaki and stood near Tūrangi, with [other mountains] Ruapehu, Tongariro, and Pihanga. Pukeonaki and Tongariro both loved Pihanga and fought over her. But Tongariro was stronger and Pukeonaki (Taranaki), bearing the scars of battle, withdrew underground, carving out the bed of the Whanganui River on his journey to the sea. When he surfaced he saw the beautiful Pouākai range standing inland and he was drawn towards her.

Pouākai and Taranaki's offspring became the trees, plants, birds, rocks and rivers flowing from their slopes.[5]

I've known versions of this story all my adult life, and thought of it, with all due respect to the mounga, as just a story, since even though I find it easy to see mounga as living entities, mountains clearly cannot move, no matter how angry they are. But of course, even of this I can't be certain, and five minutes online researching this story reveals how it's best not to make assumptions about things that appear to be very solid and still. In 2017, New Zealand's main news site reported that, according to a geology professor, 'Māori legend surrounding Mt Taranaki might explain its placement in the North Island because, scientifically, it makes no sense.'[6] However, the article goes on to say, scientists have begun to find the reason why Taranaki stands out by itself on the West Coast, isolated from his Central Plateau family. Millions of years ago, there was 'a series of unusual earthquakes that occur in an East to West line from Ruapehu to Mt Taranaki'. Unusual, because they happened 52 kilometres beneath the surface when most quakes in the area don't happen below 15 kilometres. This all sounds suspiciously like the kind of seismic activity that could forge a river or move a mountain. We can wonder at the remarkable accuracy of the tribal story even if we read it only as metaphor: how did our ancestors know that Taranaki's presence in the west is directly related to subterranean rumblings and turmoil that began aeons ago near the mountains in the centre of the island?

It makes sense, then, that in our customary literatures, contemporary 'Western' divisions of genre didn't exist. Jane McRae, who documents and categorises the types of Māori oral literatures that existed prior to European contact, states that, while 'there was no exact parallel in Māori oral tradition for the classification of fiction or non-fiction', there were debates on the accuracy of certain accounts: 'The oral texts, however, may well combine fiction and non-fiction, as these are understood in literature, by bringing the imaginative and spiritual into the explanatory or documentary. This is a mark of the thinking and reasoning of Māori in the old world.'[7] Indeed, the spirit of speculation was fully alive in the literature, as was the fluidity, interconnection and imprecision that Mika champions.

How does this non-division between fiction and non-fiction and poetry work in practice? It means that at any one moment there are multiple worlds in our writing, multiple times, multiple versions of stories, that our ancestors are alive even at the same time that they are dead. As Mika points out: 'Indigenous holistic thought does indeed suggest that apparently different stages of time are, in fact, co-instantaneous. Events do occur separately, but they are contained within a certain potential, and that potentiality is of utmost consequence for indigenous philosophy.'[8]

While writing this essay, I looked up my great-great-grandfather and found a conversation he had had in his old age with a researcher, which was subsequently published in the *Journal of the Polynesian Society* in the 1920s. When asked about albinism (kōrakorako) among Māori, he said with a confidence questioned by the researcher that such children are the result of a union between human and patupaiarehe, fair-skinned supernatural beings with blond or red hair, who are described as 'fairy people' in various accounts, though this term is misleading. Suddenly, my ancestor is here with me as I write this essay, and I find I am very pleased to be in his company, and his confidence in ancestral patupaiarehe seems as right as any other way of seeing the world, and who is that researcher to question it? It is the truth of the world my koro inhabits (yes, in the present tense, for he is still there, and he is also here in some way), the reality of it. We can turn somersaults around the metaphysics of this world view, and Mika can help us in those contortions, but as he shows us, to stand apart from this and judge it as if it is separate from us is a deeply colonial perspective. Positivism itself is only one way of seeing the world, and not necessarily one that allows us to see all of it, dividing as it does those things we have decided are 'real' from those that we've decided are not. In the world I inhabit, as a writer and as a Māori at the foot of my mounga, the multiplicity of all things is present in everything I write, so that I cannot tell the story of writing this piece without telling the story of Parihaka, without showing you how I am that mountain, and how he is me, without also telling the story of the many apocalypses, particularly the one we face now, without telling an older story of the mounga from the time before he settled and we settled around him, without meeting my ancestor on the road and hearing his voice, without noticing the many tohu. All of these stories are true.

Who is to say that the only time that really exists is the present moment, particularly when one exists in a state of such openness to potential?

> Time is hence an untidy and non-constraining phenomenon in indigenous holistic thinking, and its nebulousness would mean that parallel dimensions existed alongside the one currently being experienced. As unconventional and undesirable as this might sound to stalwarts of academic orthodoxy, it is highly plausible for indigenous metaphysics but it loses potency when explained in specialised academic language—destined, perhaps, for science fiction or new age-speak.[9]

Or, indeed, creative nonfiction!

Me? I do divide my writing quite clearly between nonfiction and fiction, because the Western system raised me, and such things are deeply ingrained, but I also carry with me this other world, or in Mika's terms 'worlding'. And while I sound quite confident that there is a line between fiction and nonfiction, I could not define for you where that is—it is certainly a very fuzzy line, a constantly shifting line, a line that has its own way of shaping things.

I turned to creative writing due to the inadequacy of other academic fields to encapsulate, or even allow for, the state of speculation that Mika asserts is the basis of Māori thinking, and is certainly my experience of the world. Obviously, fiction, and also not-so-obviously creative nonfiction, allow space for a speculative approach. The great pleasure in creative nonfiction, for me, is the paradox that confronts me every time I write; as I attempt to find more precision and more elegance, more accuracy, as I try to pinpoint any one true thing, I am often frustrated. To solidify something in words is only to omit that aspect of it which defies definition, the 'nothingness' which underlies the thingness. It is in meeting my failure on the page that I come into contact with that which underlies all creativity and creation: Te Kore, the first state in our creation whakapapa, which I think of as the nothing and the not-nothing, the field of pure potentiality. The nonfiction page therefore becomes a place where I encounter the greater mystery of creation itself.

First published in *Bending Genre:*
Essays on Creative Nonfiction (2023)

An Englishman, an Irishman and a Welshman Walk into a Pā

Origins

This is the way of it. Before I have memorised her in a way that will last forever, my mother is gone. If someone asks me to recite my first memory, which consists of chickens in a yard and an old farmhouse and an outside toilet, it will contain this absence. For the rest of my childhood, I don't think it matters.

When I was small I was provided for, though most of the time I found it necessary to keep my head down. I didn't walk out of my childhood bruised or broken in body, but there are other ways a child can be wounded. Films featuring children always worry me. I want to believe a protected childhood is a thing that can be taken for granted, but there's a delicate balance—it could go either way. In the next scene, the mother might look away or the father might lose control and the childhood could be ruined. There are no guarantees.

There were some things bestowed on me by my upbringing that don't make sense. From the earliest I learnt that people come in categories, separated by skin colour and gender, and norms of culture and behaviour defined by what we called Europeans. We were Europeans, mostly, I was told. But there was nothing European about us. We were the straggly descendants of white people who came here generations ago looking to lose themselves, and promptly did. They were running from whatever it was their own cultures were doing to them at the time, running towards some beautiful possibility in another land. That new land was lush, fresh, empty for the taking. When they discovered it was not quite so empty, it was better to put their heads down and keep working. Like most of us, they couldn't let their mythologies go. The cost would have been too much. Great white man at the pinnacle of civilisation. Everything made to bow to that narrative, even if force was needed to keep the narrative in place. They worked hard, my white ancestors, but didn't rise much higher, and it was better not to question the whys and wherefores of that. Better to be a working-class man in New Zealand than elsewhere. Meat and cheese and milk flowing through the streets. Besides, poor people are inherently better than rich.

There were other mythologies we stuck to: Europeans brought order and civilisation with them; good Maoris are happy-go-lucky, bad ones ungrateful; men have no restraint; women are slippery untrustworthy witches. I rather liked the idea of that, but could never quite get over the man thing, even when experience suggested otherwise.

I find I disagree with most of this inheritance, but it is inherited just the same.

Grandmothers

I became one of those girls who take great inspiration and comfort from the stories of grandmothers and great-grandmothers. These stories were missing when I was very young so, while I did not think I was much in need of a mother, I thought the world a bland and frustrated sort of a place. Something was missing, I knew. It was as if I had access to only a watered-down version of things—washed-out pastels and black-and-white surfaces.

As a teenager I became reacquainted with the mother I had never known and a heritage that was richer than I had imagined. Mothers brought with them whole tribes, I discovered. Aunts and uncles! A grandmother! And stories about the people who had gone before. There was the one about the great-grandmother who taught her son to pig hunt in the bush because her husband was too busy with the drink; the one about the great-great-grandmother who bestowed her land to the hapū and took my own grandmother to look after when her mother died. We have a sepia photo of this kuia from a film she was in—fierce brow, sharp-looking but nearly blind eyes, strong chin jutting forth a challenge. I named my first daughter after her simply for the staunchness that emanated from her image. You needed that kind of kaha, I thought, to get by in this world. My grandmother, of course, followed in her footsteps. Having been whāngaied by others, she looked after everyone, her own and not her own, spending lifetimes between marae and courts and social workers, until her heart gave way.

There were countless ancestors like them, these immediate grandmothers: providers all, warriors some, women who spent their days in service and survival, leadership and sacrifice. They were extraordinary women to look up to. My life has always been too soft and comfortable to make me their equal. These grandmothers brought me a world shot through with bold colour—the world that my white ancestors couldn't acknowledge for fear of losing some part of their own mythology. My grandmothers showed me origins that ranged from earth, sea and mountain, to the vastness of space: Te Pō, they whispered, Te Korekore. Sometimes they gave me access to Te Ao Mārama—the world of light, where one can see clearly.

Still, nature and nurture continue to tug at each other and negotiate some sort of uneasy truce. I'm learning to live with the discord between one inheritance and the other. 'The universe is a contradiction,' says filmmaker Shekhar Kapur. And, even though 'all of us are constantly looking for harmony [. . .] the acceptance of contradiction is the telling of the story, not the resolution.'[1]

What Will Be Remembered

Every day and night I'm in Auckland, I walk past a woman who lies and sometimes sits on a Hello Kitty™ duvet on the street. She is usually in the same doorway, quiet, innocuous, staring. Occasionally she asks for change. I walk past without looking too hard and offer her nothing. There are assumptions about homelessness I measure each time I pass. She looks reasonably healthy and sane from the corner of my vision. I think she must be incredibly tough. I think she must have other options. I wonder where she pees and what she eats. I wonder where the rest of her stuff is. I'm aware then and forever afterwards that everything I think and do in response to her presence says more about me, my sanity and my health, than her.

We stay at a very fancy hotel. I am surprised that while it's a novelty, the opulence of the place does not disturb me as much as I might have predicted. Perhaps poor people aren't inherently better than rich. Perhaps it's okay to play at richness, since this is not our real life. I make jokes about the sumptuous furniture in the lobbies—ornate couches that are rarely touched and finely crafted sets of drawers that will never hold anything. We could set up our living room there, I suggest, no one's using it. But I can't sleep at the hotel. There's no rest to be had in such a place.

My partner and I both enjoy the storied space of graveyards—how a city tells its history through its dead. One of the things we do before we leave the hotel is cross the street to walk through the cemetery. A man overhears us discussing where to go and launches into a strangely friendly rant about how the gravestones have been vandalised by druggies and taggers. We realise the extent of this when we see empty bottles and cans littering a grave. This graveyard has been sliced through to make room for a motorway, like Bolton Street Cemetery in Wellington. We walk down and read of the bodies disinterred and placed in a mass grave. Back up by the street, we're both curious about some very old brick buildings, but curtail any investigation when we see that some people have left their belongings there, where they sleep. As we leave the graveyard and wash our hands in a public drinking fountain, I wonder what kind of story this tells: the way a city treats its living and its dead.

Ornate and empty hotel furniture can't compare to the riches of well-worn family drawers and cabinets, and cemeteries. Sometimes people still espouse that old prejudice: the history of New Zealand is so recent, so limited. So poor, is the implication. Have they looked, I always wonder, really looked? Whenever I peek over the brim of the last century to the one before, I am staggered by the stories there, the cluster of voices clamouring for attention. Most of them have never been heard, and they seem much more quirky and lively and bawdy than the accepted histories suggest.

On our last day in Auckland my partner offers the woman on the Hello Kitty duvet a couple of apples. She'll take just one, she replies, reluctantly. Later, when I write about her, I wonder how to convey the strength and dignity in her voice, my own inability to comprehend her place in the world. I wonder what her story is, and I wonder why I didn't ask.

Grandfathers

When my first daughter was a baby my mother made a composite photo for her, comprising photos of six generations of women in her maternal line, uninterrupted since her namesake kuia in the early 1900s, with our marae in the background. A powerful legacy in the face of which the story of male ancestors held much less fascination. Until last year. I was on the trail of another great-great-grandmother, on the other side of the family. I soon discovered it was not her but her father who held the mystery, for we could discover nothing of him but the name: Haimona, a fairly common transliteration of Simon. Every other line in the whakapapa travels back much further, origins and migrations recorded in detail. We wondered if Haimona was the Moriori link. The obliteration of his history seemed to support this theory.

Looking for Haimona meant exploring the whakapapa around him. I discovered more ancestors, more family stories now reaching back seven generations or more. It meant just as much to learn the women's names as the men's, but this time it was the stories of the male ancestors that claimed my attention. By now I had come to understand the kinds of lives my grandmothers had had. Their stories had dominated my imagination for a long time. But I knew little about the men. What kinds of lives did they have? Why were more of them Pākehā than I'd realised, and how did they come to earn chiefly wives? And why did it matter to me?

A loss early in life can be a defining thing. If we want to go to the source of a person's obsessions, perhaps it is best to take a journey through their early years. After all, some things, once taken out of a childhood, cannot be put back. For me, the picture of what a family or culture consists of was never complete. I hungered for stories of origins, and stories of how people make families. 'Stories matter,' says the novelist Chimamanda Ngozi Adichie, 'lots of stories matter':

> It is impossible to engage properly with a place or person without engaging with all of the stories of that place or that person. The consequence of the single story is this: it robs people of dignity. It makes our recognition of an equal humanity difficult. It emphasizes how we are different, rather than how we are similar.[2]

And what if you don't know all your own stories?

I took what I had learned about Haimona and his in-laws, and I charted the whakapapa. I made copies of this chart and gave one to my mother for Christmas.

The Englishman

The first time I encounter James Worser Heberley is in a picture in Trevor Bentley's 1999 book *Pakeha Maori*. He frowns at the camera, his hand clasped protectively over that of his wife, Te Wai, who sits on a chair beside him. Her face is blurred, though her body is not, as if she were shaking her head slightly when the photo was taken. Heberley sports impressive sideburns that grow down like a beard, in the style of the time, but the front of his face is clean-shaven. His nose is broad and his lips as wide and full as his wife's. Bentley says that Heberley was one of Te Rauparaha's 'original Pakeha toa' and that as a young man he 'joined Ngati Toa in their intertribal musket battles'.[3] The Heberley name stays with me for a while before I realise where I have heard it. I pull out the whakapapa chart I created only weeks before and find the Heberley name immediately, just above my great-great-great-grandparents—Sarah Heberley and William (Pire) Henry Keenan. James 'Worser' Heberley and Maata Te Naehi e Wai (Te Wai) were Sarah's parents. With ancestry that was Māori, English and German, Sarah, born in 1840, married a man who also had mixed blood, an Irish-Māori.

Heberley's eyes are penetrating and troubled. They seem marked by sorrow rather than anger, but I am not sure I want this man to be my ancestor. Bentley's book is full of bloodshed and cannibalism, thieves and mercenaries. His Māori are bloodthirsty opportunists, his Pākehā variations of disreputable anarchists. To be fair, he doesn't demonise either group. They both, it seems, brought with them unsavoury as well as honourable practices. But the Aotearoa he describes is not one I recognise. Bentley seems to highlight every cannibal feast, every juicy narrative. According to *Pakeha Maori*, Heberley would have taken part in some of Te Rauparaha's most vicious raids on South Island tribes.

I have not read every historical account Bentley references, but of the other sources I've found, none asserts Heberley's allegiance to Te Rauparaha. They tend to emphasise Heberley's more famous pursuits: he helped the German naturalist Ernst Dieffenbach climb Mt Taranaki, thereby becoming the first man known to gain the summit;[4] he was the Wakefield family's pilot on the *Tory* and later the first pilot of Wellington, bestowing his nickname on the bay where he lived and worked: 'Worser'. The name is usually attributed to 'his habit of warning that the weather would get "worser and worser"'.[5] This story may be only legend, however, since Worser's own journal states that he was teased about living in a Māori raised storehouse, or 'whata', before he had built his own house. 'Tangata Whata' soon became Europeanised to 'Worser'.[6]

Heberley's own account is also unclear on his loyalty to the warrior chief. For the most part, his early stories of life in Queen Charlotte Sound consist of making do as best he can. He describes several skirmishes, and the necessity to flee from his home at Te Awaiti. He uses the term 'we' often, though it is unclear whether he is referring to himself and his family, his Pākehā cohort, which includes fellow whaler and employer Jacky Guard, or the Māori tribes they are living with. Perhaps at different times he means all, or different combinations of these groups. When they flee attacks, they often return months or weeks later to find all their homes destroyed.

There are two revealing references to Heberley's relationship with Te Rauparaha, aside from his matter-of-fact observations of ritual feasts. His obituary states:

[Heberley] well remembered his return with 500 prisoners from the famous raid to Kaiapoi 67 years ago; witnessed the murder of the prisoners, and the cannibal orgie that ensued. He afterwards owed his life to that same Rauparaha, who threw his cloak over him just in the nick of time to save him from a Waikato tomahawk upraised to brain him.[7]

34

This latter event occurred soon after they had fled the Sounds for Te Rauparaha's northern stronghold:

> We took our Boats and the Natives their Canoes, the Southern Natives followed us but they could not catch us, for we could outpull them, we went across to the other island and stayed at Kapiti, the Natives were at war again [. . .] so I took my boat and two natives to pull with me to a place called [Waikanae] to land my wife and child among her own tribe, I came back to Kapiti [. . .][8]

Heberley also records that he paid Te Rauparaha with tobacco for the protection of his cloak. He seemed to have a distant allegiance to the chief, owing more to the necessity of survival than a taste for warrior life. Later, he is bolder in his descriptions: 'he was very troublesome [. . .] we were not sorry when he took his departure.'[9]

Bentley's narrative, often derived from Pākehā-Māori returning to 'civilisation' who could make a good bob or two from stories of savages and feasts of human flesh, makes early New Zealand seem a relentless, nightmarish world. While there is plenty of evidence of this in journals like Heberley's, it doesn't always reflect the reality of ordinary people trying to survive troubled, rapidly changing times. So many must've been trying to get by in their own peaceful way—engage in commerce, stay out of the way of that uncle or cousin who was on a rampage, make a deal. Clearly, Te Rauparaha's reality and his legend must have been similarly disparate. The more mundane details of history are not the parts that are remembered. Things didn't always work out—history tells us that. But quiet friendships also don't make as exciting a story.

On balance, Heberley's narrative is for the most part about

trying to find a way to live in an unforgiving world. Back in Britain, he was sent to work at the age of 11 and served for years at a time on ships sometimes captained by 'tyrants', sometimes by men who found him destitute and offered him food and shelter. He doesn't expand on the hardships in great detail, apart from the beatings with frozen rope or dogfish tail that sent him from one ship to another. It must have been a grimy, frightening business for a boy to grow up in. There was some light relief when he began whaling as a young man, the rituals of cutting in being quite festive: '[T]he Steward sang out Grog O—and we began to cut in the first whale [. . .] we began to get pretty merry [. . .] they danced away, although the Decks were greasy with the Blubber, every one got drunk but not so far, as to neglect their work.'[10]

When at last he came to Queen Charlotte Sound in 1830, he was told 'there were plenty of Houses in Te Awaite and Native Women, and that we had nothing to do but to go in our Boats and catch Fish'.[11] It was not that simple, for there were no houses, and the next ten years were filled with conflicts between warring tribes that Heberley found difficult to avoid. He must have liked the place and the people, though, since he stayed among the tribes. In Port Underwood he soon found himself a wife, Te Wai of Te Āti Awa, who 'clearly had important chiefly connections'[12] and 'reared a large family'.[13] Says Bentley: 'There is an important Maori woman in the story of every known Pakeha Maori.'[14] On that detail, we agree. He also quotes Edward Markham, an English visitor, from the time: 'In fact it is not safe to live in the country without a chief's daughter as a protection as they are always backed by their tribe.'[15] Multiple wives were not uncommon, though Heberley seemed protective of and content with one, and of course 'Māori wives were rarely compliant or servile partners'.[16] Like the other ancestors in this story, Worser and Te Wai have hundreds, if not thousands, of descendants.

The Irishman

When my mother tells me about our European ancestors, it is with the same pride that she describes our tūpuna Māori. Her pride in being Welsh and Irish is at least equal to that of being Ngāti Tūwharetoa and Te Āti Awa. Henry Eagar and Jackson Keenan were among the first ancestors she introduced me to. Eagar is from her mother's whakapapa, Keenan from her father's. She has photos of each, and speaks of them with a fondness I suspect most Pākehā families would retain only for family members they had known in their lifetimes.

It should be said that in the robust Keenan line there are many family historians more knowledgeable than me.[17] I can only touch on those elements of our original Irish ancestor's story that correspond with the experiences of my other ancestral Pākehā-Māori. Jackson's grandfather, William Henry Keenan (Te Puponga), was said to have been from County Cork, Ireland, but in fact was born in Sydney, in 1806. He first landed in Taranaki in the 1820s, and was among the group of Pākehā, including Dicky Barrett and John Love, who assisted the local Ngāmotu people when Ōtaka Pā was attacked by Waikato tribes:

The siege was pressed with great vigour, and the pa would have fallen before the overwhelming number of the invaders, had it not been for the heroic stand made by the whalers. Time after time the enemy succeeded in gaining an entrance, but they were in every case driven out with loss.[18]

The whalers had taken their chances inside the palisaded pā, and emerged, with their hosts, victorious. Their fates were now linked. Although they won the battle at Ōtaka, Taranaki tribes still faced immense pressure from others, and in 1832 they began to migrate south. 'Also in the migration were the people of Ngāti Mutunga [. . .] and Te Puponga (William Keenan) from New Plymouth.'[19] During their journey, fighting broke out at Whanganui, 'and in the feast that followed, Keenan inadvertently partook of some human flesh, greatly to his disgust. The natives were highly diverted at this mistake and Keenan came in for a great deal of "chaff" over it.'[20]

Māori names and wives were bestowed on most of the original group of Pākehā at Ngāmotu. Tribal protection was returned to them for the efforts they had expended to protect the tribe. Keenan had the good fortune to earn the hand of Katarina Hikimapu Takuna (Catherine). Both the Keenans and the Heberleys married the Māori way, had several children, then obtained Christian marriages and christenings for their children when a minister passed through the area. Both settled in Queen Charlotte Sound and, in the late 1850s, saw their families linked through marriage.

The families were, of course, also linked by whaling, and by their presence in the area prior to active colonisation. Keenan's 1880 obituary is effusive and revealing of the time:

Another of the links has been destroyed, and the chain that binds the present with the past is becoming gradually weaker [. . .] With the gift of a fluent tongue and retentive memory what tales he could have told about the manners and customs of olden times, before the advent of any but European adventurers in the colony; when the early comers were more Maorised than

the Natives themselves, and might, not right, ruled this fair
land [. . .]

Few residents in this part but can call to mind the tall upright
figure that was conspicuous, especially on regatta days, his curt
sentences, as if he was afraid to use two words when one would
answer the purpose, and his curiosity in inquiring into the use
and meaning of anything new or strange [. . .][21]

It must have been this combination of curiosity and
reserve that allowed Keenan to succeed in his new home. I
can imagine his horror at the scene in Whanganui, his desire
to fit in with his hosts almost undermining his European
sensibilities. But there must have been immense, sinewy
toughness too. Keenan and Heberley both lived long lives,
despite, or perhaps because of, the challenges they faced.
Although I don't know about the first Keenan's appearance,
his son, William Henry (Pire), was said to have had red hair,
fathered 20 children, and been 'dogged by misfortune'.[22]
These were men who lived by the fortunes the sea bestowed
on them, and the fortunes bestowed on them by the tribes
they married into. It is difficult to tell whether the red hair or
the many children contributed to William Jnr's misfortune,
though it is known that his second wife, Piki Love, saved him
from drowning when all others had failed. Perhaps he was
lucky after all, in marriage.

The Welshman

The photo my mother has of Henry Francis Eagar shows a
thin and well-dressed man with a long straight beard that
reaches to his chest. His pocket watch is prominent, his back
straight. He stares into the distance with an expression that

gives nothing away. With him are his daughter, Riria, and his grandson Keremete.

The day I look for Koro Eagar at the cemetery of Rangiātea Church, it is windy and cold, but not raining. It has been stormy for days, frequent thunder and lightning sending the dog spinning on her heels, barking madly as if to scare off her tormentor, hackles raised. As soon as we arrive, a light rain begins. We look at all the older headstones, especially the ones with clasping hands, of which there are many. According to my mother, Koro Eagar has this image carved on his headstone. A gravestone historian might be able to tell us the exact significance of the relief-carved handshakes, though the symbolism is fairly self-evident.

We don't find my ancestor immediately, and the rain becomes heavy. My family take shelter while I continue my search. When I think I have exhausted other possibilities, I go up the hill. The downpour becomes wild, rain biting at my skin, and I wonder whether I am being told to leave, but I am determined to look. I quickly survey the stones on the hill and then begin my descent, looking at the last few headstones on the way. 'Well, I give up,' I say, when I reach my family. The rain has lightened. 'Have you looked at that one?' my partner asks, pointing to a monument behind me. I doubt it is Koro Eagar's. We look towards the large freestanding obelisk-shaped memorial, separate but not too far from the other headstones. But there are the two hands clasped in a high-relief handshake at the centre of the stone pillar. Better take another look. I jog over, see the words in Māori first: H F IKA. Then I know. It's him.

I am surprised at how grand his memorial is. Perhaps this was why I didn't look at first. Sometimes a large headstone suggests ostentatious wealth. But many things about Eagar's stone suggest his memorial is indicative of high esteem, rather than pretentiousness. It reads:

in

loving memory

of

H F EAGAR

TENA KOE PAKEHA

E TAPU ANA TENEI HEI

WHAKAMAHARATANGA

MO

H F IKA

I MATE IA I TE 13 O AKUHATA 1911

On the plinth at the base of the memorial are the words:

HE TANGATA WHAKAPONO, AROHA HOKI KI TE IWI
MAORI ME NGA PAKEHA TAE NOA KI TONA MATENGA
HAERE RA KI TO MATUA I TE RANGI

There are two things that strike me immediately about this inscription. One, there has been much effort expended to tell this particular story about Eagar. He was 'a man of faith' and also had 'love[23] for the Māori people and the Pākehā until his death'. Secondly, with the exception of the first part of the inscription, the memorial is written in Māori. Particularly affecting is the engraving of his habitual saying 'Tena koe Pakeha' inscribed above the handshake, which is almost three-dimensional and stands out in white stone.

Official records do not detail Eagar's involvement with Māori communities, apart from his status as the first secretary of the Ōtaki-Māori Racing Club, whose website proclaims it is 'the only Māori racing club in New Zealand, and possibly one of a few truly indigenous horse racing clubs in the world' and names Eagar 'the most important individual in the early years'.[24] He was also secretary to the early Ōtaki Library, and:

> Harry Eagar was the clerk to both [Te Horo and Otaki Road] boards, also secretary of many different concerns. Dust inside and on the papers of the shelves did not impair the efficiency of the clerk, nor dull the greeting of 'Tenakoe, Pakeha', which was usually accorded a local visitor. Eagar's funeral, which took place on August 16, 1911, was very largely attended.[25]

Says A.J. Dreaver in *Horowhenua County and its People: A Centennial History*: 'The Cyclopaedia [1897] called him "the veritable Pooh-bah" of Otaki.'[26]

Ōtaki at the time was a metropolis of 836 citizens. This might not be impressive now, but back then it had promising prospects:

> OTAKI, the largest township since setting out from the Capital, is well situated, and near the sea coast, and although under Maori rule, as it were, is yet destined to become an important town for [. . .] the town and district have many elements of prosperity [. . .] Otaki will become a resort for invalids, globe-trotters, and people seeking relaxation from the cares of city life.[27]

The community was emphatically bicultural, more Māori than Pākehā, and retains that strong, culturally distinct personality today. There were shadows in Eagar's life, as there are in any. I do not know what to make of the absence of his wife in our knowledge of him. Apparently he had caused offence to his in-laws, but I don't have the details of that, and with regard to some whakapapa, it is best to tread lightly over unsettled ground.

From the history I can piece together, I can't say for sure what any of this tells us about Koro Eagar. We know him as the Welsh ancestor, though he was born in Sydney and his name is Anglo-Saxon. He was obviously a hard-working community man, but I can't tell if I would've been on his side around the committee table.

What I am left with is a sense that he walked between two cultures, and that he did what he could to integrate both. He wasn't like my older Pākehā-Māori ancestors—though he married into the culture and adopted the language just as fast. His was a world that was rapidly becoming Europeanised. Those who paid attention still did well by engaging and adopting Māori views and ideas, by nurturing Māori friends and families. Perhaps Eagar was one of a new kind of citizen: accountable to both Māori and Pākehā worlds. Rangiātea urupā carries testimony to this: a pointed memorial, hands clasped in friendship, the cheery greeting—*Tena koe Pakeha*.

Keeping Company

We are always looking for what was lost, always trying to map connections. Once I thought I could be an archaeologist, but now I see that what I might become instead is an excavator of stories. Sometimes these stories can be dug out of family graveyards, sometimes found in the wilderness imagination; sometimes it is tempting to pick on the living, but I can see that they won't be happy about it and I'd prefer to go on being loved, or at least tolerated.

I wonder whether my preoccupations are connected to that first, primal, lost relation in my life, though I wouldn't like to place too much weight on this conclusion. There are no straight lines, no clear path. Excavation is the clearing of dirt, the patient brushing away of layer after layer of dust, the use of fine tools. A light tap, a slow chipping away. Careful! You don't want to damage the last remnant. Have you done the right karakia? Are the gods on your side?

'Stories define the potentialities of our existence,' according to Kapur.[28] Tangata Whata, Te Puponga, Ika. That these Pākehā were given Māori names, even in jest, shows the intimacy they shared with Māori. These first European settlers chose to see what was here already. They looked to the land and seas and peoples they encountered, and decided to bind themselves to the lives and customs that already existed. They didn't try to superimpose their world on the land they found themselves in.

Of course, like many good stories, this one touches on the challenge of prejudice, the mediating power of sex, and the triumph of mythology. From the first I was made aware that I came from two peoples, and that these two peoples had a lot of unfinished business. Like many mixed-origin people, I've encountered prejudice from both sides, which is to be expected, since each feeds the other. What made me interested in the stories of my Pākehā-Māori ancestors was this: if we have been inter-marrying since first European contact, and if our earliest white ancestors in New Zealand were willing to approach their ethnic identity in a fluid and adaptable way, why wasn't the development of New Zealand culture more representative of the experiences and approaches of these men? Why, when I think of the stories I was bestowed by the Pākehā side of my family, do they not include the white men who became Pākehā-Māori? Did the absolute insistence on a 'European' identity come much later in our story than we like to think?

Perhaps a new approach lies in the convoluted mass of stories from our collective past. My heritage has only ever consisted of a multitude of messy, conflicting, surprising stories. The more of them I discover, the more I am content that my personal story of loss and confusion and strange beginnings is not so unusual. I've sought them out, these fiercely independent, alternative-lifestyle Pākehā grandfathers, to keep me company. To keep company with the kauri-brown ancestral wāhine toa I like to visit often. I bet they like it here. They know their place, and it's better than where they came from. They've paid the prices that were asked of them, adopted the reo and tikanga, earned their turf through work and war and the making of babies. Their stories represent an earlier whakapapa, an alternative form of settlement. While Pākehā-Māori had their own issues, could their stories represent another model of intercultural relationship for all of us? Could the story of Aotearoa New Zealand develop differently if we recognised all the stories, not just those of conquest and confiscation, laws and land courts, but the unexpected, the unpopular, the unwritten?

First published in *Sport* 40 (2012)

Tōtaranui—Queen Charlotte Sound

We lived all over the North Island, and we moved around a lot. I spent many hours atop a mattress in the back of a station wagon, or lying on the back seat of a Hillman Hunter, breathing secondhand smoke, the windows down.

Outside I saw treeless hills, sheep and cattle and fenceposts. What trees I saw were lined up along fence lines, macrocarpa or pine or some English relative of these. In my memories the landscape of my childhood is a physical wasteland, as well as a cultural one. I don't know how much of this is true; I only know that this is what I remember. I had no heart for it.

Sometimes we lived on farms and I walked the hills looking for adventure. The ground seemed parched, denuded of trees. It was all stubby grass until torrential rain turned everything to mud. I don't remember ever seeing a pūkeko, or a kererū. Even tūī were rare. We had a black-and-white cat.

I was 17 when I first went to the South Island. Coming into the Sounds on the ferry, I was astonished. This is where they'd been keeping the trees! All of them, it seemed. I understood something then, about our country and what we'd done to it. It wasn't until that moment that I realised what exactly had been missing. It would be many years before I learnt how significant my ancestors had been in the area, and how this

was the home of my bones long before I understood it to be
mine. But Tōtaranui sang to me, on that first trip, and it still
holds me in awe each time I am there. The cultural wasteland
is long since gone, now that I know how to go home.

First published in the *New Zealand Listener*
(Summer 2019/2020)

By Your Place in the World,
I Will Know Who You Are

Around 2013, I attended a hui for a new job and was among a group of people who were, for the most part, unfamiliar. I knew a handful of attendees, so in one of the breaks I greeted an old acquaintance, and she introduced me to the other people in her group.

She said something like 'Tina is a writer' by way of introduction.

'Oh?' said one of her group, then she looked at me intently, curiously, and without recognition. 'Where are you from?'

At this point I did what I always do when faced with this question. I stumbled and stuttered, and muttered something about being from all over the place, but currently, up the coast.

'The East Coast?' she asked, her interest piqued.

To which I replied, 'Uh no, Kāpiti Coast,' and stumbled around further, trying to find purchase in this exchange of niceties that is quintessentially Māori.

What I like about this encounter, despite my discomfort, was that the woman enquiring of my origins was blonde and had very Pākehā features. I had thought she was Pākehā, and perhaps she was, but when she spoke, her intonation and her question immediately revealed something about her cultural origins or associations. Her expression was one I have only encountered from Māori seeking to make connections. And her question meant: 'I will be able to place you if I know where you're from. By your place in the world, I will know who you are.'

As soon as this happened, I felt culturally inadequate, but that had nothing to do with skin or features or any outward expressions of identity. It was about knowing your place in the world.

Each time I encounter this question, I feel like I fail a small test, no matter how hard I work to come to terms with the lack of precision and definition in my answer.

Sometimes writing a personal essay feels like a constant argument about place—the place I belong, how I place myself, my place in-between cultures—a constant wrangling between two sides that at its simplest is embodied by my Māori and Pākehā parentages. The marriage between my Pākehā father and Māori mother didn't work, and they separated when I was still a toddler. My sister and I were brought up by our father. It's not important to go into the details of that, suffice to say I still remember the exact moment when, as a teenager, I began to see my parents' relationship as a microcosm of the historical relationship between Pākehā and Māori. This analogy was of some use to a confused young woman, although time and maturity eventually caused me to view my parents, and history, as more complex creatures. However, the outcome of all of this was something that doesn't make much sense, something paradoxical if you will—a Māori who doesn't come from any place in particular. Tūrangawaewae or papakāinga are widely held by Māori and Pākehā as defining features in placing who Māori are. As Indigenous peoples, as Treaty partners, as tangata whenua, knowledge of and relationship to ancestral land is paramount in explaining and maintaining not just personal but political and economic claims to tino rangatiratanga, or sovereign status. Knowing where you come from really matters.

But if I am asked where I come from, I can't give a direct or single answer. This is particularly problematic when meeting other Māori, for whom it is more common and polite to ask where you're from than who you are. Not only was I brought up without any knowledge of my papakāinga, but we also moved places every year or two. I do not have a 'hometown', even in the Pākehā sense.

This void or absence shouldn't be confused with not having any relationship to homeplaces. I do have multiple papakāinga; that is, I have several mountains, waters, lands and marae that I connect to via whakapapa or genealogical and familial links. These are my 'places to stand', and I can go to any of them at any time and find myself 'home'. I don't mean some ephemeral, non-experiential sense of home—I mean that they quite literally, physically embody home spaces for me. One summer several years ago I was doing novel research in Waikawa Bay, Picton. I hoped to find evidence of stories I had heard about my ancestry that had inspired the fiction. Waikawa is my grandfather's marae, and therefore very much mine, but I had not been there for approximately a decade and we knew few people who still lived in the area. My first stop was the urupā, where I could greet my ancestors and seek the ones related to my story. It is an extraordinary place at the height of summer, high on a hill above the Sounds, and I always feel as though the tūpuna get a pretty nice view to watch over for all of eternity. I took my children exploring with me, and told them what I could of our connections, and as we were leaving we visited a second spot with additional graves. Here, an aunty who was also visiting her people took me in hand. Who were my people? she asked. I told her my grandfather's name. Oh, you're one of ours. Are you coming to the marae? There's a tangi, one of your relations. Come have a kai. Do you have somewhere to stay? And so, even though I hadn't told anyone we were coming, even though I wouldn't have known who to tell we were coming, there we were, home, and not one person looked at me like I was a stranger, even though I kind of was. I was theirs, they were mine—that was my place. It is possible for me to do that on six marae, maybe more. Nothing I write in this essay and none of my discomfort refutes the fact that they are inexorably my places. But I wasn't brought up near them. I did not spend my childhood playing around the marae ātea of any of them, or sleepily looking up at the rafters of the whare while hui went on for days. Most Māori identify more strongly with one or two places, one or two iwi. Mother and father. Even if we leave out the fractured beginnings and the Pākehā upbringing, I have trouble claiming just one or two of these marae as my main places. Where are you from? For me, the answer is at least a paragraph, if not a page. Never a sentence.

It feels somewhat ridiculous to be concerned about this—six marae, maybe more? Surely I am drowning in cultural riches. But the ahi kā, also known as 'keeping the home fires burning', is a tikanga that can't be discounted. If I don't live by these marae, if I don't contribute to them regularly, if the people there don't see my face each month, or even year, how can I maintain my place there? I'm a townie. I live where I hope to make a good life for my children. I choose to expend my cultural energy in writing and urban cultural activity, for the most part. I operate in the wider world as Māori even though I don't always know how to 'be' Māori when Māori are by definition tribal. For example, I can't choose between my western or central dialect: should I say 'whakapapa' or 'w_akapapa'? There is whakamā in all of this.

Put simply, there is an expectation that Māori know where they come from, yet I write as a Māori who doesn't have grounding in just one place, one tribe, or one culture, but is still Māori. I am Pākehā too. I am not part Māori and part Pākehā; I am both Māori and Pākehā.

One great solace and encouragement is that while the specificities of this story are uniquely mine, the outcome is not: we, whatever we are, are everywhere. There are labels— variations on hybrid, urban Māori, ngā awarua. There's even a movement to reclaim the term 'half-caste'. It really shouldn't be such a big deal anymore, except I still can't answer the simple question 'Where are you from?' and I still meet young people who are deeply conflicted, even ashamed, about their multiple heritages.

I often think of writing in terms of paradox.

How can two seemingly opposite ideas exist in the same place?

Do they actually exist in the same place? Are they actually opposites? How can someone be from more than one place and from more than one or two or five peoples?

The place I write from consists of two opposite and conflicting ideas: one, that I absolutely belong to multiple places in Aotearoa, that I have inalienable rights to those places as mana whenua; and two, that until I was almost an adult, there was a void in my life where papakāinga or homeplaces should have been. A void which also should have been occupied by cultural and familial knowledge, and which is no longer unusual among either Māori or Pākehā.

This paradoxical place is extraordinarily powerful to write from: teetering on the edge of the void, buoyed constantly by absolute belonging and knowledge subsequently gained as an adult. It is the pain and loss and discomfort of the void thrown up against the wealth of what I now know that informs what I do. It's something I'm grateful for every time I write, because writing is itself an enactment of that very same tension: what we don't understand, what we yearn for, what we seek, and what we know utterly at the level of bones.

I have written about Māori versus European conceptions of the universe, Pākehā-Māori ancestors from the 19th century (the original hybrids), and about loving museums and being confused about their history of containing and misrepresenting, even of maiming their collections, including people. I've written about how crucial it is to use Māori words in English-language stories, the strange rightness of a carved tauihu in a European museum, the feeling I sometimes have that ghosts linger in my writing, or maybe that is just a way to explain things. In each of these essays, there is a tension from the very first sentence—this is how I know I should keep writing. Even now I feel it, the impossibility of making what I'm trying to say clear, transparent, sensible, straightforward even. It isn't. Māori and European systems of understanding the universe are surprisingly similar, except in the ways they are not. Pākehā-Māori were Europeans who assimilated themselves into Māori culture by choice and desire, except they were still Pākehā. A carving from a 19th-century waka should not belong in a museum in Frankfurt, except that somehow it does.

The essay is the perfect site to explore paradoxical questions because an essay is supposed to be nonfiction, which means it is supposed to be about a knowable truth. And yet the essays I enjoy circle around the unknowable, constantly searching for answers to questions the writer knows are, at some level, unanswerable. Fiction does this too, but fiction has permission to do anything it wants. Don't know who you are? Make something up! With nonfiction there is a tension already on the page from the moment we touch pen to page or fingers to keyboard. The tension comes from nonfiction's imperative to 'write something true' when we don't even know if that is a thing that is possible. Essays ask us to achieve the unattainable, like being multiple things and coming from multiple places all at once. How do I understand the complexities of a simple encounter like the one at that work hui, with all its layers of culture and nuance, differing understandings about the significance of not just physical but cultural place, and appearance? I write a personal essay, though I'm not sure I will find my way to any particular answer by the end of it.

I love the challenge and the impossibility of the form. I can gather evidence. I can draw pictures and diagrams, I can problem-solve, I can quote the greats. Occasionally, I can capture a reflection, sample soil or draw blood. I might even get satisfaction from evoking a sense of how I understand the world, but what I can't do is present what I have written as 'the facts'. The Way Things Are is changeable, difficult to corral into tidy yards. Things like place and identity can't be captured, but fleeting glimpses of them can.

I struggle with those personal pronouns at the centre of the personal essay—the 'I' and 'me'. But what I'm really talking about, by extension, I hope, is us. How does it work for any of us? What does tangata whenua mean in this moment? Suffice to say that the essay is a place where we can make, as Albert Wendt pointed out in his iconic 1979 essay 'Towards a New Oceania', our individual journeys into the Void, where we can explain us to ourselves. I have used the essay as a site to make ancestral journeys, and these explorations have only complicated my understandings of where I come from, rather than simplified them. There has been no single path, no single people, no single place that takes precedence in these stories. But knowing the stories, getting closer to the heart of the contradictions, has taken away some of the whakamā. I can only view the complexity of what the tūpuna have left behind as a gift, a place that offers comfort even where it does not provide certainty.

Postscript

A new question arises now, one I had not understood to ask when I first wrote this essay as a talk for Ingrid Horrocks and Cherie Lacey's colloquium 'Placing the Personal Essay': what does mana whenua mean in this moment? A week after submitting this essay, I returned to Waikawa for a long weekend with my family-in-law. The trip had been planned, serendipitously enough, by a sister-in-law who knew nothing of my connections there. I knew we would be staying close to one of my homeplaces. In fact, our cottage was nestled under the hill where my ancestors rest. We went to see them. We passed the marae each day. In the new whale centre and the old museum my great-great-great-grandparents were alive in black-and-white stills.

I can't remember who said it first. *We could live here. We should live here. Look at the hills. Look at the sea.*

It had not seemed like a remote possibility before. Imagine living in a place where the tūpuna are everywhere, we said. Making a real contribution to the marae. Imagine how it would feel to have that much sureness when your feet touch the earth.

I could see that one day I may be that person. The young ones will come to visit from the city and think there's no way they could live in this small nowhere town no matter how beautiful it is. They probably won't ever live near one of their marae. This is what I thought. But no matter how much you and your whakapapa wander, the homeplace calls.

Post-postscript

Nine years later, as I prepare this collection for publication, we are finally becoming kanohi kitea at Waikawa, working towards our collective papakāinga moemoeā. Even as I wrote the final words to this essay in 2015, I could not have imagined where we are now. I join a stream of whānau returning. Fires can always be rekindled. With all the whakamā in the world, you can still go home.

First published in Extraordinary Anywhere: Essays on Place
from Aotearoa New Zealand (2016)

Twitch

Like most people, as a child I would ask my father where I came from. Discussions of human sexuality were strenuously avoided, but there remained complex and puzzling questions about our presence in the universe. I have a distinct memory of being taken outside one night to look up at the full and startling moon. It was the late 70s, and I was four years old. What I saw in the moon was one of the warrior gorillas from the TV show *Planet of the Apes*. I carried this as a true memory right into adulthood, though it is obvious now that this could not have been what I saw. I'm not sure what I was meant to discover that night as I looked up at that luminous sphere cloaked in cool darkness. But I see now that my imaginative world of TV shows and plastic gorillas out of cereal boxes must have been just as real to me as what was 'out there'.

The internal world: the external world. How do we know our place in the universe? The answer that comes to me immediately is whakapapa. It doesn't sound very scientific—'genealogy'. But in the Māori world view, it takes you right back to the beginning of time. Right back, in fact, to before the Big Bang.

There are some people who can trace their whakapapa back to Māui. I am not one of those people. I don't claim to be any expert in these matters, but the little I do know is enough to paint a startling picture of creation—a picture that is surprisingly in tune with conventional Western ideas about how the universe began.

One story says Māui was a demigod. His grandmothers were goddesses, and one of them was the first fully human being to exist—Hinetītama, the dawn maiden, who later became Hinenuitepō, the great mother of the night. Hinetītama was born of Hineahuone, the earth-formed maid, and Tāne, the god of forests, who became the progenitor of many living things. So, Hinetītama was created through a combination of the earthly and the celestial. Tāne himself came from the marriage of Papatūānuku, the earth mother, and Ranginui, the sky father. If you can trace your whakapapa back to Māui, you can connect yourself to the gods. Ranginui is the heavens—so you have found your connection to the universe the way we think about it these days, up there, in the sky.

Perhaps you choose not to believe Māui was part god. Some of us don't really know. Perhaps he was a great and illustrious explorer, whose exploits were so extreme and world-changing that he is remembered throughout the Pacific. It is not outside of the realms of possibility that Māui was a real man so revered by his descendants that they have maintained the woven strand that links them to him for centuries, remembering him in legend and genealogy. Allow for the possibility. But what of the idea his grandparents and great-grandparents really were the initiators of the human race, and if you go further back, the order of our universe as we know it? That is a story, and what is important about it is not that we believe it is true, but that we understand what it stands for.

It is interesting that even writers of Western science, or popular books about science at least, describe creation in evolutionary terms that sound almost genealogical. Note here how our cosmological beginnings are described as a birth: 'The true picture of the Big Bang is one in which space, matter and, crucially, time were born,' write the authors of *Bang! The Complete History of the Universe*. 'Space did not appear out of "nothingness"; before the moment of creation there was no "nothingness".'[1] This is similar to Bill Bryson's description of the 'singularity'—in which 'every last mote and particle of matter between here and the edge of creation' is squeezed into an infinitesimally compact spot that preceded the Big Bang: '[O]utside the singularity there is no where. When the universe begins to expand, it won't be spreading out to fill a larger emptiness. The only space that exists is the space it creates as it goes.'[2] If we look at one of the many Māori versions of creation (there are tribal variations, but they all conceive of the universe in terms of whakapapa), we find extraordinary similarities to scientific ideas of what preceded and followed the Big Bang:

Te Korekore—a double negative, the Absolute Nothingness.
Te Korekore Te Rawea—the Absolute Nothingness which could Not be Wrapped Up.
Te Korekore Te Whiwhia—the Absolute Nothingness which could Not be Bound.
Te Korekore Te Tamaua—the Absolute Nothingness which could Not be Fastened.
Te Kowhao—the Abyss.
Te Po—the Night.[3]

In this Ngāpuhi account, Io-Matua-Kore: Io the Parentless who was Always Existent without beginning or end, lived eternally in Te Korekore. Io is sometimes thought of as the Creator, though Io might be characterised as something like a divine animating spark that begets life. Among the Williams Dictionary definitions of the word 'Io', we find 'sinew, muscle, nerve' first, and 'twitch' later.[4] I may be stretching things, but it might even be possible to describe Io as a 'singularity'.

Māori Marsden describes the meaning of Te Korekore as

[. . .] not simply 'non-being', or annihilating nothingness, though it includes this meaning, but it went beyond this. By means of a thorough-going negativity, the negation itself turns into the most positive activity. It is the negation of negation. Te Korekore is the infinite realm of the formless and undifferentiated. It is the realm not so much of 'non-being' but rather of 'potential being'. It is the realm of Primal and Latent energy from which the stuff of the Universe proceeds and from which all things evolve.[5]

As one author explains: 'This was the space-time framework, the space (void and abyss)—time (the nights) continuum, in which the cosmic process could begin to operate.'[6] Which leads us to wonder how a people considered 'stone-age' had this level of understanding of what lay behind the observable phenomena of the night sky and the physical world.

*

In *A Short History of Nearly Everything*, Bryson does an impressive job of describing the Big Bang—more a sudden expansion than explosion—in such a way that it becomes accessible and, almost, imaginable:

In a single blinding pulse, a moment of glory much too swift and expansive for any form of words, the singularity assumes heavenly dimensions, space beyond conception. In the first lively second [. . .] is produced gravity and other forces that govern physics. In less than a minute the universe is a million billion miles across and growing fast [. . .] In three minutes, 98 percent of all the matter there is or will ever be has been produced. We have a universe. It is a place of the most wondrous and gratifying possibility, and beautiful, too.[7]

Again, if we look at various Māori traditions, we find many similarities:

Te Kore,	The Nothingness,
Te Pō,	The Night,
Te Rapunga,	The Seeking,
Whaia,	Following,
Te Kukune,	The Conception,
Te Pupuke,	The Swelling,
Te Hihiri,	The Elemental and Pure Energy,
Te Mahara,	The Subconscious,
Te Hinengaro,	The Deep Mind,
Te Manako,	The Desire,
Te Wananga,	The Wisdom,
Te Ahua,	The Form,
Te Atamai,	The Shape,
Te Whiwhia,	The Possessing,
Rawea,	The Being Bound,
Hopu Tu,	The Possessing Power,
Hau Ora,	The Breath of Life,
Atea.	Space.[8]

The language used above to describe the most ancient genealogies of creation emphasises expansion—seeking, following, conception, swelling, the development of pure elemental energy or power out of which all physical things will spring, much in the same way that Bryson and other writers describe the Big Bang as a massively creative moment. Finally, form, shape, power and life come into being, resulting in Space and 'all the matter there is or will ever be'.

The aeons of time that followed the burst of creative expansion we call the Big Bang are described by Māori in terms of night, and these descriptions reveal a poetic temperament determined to explore and reveal the different qualities of the '300,000 years following the cataclysmic period of inflation'.[9] Here we encounter Te Pō tē kitea / the unseen night, Te Pō tē whaia / the unpossessed night, Te Pō tē wheau / the fleeting night, Te Pō tangotango / the night of utter darkness, Te Pō tē whawha / the untouched and untouchable night.[10] The twitch of Io in the realm of Te Kore has created the conditions that make the development of the universe possible. These different Māori traditions bequeath us a legacy of descriptive language with which to come to terms with more esoteric scientific theories:

> The Universe became a less violent place. As the temperature dropped, so the protons and neutrons began to slow down; however, radiation and matter were still linked [. . .] the biggest difference [. . .] is that in those very early times [the Universe] was completely opaque [. . .]
>
> However, when the Universe had cooled to a mere 30,000 degrees, around 300,000 years after the Big Bang, a sudden change took place [. . .] The first neutral atoms were formed [. . .] A large expanse of space between each newly formed atom therefore opened up, and photons were suddenly free to travel for great distances. In other words, matter and radiation were

separated, and 300,000 years after the Big Bang the Universe became transparent.[11]

The picture is completed hence:

Te Pō namunamu ki taiao	the night of seeking the passage of the world
Te Pō tahuri atu	the night of restless turning
Te Pō tahuri mai ki taiao	the night of turning towards the revealed world
Te Whai ao	the glimmer of dawn
Te Ao mārama	the bright light of the day[12]

Those neutral little atoms creating space for transparency— that's the letting of light into the universe, making way for Te Ao Mārama, literally 'The World of Light' ('mārama' can also mean transparency and illumination). In the Christian tradition, this is the moment God said 'Let there be light'.

*

Most New Zealanders know a little about the story of Ranginui and Papatūānuku, tightly embracing at the beginning of time, bringing forth children who were gods in their own right, but were miserable in the clammy dark between their parents' bodies. Many are familiar with the story of how the children of Rangi and Papa debated and quarrelled, arguing whether to kill, or separate, or leave their parents alone. In the end it was decided that separation was the most humane option for all involved, and there followed a number of stories around how this was achieved. Eventually Rangi was established in the heavens, with Papa lying below him, her face turned away in her sorrow, no longer clasped in her husband's embrace, but bathed in his tears. And, as I described earlier, the descendents of Rangi and Papa eventually produced Māui and his generation of people, who in turn produced te iwi Māori.

What would the scientific account make of this? Bryson gets to the heart of things quickly and succinctly:

> About 4.6 billion years ago, a great swirl of gas and dust some 15 billion miles across accumulated in space where we are now and began to aggregate. Virtually all of it—99.9 percent of the mass of the solar system—went to make the Sun. Out of the floating material that was left over, two microscopic grains floated close enough together to be joined by electrostatic forces. This was the moment of conception for our planet [. . .] In just 200 milllion years, possibly less, the Earth was essentially formed, though still molten and subject to constant bombardment [. . .]
>
> For the next 500 million years the young Earth continued to be pelted relentlessly by comets, meteorites, and other galactic debris, which brought water to fill the oceans and the components necessary for the successful formation of life. It was a singularly hostile environment and yet somehow life got going. Some tiny bag of chemicals twitched and became animate. We were on our way.[13]

For a long time, it seems, the Sky was a lot closer to the Earth than he is now. He touched her passionately, sending her way the elements that would shape her and allow her to bring forth life. They were locked together in a tumultuous embrace that brought about the right conditions for life to exist. But, in the beginning, those conditions were hostile, tempestuous, and not easy to live in. It was not until the Sky and the Earth separated that the atmosphere calmed and strengthened and cooled, and light became a constant and reliable presence.

*

I have a tendency to revere my ancestors, all of them, the Māori, Pākehā, Moriori. Still, it astonishes me that the visions of creation from my tūpuna could have been so accurate. Perhaps this is because it took conventional Western science up until at least the latter half of the 20th century to figure most of this out, and we like to believe that Western science is the most advanced of all. So how did the old people do it? Of course, I can only guess. I see the advantages in being 'stone-age'—that in the evenings, you only had the night sky to look at, and stories to tell. That, over generations, stories built upon older stories, certain people with particularly clear vision saw patterns in the night sky, or noticed movements, a distant star going supernova perhaps, or the blinking out of light from a long dead sun. It is possible they looked inward as often as out, travelling the complex pathways of the mind and spirit, touching ancient wisdoms about our origins only dreams can offer. And, in the darkness with only natural light from the Milky Way to see by, they began to understand what lay behind the stars, what went before them, the place of potential, Te Korekore, with Io twitching into life.

I love the Hubble Space Telescope pictures: how can you not be floored by the 'Pillars of Creation'? Google it, you'll see what I mean: 'These pillars of interstellar gas and dust are a chrysalis for new stars [. . .] Several of the newly formed stars can be seen emerging at the tips of spine-like features.'[14] The names don't prepare you for the astounding display of colour and light suffusing space dust and gas you'll witness if you go in search of the Orion, Dumbell, Helix, Flame, Horsehead, Eight-burst, Little Ghost, Spirograph, Twin Jet, Blinking Eye, Elephant's Trunk, Cone, Ant, Cat's Eye, Red Spider, Lagoon, Rotten Egg, Cat's Paw, Swan or Boomerang Nebulae. And then there are the spiral galaxies which, as Nicolas Cheetham writes,

> owe their elaborate anatomy to an ephemeral light show that traces the progress of a density wave churning through their discs. The crest of the wave is illuminated by a surf of massive, short-lived stars sculpted from the interstellar medium by the shock of its passage, as well as by existing stars bunching together as they slide over its peak.[15]

There are whirlpool galaxies, some we have only seen side-on or at an angle so that they look like ethereal Frisbees, and one that is apparently spinning backwards. Some galaxies cluster in groups or pairs and some have tails like mice. The cosmos is full of dazzling spectacles we can only wonder at. Paradoxically, it is in mystery itself that I also find my place in the universe. It is here I find comfort—for all we think we know, there is infinitely more we don't. I may not be genealogically related to the universe, but it's just as likely that I am. It's not that we must believe the stories, but that we understand what they tell us. What they say is that we are connected to all of creation, and science doesn't deny that:

> Whatever prompted life to begin, it happened just once. That is the most extraordinary fact in biology, perhaps the most extraordinary fact we know. Everything that has ever lived,

plant or animal, dates its beginnings from the same primordial twitch. At some point in the unimaginably distant past some little bag of chemicals fidgeted to life. It absorbed some nutrients, gently pulsed, had a brief existence [. . .] But this ancestral packet did something additional and extraordinary: it cleaved itself and produced an heir. A tiny bundle of genetic material passed from one living entity to another, and has never stopped moving since.[16]

That's whakapapa.

*

Google. Hubble. It may not be necessary to use technology to view a picture of a spiral galaxy or the wonders of creation in space. Next time you are at a museum, or if you are able to visit a marae, find a wharenui, pātaka, or waka taua. If the structure is a house, look to the lintel above the doorway. If it is a canoe, look to the prow or stern. You will see figures carved there, and spirals carved between them. The double spirals may be carved in such a way that there are gaps pierced between the lines of the spirals, allowing light to filter through. This is the takarangi. What you see depicted in the carving before you is Te Kore, Te Pō, Te Ao Mārama—a spiral universe of potential being, darkness and light in a swirling, dynamic dance, the Earth and Sky separated yet linked. It is a good enough way to view the world. Either that, or take the kids outside during the full moon, so that you can all look up in the cool dark at the mystery of the heavens, and ask them what they see.

Winner, RSNZ Manhire Prize for
Creative Science Writing, Nonfiction, 2009

Pudding

It must be summer. The ground flat and parched; what little grass there is, brown. That's how I remember the farm and that whole year, 1983. I think it's summer because I can't remember going to school that week, the week of the pudding. But in fact it could easily have been autumn or spring, those school holidays we had in between school terms. The pool isn't even there, in my memory. In summer the small round Para Pool is always up, its corrugated-iron sides interlocked, rubber lining stretched over and held in place by plastic tubing. Big enough for me to swim around and around most days, pretending to be a mermaid, but only the radius of my nine-year-old body, plus a nine-year-old arm's length. Once the green algae start to colonise the pool floor we'll dismantle it for cleaning, pulling off the tubing and separating the interlocking pieces so that the rubber lining sloshes its contents onto the lawn, causing a wide and improbable puddle over the grass until it sinks in. But before the green sets in there are weeks of play, the cool water a respite from that relentless and angry sun, and the sunburn obtained from many hours under it, sunbathing on scorching paths made tolerable by the application of soaking wet bodies.

But the pool isn't there, on the lawn we cross to get to the letterbox, so maybe it is autumn. That makes sense. I feel like there is a too-tight woollen jersey constricting my neck, its cuffs too high above my wrists. I'm growing fast.

No one goes clothes shopping, much. Dad's a shepherd, always working, and not well paid, though there is the free mutton. The weekends are for watching sport, cigarettes, beer. A man's got to have something. And we have the outside. *Go outside and play.* Though outside is boring. I exercise every ounce of my imagination to make it *something*. But that parched earth. No bush. I try to make something of the macrocarpa windbreak, hunt every inch of it for hidden treasures and huts. Try to make the fairies appear, or the pop stars. Either will do.

Every second Friday night there is food shopping and fish and chips in town, and this is the highlight of the fortnight. In town, there is the possibility of glamour, even in Central Hawke's Bay. Girls at school have leg warmers and bubble skirts and Wham! records, potent symbols of fashion and the secret elixir of adulthood. At Lisa's ten-year-old birthday sleepover we discuss sex, what it is and how it's done and the noises Lisa's mother makes when her parents do it. Lisa's parents are young and good-looking, and that makes it easier to imagine they'd want to do it, but when Lisa imitates the noises I argue loudly that she can't possibly be right. I've never actually heard anyone have sex but logic tells me it wouldn't sound like that. And then I attempt to make other noises, imitating an activity I have never heard and know little about. No one says anything, but I remember their faces.

I'm not sure if it's then or later that I begin to lose my friends. Early on, when I moved to the area, we were so ardent in our friendships that we whispered 'I love you' to each other in the reading corner at school. But somehow I cannot maintain my grip on these relationships. I can't keep up with the leg warmers and bubble skirts, the baubly hair ties and pigtails. My hair is cut short so that it's tidy and doesn't require too much attention. My wardrobe only grows more sparse, and one day I go to school in bare feet rather than wear the cheap Roman sandals my father has replaced my too-tight sneakers with. No one is fooled by this move. Kids' instincts for shame and embarrassment are just too finely tuned. I think even then I understood that they weren't laughing at my sandals so much as my inept attempts to pretend I was something else. This was before all of us were forced into the same ugly sandals at high school anyway. School uniforms saved my life.

Anyway, Friday nights. Food shopping; fish and chips. Even better if we can eat them on the way home, but sometimes we have to wait. The drive home takes about 20 minutes, and during that time I lie on the back seat of our Hillman Hunter and imagine I have the power to become invisible, or to freeze everyone around me. This last is a favourite, but both fantasies have the same objective: power. In such a world, I imagine, I would be able to travel around freely, help myself to all the lollies and all the clothes I want. Live in the best houses. I'd definitely live in town, or somehow go overseas. I'd have to figure out how to drive. And I'd be able to snoop into people's lives. Undress movie stars. Eat anything I want. Get as much money as I want. When I felt the need for company again, I would unfreeze everyone and they would find me transformed: wearing the coolest clothes, in possession of large amounts of money, the better to continue my lavish lifestyle. Surely someone with that power wouldn't even need parents anymore. Somehow with this wealth I might also transform my looks: rid myself of the curly red hair and freckles, grow suddenly slender. *Annie* the musical is huge, and nobody looks more like Annie than I do, but I am not fooled into thinking that her charms have anything to do with her looks (and I am neither precociously charming nor a great singer).

I'm always dreaming of escape. Always imagining myself away from whatever pain I'm experiencing at the time: rejection, shame, boredom, parental anger, the depths of my discontent with the world and everything in it.

Sometimes Dad runs out of money completely. This means driving the 20 minutes home on empty. On empty means there is some petrol in the tank but only a little so the dial on the dashboard can't detect it. On empty means you're never really sure you'll get home. But we always do, somehow. Dad's pretty clever. He turns off the engine and cruises down all the hills. This saves a bit of petrol but there are no guarantees. Over the weekend he siphons a bit of petrol out of the Landrover he uses for work on the farm. Enough to get the Hillman back into town when he gets paid again. This is how I first learn that a good car, like our Hillman Hunter, will *run on the smell of an oily rag.*

The particular week I'm thinking of, Friday night shopping doesn't happen. For some reason Dad hasn't been paid. Maybe a problem with the bank. The farmer Dad works for is rich. Not a showy kind of rich, but he can ride out the odd blip in cash flow. He can even ride out the odd drought. He has enough money for a new ute every year. He owns hills and hills of sheep. One day I am allowed to go inside his house and I understand that it is old money that runs his farm. Inherited wealth. Everything in the house is old, and now, in my memory, it is reddish-brown, the colour of ornate carpets. There are old ornaments in there, grandfather or grandmother clocks, mounted animal heads. It doesn't seem a place for children, but Dad tells me the stuffed mongoose entwined with a snake that sits pride of place on a side table represents the story of Riki Tiki Tavi. Do I know that story? No, I don't, I say, and after he tells me I spend a lot of time wondering how a small mammal can be fast and fierce enough to kill a snake. The farmer has two young boys. One day Riki Tiki Tavi will be theirs.

But *we* don't have enough money to get through the odd blip in cash flow. Sometimes we can barely make it through a week with the expected cash flow, so not getting paid is an issue.

Dad gets a roast out of the freezer and puts it in the oven, goes out to give the dogs a run and organise scraps of carcass for their dinner, and thinks about what to do. He's good in a crisis. That's when he snaps into gear. He's not good when he has time to ruminate, too much time to sit in the La-Z-Boy with a drink, too much time to work his way from loneliness to anguish to rage. But when there's a problem to fix? He's on to it.

So, there's the roast, and whatever is left in the fridge and cupboard, but no shopping this week. Luckily, bread and milk is delivered to the gate by rural delivery, along with the mail. A stroke of good fortune means the deliveries won't stop and it'll be payday again by the time the bill is due. At least we have that. I don't see Dad come up with the brilliant plan, but the next day we're collecting the bread and milk at the gate and using the last of the money to buy up enough sugar, butter and raisins to last a week or two.

'Have you ever had bread and butter pudding, bub?'

I don't think I have.

'Oooh, it's good. Just made out of bread and butter and milk and sugar and raisins. That's all. Do you want to help me?'

I nod along, and follow him and my big sister, who is always his right-hand man in daily concerns and operations. We butter the bread, layer it with the sugar and raisins, then cover the lot with milk. Bread soaked in milk doesn't look good to me. Do I say this?

'Just wait until it's cooked.' He rubs his hands together. 'It's really good. And guess what? We can eat pudding every day for dinner for the rest of the week!'

I'm doubtful. But something in his voice is utterly convincing. He makes it sound like an adventure. Bread and butter pudding every day! Pudding instead of regular food? Instead of vegetables? Even if it is made primarily out of bread and milk, this seems like a good deal.

And when it comes out of the oven, after an infuriatingly long time, it's delicious. There is a rich crust, and the milk-soaked bread has a wonderful consistency, more firm than instant pudding. The raisins are fat with absorbed juices, and the butter has done what butter does best, infusing everything with rich salty-sweet flavour.

We eat our fill. And eat our fill again the next day. Dad is a genius. Every day he waits to see if the money has come in and when it hasn't we make another pudding and he makes a game of it. By the end of the two weeks we've all had enough of bread and butter pudding, and I don't think I'll ever eat another one, but it's okay.

I don't remember Dad being angry during those two weeks. He is determined to make it fun, and we are determined to play along. The world isn't being kind, but out here—far from everyone else—we are all on the same side. Then the second Friday comes around again and there is money in the bank, food shopping, eating fish and chips on the way home, cruising down the hills.

First published in Landfall 237 (2019)

Gods and Ghosts

I have never seen a ghost. My mother sees them. She used to have an unnerving habit of looking over your shoulder when you were speaking to her and smiling at whoever she saw there. But I didn't inherit that skill from her. I don't believe in phenomena I haven't experienced for myself. So I understand if this ghost thing seems a bit far-fetched.

The first time I sat down to write about my grandmother, who died when I was 20 years old, I worried that there was no way to write the true story without using my imagination, perhaps even *fictionalising*. I knew the bare bones of the story, but it was about something that happened when she was three years old. That would have been the 1930s. Later, thinking about how I wrote that piece, I noted:

> As I sat down to write the first lines of this story I thought about our papakāinga at Lake Taupō and my grandmother as a three-year-old. I could almost hear her voice, the things that fascinated her, the smells and rhythms of her life in this isolated place. I felt like I was watching her, a ghost of her future eavesdropping on her past. In turn, I felt like my nan as I knew her was watching over my shoulder, and I found myself having a conversation with both her older self and the reader.

The sensation of watching my grandmother as a toddler while her older self watched over me was tangible. Sure, I had engaged my imagination to find a sense of what she would have been like. I saw quite easily where she had lived, because it has not greatly changed from that time. I saw her because I am sure she bore some resemblance to me and my own girls as toddlers. But it was more than that. There was some sort of alchemy in the feeling that my nan as I had known her was present in the room. First, I felt a tremendous sense of focus: a responsibility to get the essence of her experience right. And this focus, along with her presence, brought confidence to the writing: if it wasn't right for me to be doing it, she wouldn't have been there. I took it as a blessing.

Writing is best when it's intuitive. It's the most fun when words arrive on the page without too much thinking, and that's also, in my experience, when the best work is produced. I get a hunch, I follow it. Sometimes a line arrives in my head fully formed, so I write it down and take the concrete path or dirt track it reveals. I trust the words, the inner music, the story unwinding itself in the background of things. I find a way to tune myself, like the string of an instrument being wound to the sound of a tuning fork, into the code of human narrative, simultaneously particular and universal.

This all sounds very grand and romantic, but these are only the best times. The rest of the time it's just my lowly brain trying to find the right word from my paltry vocabulary, my poor grammar-stunted ear trying to make song from a collection of rudimentary sentences, my opinionated, bossy ego trying to muster words into some formation of character and plot. Such things can't be forced, but I do my best to force them anyway. And that doesn't work good. So I can't think of anything better than when a character starts making their own decisions. Or when a random line of language leads me to a story I didn't even know was in me. Or when I feel

that one of my dead relatives is watching me work. Is it real?
I don't know. Does it matter? No.

The story about my grandmother was good. It had voice.
It was the goodest thing I had ever produced to that point, as
a still unpublished writer. I have no doubt that this was due,
in part, to Nan's presence, or to my decision to surrender
to her story—not to impose too much control on what was
happening. Sometimes writing is about removing barriers.
What do you really think happened? What would happen if
you wrote the next words that came into your mind, without
second-guessing yourself? Whatever it was, I don't think
I would tell you now that the story was nonfiction. I had
crossed the invisible line into the world of fiction. At the
same time I still believe that something about that story was
true.

Nan's story won me a small prize and entry to the MA Creative
Writing programme at the International Institute of Modern
Letters in Wellington. That year I wrote a collection that took
as its starting point Māori creation stories. I was prompted
by a classmate to think about mythological characters, and I
remembered an old obsession with mythical stories. Without
rereading the stories I knew, I decided to transplant the gods
of old into a contemporary timeline, where the old stories
would unfold in a new way. I had to try to make it work in
present-day terms, at the same time re-casting these mythical
beings as human, with human motivations.

There is a great deal of similarity between working with
creation stories and working with true stories: the framework
is there; the characters are pre-formed; you can play with all
the elements of story but you have to decide how far you can
go before you've wandered too far from the original material.

Working with the gods gave me the same sensation as working with ancestral stories—things flowed smoothly, I felt guided. Most importantly perhaps, I took risks I might not have taken if it weren't for the fact that mythology is such a strange and distorted version of reality to begin with. I could go places I would never have gone by myself.

Sometimes I thought Māui got a bit of a bad rap in my hands. But I figured he could take it. He is usually the star of the show, the centre of attention. I focused more on the perspective of his illustrious female ancestors. Even so, I wondered why he kept showing up in so many things I did. A year later, when I wrote about the Big Bang in a piece called 'Twitch', there was Māui in the middle of it all. I had not intended to write about him at all. Then, halfway through the first page, he appeared. In an essay about the creation of the universe, he had managed to make himself central to the story. He was the ancestor, I found myself suggesting, who connected us to the gods and therefore to the universe. Maybe, in a way, this was payback. I had had tremendous fun playing with creation stories, and like my grandmother's story, they were well-received. But by writing them I had formed a relationship with my characters. I had a responsibility to the gods and goddesses now, to do them justice. Perhaps Māui's appearance in 'Twitch' was his way of evening the score.

As I write this, I am again working with an ancestor on fiction that has its beginnings in true stories. When I started in 2009, I began journaling the process of research and writing, and was surprised and very happy to meet my great-great-grandmother on the page soon after I began my first entry:

I feel like she is leading me into the story, even though she may not *be* the story. She is taking me towards it, she is standing behind the door, opening it just a crack now, looking at me, a visitor. Should she let me in? The house is shadowy behind her, an old colonial villa. She's squinting out at me, here in the glaring sunlight.

In there, in her house, it's the turn of the 20th century. I look strange to her. White skin, freckles, jeans. I don't look like her kin . . . except, there's the red hair. Maybe I look like the daughter she will have one day.

The other relatives, the old people, are in her kitchen, and out back. Some refuse to come in, refuse to enter the alien house. They might be found at the bottom of her garden, or beyond, if I were to walk through her house and exit out the back door. My elusive ancestors. Will they deem me acceptable? Is worthiness something they expect of me? Will my ancestress feel the weight of my spirit in the palm of her hand? What will get me through the door?

I'm a veranda baby now. That's where I'm at. Up the steps. In between her world and mine. I know nothing of her furnishings or the colours on her walls. I don't know the smell of her kitchen or how many chickens she keeps in the yard. Tomorrow, or the next day, she'll let me in. I think she might be a wonderful storyteller. She'll deny it, tell me she has nothing to share. But then, after we've caught up on the family gossip—who married who, and what happened to the land. Then. She'll begin.

I had no idea when I began to write that my ancestor and her house would appear to me. When it did happen, I had the same sense of thrill I'd had in writing the other pieces I've mentioned here. If ancestors or gods or any kind of seemingly autonomous being makes an appearance, I know it is a good sign. It doesn't happen all the time. It does happen often enough for me to recognise it and appreciate that it occurs at all.

I have already found out that the story our family carries may be quite different from the one that actually happened. Apparently, that's okay. How do I know? Because that's what she tells me. But is it real? It doesn't matter. It works. Wherever it comes from, it works.

First published in *Hue & Cry* 4 (2010)

A Strange Leaving

You rang this morning when I was meant to be packing my bag to go to Toronto. I thought how perfect your timing, how you always know when something's up, but then you said you were checking whether you still had my daughter's number to wish her happy birthday. I didn't tell you I'm going to Toronto. I've gotten into such an abiding habit of not telling you anything; it's more peaceful this way. Our relationship exists in its own space apart from my life, which I protect fiercely, as always. So it must seem incomprehensible to you, this public act of writing, when we've never spoken to each other of these things.

You asked when I'm going to send you my new book. I said I didn't think you'd like it. I know you won't. It gets explicit, for a start, and not all of the characters are straight. I won't get into the cultural politics of it. But you're in there, just like you're all through this book, though not as directly as here. You're there like you're everywhere: the person who made me strange, and made me see the strangeness of the world, and helped me understand how the things that are good in us are so often intimately and painfully linked to the things in us that are bad.

I don't know how to explain to you why you are here, in this book I am writing now, so much. I didn't intend it, but it seems I can't write anything about life without coming back to origin stories, so there you are. I can't think that you would be very happy about seeing the things I have written, but I hope you can see that it *means* something that you are threaded through everything. Writing this has become an act of knowing you again, and of understanding how all the terrible things have faded. Lorry says everyone gets off pretty lightly in these pages. I suppose that's true: I don't really have the stomach or the heart to dredge up all the old hurts, and what would it achieve? But still, maybe there are things you won't like in here. I can't imagine you ever expected your private life to be public.

Today on the train, just before Paekākāriki, I saw the stiff, still hooves of a horse sticking up in the air, the round of her belly beneath. She was lying on her side in a field of very long grass, and I wondered if she had eaten too much and gotten colic and died, which is a thing you once told me about when we had horses. She could have been asleep, but those stiff hooves pointing straight out suggested something more permanent. I wondered if her people knew. It seemed incongruous, to see a big dead horse in a field on the way to Wellington, but it made me think of you because you would have likely known what might cause such a thing. At Paekākāriki my sister got on the train, but I didn't know it yet. We found each other only at Porirua, when we all had to disembark to catch a bus. You asked about her this morning on the phone, asked if she's okay. She is, I said, but you can't quite figure out why she doesn't tell you directly. Anything at all. And because I am not the kind of person to dredge up old hurts, and because I don't want to cause new ones, I can't tell you why we've both stayed away over the years. You have to look at it yourself, I think.

It's been a strange leaving, this one, even though I'll be back in a week. All of you have arrived unexpectedly, one way or another, and I've begun to feel like the leave-taking is too perfect, that something is going to happen to someone, all of you perfectly aligned and present, an event too unusual not to touch me with a sense of doom, or beauty. Sometimes I can't figure out the difference between those two things. We once found a bunch of flowers on our doorstep with no note, and Lorry was delighted. How nice! he said. Nice? I said, no! It's scary and inconsiderate! Who was the creeping stalker who had decided to terrorise us thus? Even when we found out it was a well-meaning friend, I wasn't repentant. Affection can be dangerous.

This morning you told me something you'd never said before—that you had wanted to go overseas when you were a young man, but 'back in those days the only way you could go overseas was if you signed up to get bayoneted in Vietnam'. Then the rest of the story, which I did know: some time after you joined up, you were given a choice: to marry my mother or go to Vietnam. By that time you'd been through training, inoculations, wisdom teeth extraction and the knee operation they'd insisted on, and things in Vietnam had turned bad. Plus there was the baby beginning to make her presence known inside my mother's puku. You got married. Cue both of us making a series of dark jokes about whether that was the right decision, considering the outcome (my sister, me, a violently broken marriage, estrangement on both sides). We didn't name those things; in fact I remember thinking mainly about how you ended up a single dad and maybe Vietnam, in its own way, might have been easier. Black humour has kept us going all these years: you, me, my sister, our children. The blacker the better. I thought that was just our crazy little fractured family unit, but I met your brother's son for the first time about ten years ago and we immediately started joking about our fathers, and death, and the blacker and weirder it got the more I knew we were true kin.

Anyway, Dad, I wish you got to see more of the world. It's morning now and I've just had breakfast in the skies somewhere above the seas to the west of Mexico. The flight map tells me we're just hitting land, so for the last 11.5 hours we've been flying over the Pacific. That's how vast the Pacific is—endless blue on the map, though the many, many islands don't show up too well on this tiny computer screen. When we left Auckland last night there was one of those extraordinary sunsets where the particular pitch of light turns the mountains in the distance into layers of silhouettes, in a haze rising off the sea. They've done the airport up, so to get to my flight I had to walk for 20 minutes but I had that skyline to look out at. I'd been reading *We Can Make a Life* by Chessie Henry, a memoir about a very different family from ours, and having spoken to you and my sister, and my daughter that morning about some things she feels sad about, that skyline and that book were an undoing. What I haven't mentioned is that to see the horizon I had to look past all the commercial planes lined up like Armageddon's death machines. Beauty and doom in a deep embrace. I don't know if I'll ever be able to see one without the other.

So it's an extraordinary life, Dad. I get to have these amazing experiences, but I don't get to do it with my eyes closed. I don't get to 'go on holiday'. I always have to be seeing. That's what we do I think, writers: we look. That sounds so silly and pretentious, as if writers have better sight than others. It's not that, it's more that we have to—we're compelled to—if we are to do a good job. Human nature is ridiculous and contradictory and paradoxical. You taught me that. Human nature is a great ugly beautiful puzzle that you can work on for days–months–years and only get a corner of it, the rest of the pieces scattered and nonsensical. Don't get me wrong—I like to look away just as much as the next person. I like the illusions we have built for ourselves. We're master storytellers, all of us, and we can make our narrative fit our needs. Even writers must look away at some point so as to preserve our ability to see. Though the more courageous of us watch things that would cause me to put my eyes out.

I'm sorry if any of this takes you by surprise, but I'm not sorry about anything else. I'm glad you're here. I know you wouldn't understand this, why I've written it down, just as I know you wouldn't understand the world I live in, just as, even though I try, I see the world my children live in slipping away from me. So I can't explain it to you, this compulsion. Only that the more I do it the more I must continue: stripping away at layers of artifice and pretence, trying to get at something ineffable and important, something I can't pinpoint even now in this most direct of epistolary notes. So here we are, Dad, somewhere in this book, if you look hard enough, in this series of strange leavings and returns.

2018

How to be a Māori Woman

I went home to my mother's house for the first time when I was 16, and I stayed. I can look back now and see that Dad believed he had done what was best for us by taking us away, and the older I get the less sure I am about the absolute clarity of his wrongness, but back then all I knew was that this whole big thing had been taken from me, not just a relationship with my mother, but a *whānau*. The immensity of my ignorance about my own family was shocking. I simply did not know they existed. Such a huge, warm, substantial group of people had been made to disappear, and my sister, by going in search of them, had made them appear again as if by magic.

All of my wonder at this was concentrated primarily around one person: my nan. I hadn't known I had a grandmother, and such a grandmother! It's impossible to know what you're missing until you find it. Mothers and daughters have things to work through, tensions and questions and desires to find ourselves in each other that can make for complicated relationships. But grandmothers offer us respite from this complexity: straightforward and all-encompassing love, deep and dependable. Wisdom that is sometimes inscrutable but gently offered. Nan had a way.

I didn't get into the art school I had applied for, so I stayed in the Manawatū. It seemed meant to be. I would find out more about who my whānau were, what our culture was, and by extension, who I was. One day I went out with Nan, to the shops or some errands, and she took me up to Massey University. I still remember the first time we climbed the steps to the Registry Building, and someone gave us the pamphlets and introduction booklets for course planning. It was already the week before classes began. I hadn't known that going to university was on the agenda for the day. She must have watched me inspecting the booklets, exclaiming at this or that course. I didn't know who I was but I was a bookish kid, I'm sure she saw that. I remember the little leaps of excitement when particular papers caught my eye, the low buzz underneath it all that said, *yes*. I'd never heard of social anthropology. By the end of the week it was my major.

I signed up for classes: anthro, beginners' te reo Māori, Māori culture, English, museum studies. It seemed meant to be. I wanted to know all about the world, which had so far proven stunningly peculiar and challenging. I didn't know how to be who I was yet. Who does, I think now, but back then I was opening the door to a world I hadn't known existed, and it was supposedly right inside me. I didn't know how to be a Māori woman.

Awe

Palmerston North didn't have much for students in the early 90s apart from a number of well-trodden pubs. There was one curry house, which had gingham tablecloths and sold three kinds of generic curry: chicken, lamb and vegetarian, with peas; a Thai restaurant that sold exquisitely fragrant and spicy meals with beautifully carved vegetable garnishes; a couple of movie theatres and two small malls, plus the usual mid-size New Zealand town staples. But it did have an easy-to-access creative community, small but not bad for a place like Palmy.

And one place I loved to go: the women's bookshop in Square Edge. I don't remember any other store in that old building, but I remember the women's bookshop vividly, right down to the arrangement of the shelves, the velveteen furnishings, the subject labels in a strident feminist hand. I used to sidle in and search through the books on each shelf, meticulously hunting for I'm not sure what: inspiration, clarity, a clue. A clue to identity and womanhood and just how to be in the world, I suppose. I always felt shy of the women who worked there; I felt I was probably not quite the right kind of person to be in this shop and that if they asked me anything I was sure to get it wrong.

There seemed to be a lot of rules about feminism that I was unsure about, and I was constantly trying to get a steady political footing. 'Intersectionality' wasn't a word I knew, but Alice Walker's 'womanism' was a sound that made sense to me, though it never came into wide use. I must have bought most of my collection of Alice's books there, including her essays, and maybe Jeanette Winterson's too. I can't imagine where else I would have bought them. And I know for sure this was the place I found Ngāhuia Te Awekōtuku's 1991 essay collection *Mana Wahine Maori: Selected Writings on Maori Women's Art, Culture and Politics.* I immediately bought and treasured it. Here was a book that addressed so many pressing questions and complexities about the righteous power of being a Māori woman in a social, political and sometimes even cultural environment that didn't recognise that power. Though even when describing the problems and barriers that Māori women face, *Mana Wahine Maori* wasn't about powerlessness. It illuminated the lines between colonial impositions, which had skewed gender relationships within Māori society, and earlier understandings and practices. As she reached into the past and drew out strands, Ngāhuia showed how diverse genders and sexualities—which had been celebrated in Māori society—were undermined, hidden, if not vilified by the warping influence of European colonisation. *Mana Wahine Maori* was the first place I encountered the word 'takatāpui'; I credit it as the text that led me to an enduring appreciation of and identification with archetypal goddesses and ancestral stories; here was a collection of stories about Māori women's lives, and it was like rewena and boil-up to the starving white-skinned post-Pākehā-Māori girl that I was.

Not only did I have no clue how to be Māori at the time, I really had no clue how to be a woman, having not been brought up by one. My ideas about womanhood came directly from television and movies, and—when those proved inadequate, which they often did—from books. On reflection I see that the women I read in my late teens, the ones I remember most, were predominantly lesbian: Alice, Jeanette and Ngāhuia (though also Isabel Allende, and in my early teens Jean M. Auel, not lesbian perhaps but certainly liberal and feminist in their depiction of women and sex). It wasn't a conscious choice. I wasn't searching for non-hetero literature. But now, looking back, I wonder whether there was any commonality in lesbian writing that drew me to it. What was almost conscious, and is certainly evident to me now, was the concentrated study I made of these writers, how I tried to map the many ways of being a woman that they depicted. It was a fantastic education. Their words and characters were liberated, free-thinking, complex, fluid (to the extent that they shape-shifted on occasion), often fighting conventional boundaries to their identities, sexualities and relationships. But their characters were also conventional, flawed, foolish, human. In these books, ancient women's mythologies surfaced and gave characters ways to transgress. Female characters experienced the worst that mankind could perpetrate, and somehow came through the pain and degradation triumphant or, at least, came through it. My immersion in gay literature didn't make me gay, but it did make me intellectually and culturally open-minded and critically equipped. For a long time I didn't realise that my expectations of womanhood were so out of sync with what might have been 'normal' then, or even now. It was the lesbians, I suspect, who gave me this sense of women's power as immense and eternal and quite obvious.

There's something that happens when one aspect of your identity evolves out of the very powerful world of myth and archetype and story rather than family. It's like being created out of sea foam, or red earth and Tāne's breath, or like springing fully formed from Zeus's forehead. Your sense of reality is skewed by those ethereal origins, and you remain unmoved and unimpressed by the fleeting prejudices of human societies, even though you still live in one.

But this is about dear Awe (Ngāhuia's chosen name), who spoke directly into my mind all the things I didn't know about growing up Māori, about living as a Māori woman, about the way things had changed and not changed for Māori through the last part of the 20th century. Not only did she gift the stories, but also the method and methodology; from her I learnt that so many of our origins have been covered by layers of anthropology and scholarship, that we have to keep sorting through the mess until we reconnect with the truths that chime with what we knew from experience, and from talking, and from what we feel in our own places. From her I learnt to trust in the wisdom of the stories and the old people, and to test all dominant beliefs about Māori against our own cultural traditions.

And it was her words I carried with me for years, through everything that followed, her words that became a waka for me to cling to when I found myself in the choppy, dark seas of identity loss and searching:

> The power, the rightness, the sheer joy of being a Maori woman. Of knowing that stretching out on either side of you like a vast, glittering fan of light are women of courage, initiative, healing, terror, and deep, deep knowledge.
>
> Whose adventures crossed mountain ranges and spanned the huge ocean; whose visions knew no bounds.
>
> Whose searching and inventiveness discovered new fibres, new foods, new richness in a strange environment.
>
> Whose very being, in these islands, left breath that fills us all. With the knowing, they were here.
>
> And still are.[1]

Keri

Keri had been there a long time by the time I went to university. She must have been my first exposure to a Māori woman's voice, as far as I could remember. And she enthralled and fascinated me, though I often couldn't quite grasp everything she was saying. I must have been 13 the first time I read *The Bone People*, and the music of it carried me through its twisted passages and spiral stairways. I read it again a year or so later, then again, then again, every year or two getting caught up in the language of it and coming away with something new.

I was shocked afresh with each reading. There was something searing in the book, as if my own childhood miseries were lanced and sealed by the fiery heat of Keri's white-hot prose. I read Alice Walker's *The Color Purple* around the same time, and from these two books I learnt that the vulnerability and powerlessness of the child is no unique thing. That my own experience had not made me exceptional, and for that I was lucky, because there were worse things. Much worse things. That people can love you even as they damage you. I struggled with this, the thing that was for me the central paradox and confusion of *The Bone People*: how could Joe save Simon and then beat him senseless even as he cared for him? Why didn't Kerewin do anything? How could the heroes of the book be so feckless and useless at times? And yet so generous at other times? Maybe that was why I kept coming back, struggling to understand. If I could understand this book, could I not also understand the contradictions in my own life?

And Keri herself was so confusing: somehow intertwined with her heroine yet not, asexual (how could this be a real thing when sexuality seemed such an immense driving force in the world?) and Māori, but fair. Like me. Her words were somehow Māori even when they were not, too. Keri's ability to defy definition was perplexing in a way that made me consider what it was to be different, what it was to be the same, what it was to be an outsider. Who was Keri *inside* with? I wanted to know what it was like to be this woman who was outside the things we were told it was important to be part of. Maybe there were other possibilities.

In writing fiction, I think I'm still learning from *The Bone People*. How much to risk. How far to let the violence go. When to let language carry you somewhere new, somewhere others might not be able to follow. I haven't had the courage to be that brave, to expose my characters' most unattractive traits so honestly, to expose myself so honestly. Still I want to make my reader feel like everything is going to be okay; still I want to create a world which is better than the one I live in. Yet I yearn to take the brakes off. To depict the world in all its brutal beauty. Maybe I don't have the poetry in me. Maybe I do. Such things are certainly uncertain.

Merata

Before I wanted to write books I wanted to write plays, and before I wanted to write plays I wanted to make films. I was brought up in front of screens—television most of the time, but throughout our childhood Dad sent us to the movies. For a couple of years it seemed like we went to the movies almost every week. This was around the time of *E.T.*, and I saw that three times. And Dad would encourage us to watch any New Zealand films or miniseries, sometimes offering little commentaries about how they related to history, or what kinds of cars the characters drove, or who had made it and why.

There were lots of ways we weren't lucky, but how we were lucky was libraries and museums and movies. Despite being anti-establishment, anti-authoritarian, anti-intellectual, cynical, and at his worst, racist, Dad was intellectually engaged with the world. He liked to read nonfiction, go to museums, discuss history and the incomprehensibility of human violence against our own kind. He was a pacifist, a leftie, always for the underdog. That Māori weren't recipients of his compassion might be one of those contradictions that can be observed wherever the white working class feel disenfranchised by the system. I'm not going to pretend to understand it, and it's possible that personal prejudices had taken seed in him during the tumultuous time between falling in love with, and separating from, my mother.

But we weren't a cultured family. A running joke between my sister and me is that culturally, on our father's side, we're white trash. I don't think the sexism ever really took hold. A man can spout rubbish about the uselessness of women, but if he's simultaneously teaching his daughters to be self-sufficient, it doesn't work. Racism is different—race can be minimised, as ours was, and stories of cultural origins can be manipulated. My sister and I were told that we were 1/8th Māori. Blood quantum and the fractionalisation of identity has no social or scientific credibility, but we didn't know that then and this one story changed everything we understood about ourselves. Our Māoriness was only a small fraction of who we were. Mostly, we were made to understand, we were white. Never mind that our mother and two of our grandparents were Māori. I don't know where Dad got the 1/8th figure from. It was a legend told whenever the question was asked: Who were we? *What* were we?

So apparently we were the 'right' race, mostly. And the pretence was that we were middle class, though we kept ourselves at a distance from other middle class and certainly all wealthy people. I can see now it was poverty that kept us at this distance (as well as Dad's alcoholism and paranoia). Back then though, we acted as if we were superior to others, on the outside by choice. Better than.

The most interesting thing about humans, I think, is that almost everything about them is inconsistent. So despite all of the above, and Dad teasing me if I used a word that had more than two syllables, he exposed us to some of the best storytelling our country had to offer, much of it subversive. *Utu. Goodbye Pork Pie. Smash Palace. Mark II. The Quiet Earth.* I saw them all, probably before it was appropriate to do so. I don't remember seeing *Ngati* or *Mauri*. I think they would have just been too Māori for Dad, or too Māori for mainstream television and not set comfortably in the past, at a distance, like *Utu*. But I do remember discussions about the Springbok Tour—who was right and who was wrong and how awful apartheid was for those Black people over there in South Africa; they had it much worse than the Maoris, eh? And my sense was that even though Dad liked his rugby, he didn't think the tour should have gone ahead. He delivered a number of anti-Nazi lectures too. He liked to read about the War and try to figure out how the Holocaust could possibly have happened. And he was interested in African American civil rights. Shows like *Roots* were my early exposure to the history of slavery. It's strange how assessments of historical prejudice can be appreciated—but also cohabit comfortably with local, present-day racism.

This is meant to be about Merata, and this is not the way I thought I would begin, but perhaps this convoluted detour is important, because what I want to talk about is representation, and how much it matters. I don't think we really have a clue how much. It seems like an extraordinary mishap, some glitch in the system, that despite all the negative, anti-intellectual, anti-Māori messages I received as a child, I became a feminist, 'intellectual' Māori, identities I chose as a teenager as an antidote to the patriarchal inheritance I had been offered. I somehow received alternative messages. These messages came through those screens as much as, if not more than, they came through books. And while Merata may not have been at the forefront of many of those films apart from *Utu,* she was there exerting pressure in the background, always. She was actively changing the culture, and the isolated Pākehā-identifying-Māori girl I was heard her.

I don't know what other kids were doing in high school but

I was watching several films a week, especially independent cinema if I could find it. In my sixth-form year I worked in a video store, in seventh form Charley Gray's cinema, and somewhere around that time I watched *Mauri*. I had, by then, met my mother again. I understood little of what I had missed throughout my childhood, but I had a visceral sense of a whole way of life existing in Aotearoa that was largely invisible to Pākehā people. The customs were different, the expectations were different, the warmth was different, the weight of history was different. I would find words for all this later. *Mauri* showed me what it looked like, how it felt. Merata's images took me closer to a world that belonged to me, but that I had only just discovered in my late teens.

Merata's work stayed with me; she seemed significant. It was some time before I found a way to view *Patu!*, but when I did see it, despite having read all about it, I was shocked to my core. Dad had been right about the police. A healthy disrespect for authority was reinforced right there. Of all the strange contradictions in this story, and in my upbringing, the confluence of Dad's anti-establishment, anti-authority leanings and the activism brilliantly and forcefully revealed in films like *Patu!* astonishes me: he was so often much closer to those he held prejudices against than he would ever admit.

Merata was significant because she was a Māori woman who made films, and that was what I wanted to be. Not only did I learn about the Māori world from her films, I learnt about being a Māori woman from her fearless and fierce approach to her work. I read about her, watched documentaries about her, and aspired to be like her. When she disappeared from the New Zealand scene (probably around the same time I did), I missed her. I had given away my film-making dream by then, but I had already internalised her stories and the way she told them.

At the 2018 New Zealand International Film Festival, we went to see *Merata: How Mum Decolonised the Screen* at the Embassy Theatre alongside every other Māori person working in film, theatre, writing or art, plus quite a few non-Māori in those fields, and the rest of Wellington too. I didn't expect to get stage fright walking into the packed cinema, but it was somehow confronting because everywhere I looked were people I admired and people I knew through creative work. Predictably, late in the film, I cried. As much for Merata's children as for my hero. Most of us hadn't known their stories of course, or what Merata and her family went through to make her work. And as her son, filmmaker Heperi Mita, said during his kōrero, one of the hardest things was knowing that *Mauri* was still the only film directed by an individual Māori woman. But there we were, all of us in that theatre and in other theatres around the country, people who had been influenced by her in small ways and large, Merata's people.

Makereti

And so here was Nan, leaving me at the steps to the university, watching me walk up. She had gone to teachers college with her sister as a young woman. That must have been in the 1940s. Then there's a space in my knowledge, but she soon met my koro and had lots of children and a fish and chip shop that everyone in Feilding over a certain age remembers. There was the marae and community work, always, more and more as time went on. And many, many mokopuna. And we were taken away, and koro died. So many losses, all her life; I can't imagine it. She had been whāngaied at three years old, after her own mother and kuia died. So many losses I can't write of them here in any detail. She worked so hard, put her shoulder against all those things, and kept going. Made sure everyone was looked after, even though that was sometimes taken out of her hands.

I wonder what it was like for her to see us come back. To see one of her daughter's wounds heal over at last. A scar doesn't hurt as much as an open wound. She led me to all these other Māori women and she taught me her own quiet lessons about how to be her granddaughter. At our first Christmas together, I watched her assemble a Christmas cake without a recipe. In my memory she did this completely by hand, scooping handfuls of flour and sugar and dried fruit. Maybe she spooned in the baking powder. Maybe she actually used a cup for the scooping, but my impression was that of a familiar dance, no written instructions, no strict measurements. I remember the continual flow of food between her kitchen and table: as soon as we'd eaten one meal, another began to materialise. These lessons were presented without commentary. This was just what you did.

As far as I could tell, women were in charge of the domestic sphere and the pā. Need heavy lifting or other errands? Ask an uncle, brother, cousin or son. I'd never seen women in such possession of their power. Women were the overseers of what needed to be done, when and how, and Nan was at the top of that hierarchy. I'd always done everything myself and found it hard to ask for help when I needed it. To command assistance as she did.

Other lessons also failed to take. One summer when we were staying at our marae at Lake Taupō, Nan went to the harakeke bush to cut long sheaths of flax for weaving. She set up in a far corner of the wharekai, a wonderful old building with a vast fireplace that always had a fire going for kai and hot water. If you leaned in beside the heavy cast iron pots, you could see the sky through the wide opening that let the smoke out. That fireplace made it into my first novel. Anyway, Nan was on the other side, far away from the cooking area. And there, in what seemed like less than a morning, she constructed a neat kete, folding the leaves in expertly, trimming and fastening. Again without pattern or paper or pause. I would not have enough time with Nan to learn the magic habits of her hands. Years later, at the first weaving hui I attended, I attempted to weave a whāriki. That's not the best way to begin. A kete or even a flax flower might have been more successful, but this was a whāriki wānanga, so I tried to follow along. On seeing my efforts, one of the expert weavers exclaimed, 'But your grandmother was such an amazing weaver!' and walked on, puzzlement still evident on her face.

I knew some reo Māori after a year or two at university, and I tried to write letters and cards to Nan. Sometimes she would correct me. My mother's generation had not been allowed the reo, so it had become the language in which old women gossiped and discussed things that weren't for children's ears, as well as the language of ceremony. Our reo had been used against my mother's generation in so many ways, but it was coming back to my generation, though I was not a good student of it. I was more interested in politics and culture and the business of helping our people. And boys. When I made an inappropriate liaison that my mother was very much against, Nan asked me why. I can't remember what I said, but I knew I wasn't in love with the boy. She listened quietly, nodded. 'Do what you need to do to get it out of your system,' she told me. She was so frank and practical that I knew right then it wouldn't last much longer. The only other advice she gave me about the opposite sex was to make sure I found a man who was my equal, who was as smart as I was.

Nan took me to important meetings from time to time, and I felt the expectations that might accompany the education I was getting, and I felt shame at all the things I could not fix. She was lighting a long-burning flame that would rise against all the many things she had seen, the ones that stayed the same and the ones that changed for the worse. Eventually, Nan got to see me graduate, and even though I still felt like I was only at the very beginning of things, I hope it gave her some joy.

A few months after that, we were at a hui. As usual, Nan was busy ensuring everything was taken care of: the pae, the kitchen, the whare, the manuhiri. I had been working in Wellington and hadn't seen her for a while. I went to her for the warm embrace I knew she would give, the awhi that I had become accustomed to seeking from her. She didn't respond. I hugged her, but she wasn't there, not like usual. And I wondered if she was okay, if she was annoyed with me perhaps, or too tired, or sick. It wasn't long after that that the news came: a different day, a different hui; she had come home from the marae for a little break, fallen asleep in her chair, and never woken. Her heart. She was 63 years old. I had known her for four years.

I have three Christian names: my sister says she named me Tina after her doll, but my father always claimed my name came from those kitsch J.H. Lynch 1970s 'Tina' paintings. My second name comes from a dear aunt—my father's sister, Robyn—and my third name was my nan's, Makereti. When I began to write, I thought about what name I should publish under and I thought about all those Māori women, the ones whose words I loved to read, and the ones who had gone before me, multiple lines stretching back to the beginning of time, rivers of them, oceans perhaps, of which I was one small tributary. I thought about my nan and how I carried her name already, even though it was a transliteration of an English name. Even in that, there is a story. Her name reminds me of who I am. Her name reminds me when to be careful, and when to take risks. Her name keeps me safe. Her name is dignity and generosity and kaha. It is something to live up to.

1981–1994

He Whare Tuhinga

~

Stories Can Save Your Life

Poutokomanawa—the Heartpost

University of Auckland Free Public Lecture
Auckland Writers Festival 2017[1]

I want to begin by acknowledging Tāmakimakaurau, who I have a history with. I lived in Auckland for five years while I was a teenager. When I lived here, I think I was like many Aucklanders. I didn't know who I was or where I came from. I knew nothing of my whakapapa. I knew nothing of half my family. Nothing at all. And though I didn't know what I didn't know, I felt haunted by that loss. I was as awkward and lost and damaged as a person can be in that situation. But I could write, even though I forgot it for a while, and I did write, and creativity kept me alive.

I tell you this now because I want you to know I do not come from privilege, even of the cultural kind. I come from not knowing, and that is how I know how important this kaupapa is. Stories can save your life.

If I could do anything in the world it would be to sit in the corner and read and write books. I would happily lose myself in stories for the rest of my life. I never planned to find myself a podium and talk on it. But here I am because when I started writing seriously I looked around me and I was startled by what I saw, and I knew we were missing something vital, and I wondered how it was we had gotten ourselves into this position.

And I'm not very good at ignoring problems. But I don't want to start there, with the problems.

I want to share with you a vision: I want you to imagine a whare tūpuna or wharenui, perhaps like this one at the University of Auckland's Waipapa Marae, Tāne-nui-a-Rangi. Because this is the University of Auckland Public Lecture, I thought Tāne-nui-a-Rangi could be the inspiration for this imagining.

A wharenui, as we know, is a house that represents the body of an ancestor, and contains within it the whole whakapapa of its people, reaching back through generations and migrations and aeons until it touches the cosmology and origins of all things. The whakairo, or carvings, along the walls and on the front of the wharenui represent ancestors and ancestral stories. The tukutuku and kōwhaiwhai often represent our connections to the natural world and each other, all through the same mechanism of whakapapa. When we go into a wharenui, we go into the belly of the ancestor, and when we engage in pōwhiri and hui and tangi, we re-enact those connections that are depicted all around us in wood and fibre and paint.

That's a generalised description. Wharenui are as diverse as their makers and their people, and there are many variations on which elements appear and in which order. It's safe to say, however, that all wharenui embody principles of connection and narrative—they tell our stories and by doing so they show us who we are and what is important to us. Patricia Grace writes about wharenui often in her novels and stories—*Potiki* is of course the most famous example of this. In her writing, Patricia often manages to encapsulate principles that are central to a Māori world view:

> We could not afford books so we made our own. In this way we were able to find ourselves in books. It is rare for us to find ourselves in books, but in our own books we were able to find and define our lives.
>
> But our main book was the wharenui, which is itself a story, a history, a gallery, a study, a design structure and a taonga. And we are part of that book along with the family past and the family yet to come.[2]

Take those words in—think on them a bit. They are at the heart of everything I want to talk about today.

I began by asking you to imagine a wharenui, and by showing you a picture of Tāne-nui-a-Rangi to aid that imagining. Now, imagine that the wharenui you are thinking of is the House of the Literatures of Aotearoa. As I mentioned, every house is the body of an ancestor, but Tāne-nui-a-Rangi embodies an atua—'god' is the closest word we have in English—and he was chosen so that the University of

Auckland's Waipapa Marae could welcome and absorb and connect all the different tribes and peoples and histories of Aotearoa. Our whare is kind of like that. It's a kaupapa whare; it's a whare that must welcome and absorb and connect all the literatures and writers and readers of Aotearoa. It's a whare for all of us.

Imagine it. The swirling, spiralling, notched lines of poetry; the strong limbs and bright eyes of fiction; various nonfictions in repeating patterns overhead. Imagine the sumptuous kōrero that takes place in this whare late into the night, the breaking away for Aotearoa's most delicious kai, shipped in from all regions, the coming together for waiata of the most melodious varieties, the drums of the Pacific like

Interior of Te Whai-a-te-Motu meeting house, showing dressed poutokomanawa at centre. Mataatua, c. 1910.

heartbeats behind our songs.

Imagine the laughter.

Imagine the tears.

And oh, metaphors to make your knees weak. We'd bring the forests in through the doors, and make the wars and warriors stay out on the marae ātea until they're ready to calm down. *Are you ready to talk about it?* we'd ask, and when they were they'd duck under the doorway, beneath Hinenuitepō's widespread thighs, and find themselves born into the belly of peace. The politicians would shuffle in too, and bear our teasing in a puzzled, proud, but generally good-natured fashion, until someone decides to speak their mind a little too loudly. Mostly it's a house for the people, for anyone and everyone to bring their stories and their songs and their children. We already know that in times of crisis—earthquake or flood or poverty—the wharenui is the place we go for solace, to warm our bellies and our souls.

Our house needs carvings.

In most wharenui, carved poupou depicting ancestors line the sides and back walls, and heke or rafters depicting kōwhaiwhai spread down from the tāhuhu or ridgepole, with poutokomanawa centre front.

It takes decades of planning to get to this point, and for our house all the greatest minds of literature have come together with our artists and designers to ensure all of the ancestors of the Literatures of Aotearoa are represented. The method is whakapapa, so ancestors who connect and represent different literatures must be chosen carefully. Each poupou along the walls represents a different literary forebear. Whare usually only depict those who have passed on, hence we cannot name any illustrious living New Zealand writers. Please add your own names to this list. After all, such a venture is not an individual endeavour. Who might we see? Apirana Ngata, J.C. Sturm (Te Kare Papuni), Kāterina Te Heikōkō Mataira, Hone Tūwhare, Arapera Blank, Rowley Habib might be a good start.

Perhaps they would face Katherine Mansfield, Frank Sargeson, Janet Frame, Margaret Mahy, Michael King, Ngaio Marsh, Robin Hyde.

And here we meet the limits of my own ignorance, for the list of storytellers from the wider Pacific must be vast, and we would invite them all into our whare, that their people might know them. Let's simply start with Epeli Hau'ofa, Alistair Te Ariki Campbell, and the beautiful, indomitable Teresia Teaiwa.

We'd have our other migrant storytellers too, including the Chinese ancestors who came to Aotearoa as early as many of our Pākehā forebears. And this is a harder story to tell, because if you can name a New Zealand Asian ancestor writer then I would love to hear of it. Some very kind people in our Chinese writing community answered my queries about this. I heard about a rich tradition of literature that didn't survive those early crossings across the vast Pacific, at least not in visible or material ways. I heard about the need and desire to work hard, and fit in, and make a life for the next generations. From this distance in time and perspective, it may seem like their presence was mainly silent, but they were certainly there, the poets and storytellers.

I would give you two names: the first, Chiu Kwok-chun, who used the pseudonym Ping Ming, from the Chinese proverb 'Bu ping ze ming' (meaning: 'On witnessing injustice one should cry out'). He founded and edited a New Zealand Kuomintang newspaper, the *Man Sing Times*. He also wrote, edited and helped to publish its Wellington branch newsletter, which appeared throughout the war. The second—who is Alison Wong's paternal grandfather—carried the extraordinary name True Light, also known as James Wong. He wrote Chinese poetry to exchange with others in New Zealand. Apparently, back in the day the Chinese Consulate in Wellington held Chinese literary classes. None of True Light's poetry has survived.

There are so many stories to unearth.

The committee would have thought long and hard about how to represent all our literatures:

There would be tohunga whakairo, who have always told our stories through the medium of wood

Tohunga raranga, who keep our stories through fibre patterns

Tohunga moko and tufuga ta tatau, who carve our stories into skin

The makers of tivaevae and tapa

The keepers of the dance, whether haka or siva

The kaiwaiata or songwriters

The keepers of whakapapa, and of oratory, the kaikaranga whose voices are the first heard in any marae in the country

The contemporary visual artists

Let's not forget the atua of our stories: Hinenuitepō, Tāne and his baskets of knowledge, Māui and Tawhaki, Nafanua and Tagaloa

It would be a very full whare.

I can't tell you all the names of the tūpuna who would be depicted in this particular house—that's more than one person can imagine; it would take all the keepers of cultural knowledges and practices to come together and decide. We'd make space for all our peoples in our whare, because we want it to be vibrant, and diverse, and represent all that we are, all of the stories of Aotearoa.

And once we'd decided all that, we'd go to the heartpost, the poutokomanawa, which sits at the centre of the whare, and must be someone who connects all these people and all these literatures. Maybe our poutokomanawa will have many figures, and through this we will show the origins of all our stories. Again, Patricia Grace gives us ways of understanding the significance of the heartpost. This, from 'Love Story' in *Small Holes in the Silence*:

> A poutokomanawa, besides being a piece of art, has an important and serious function. It connects earth and sky—or in other words it holds up the roof in an ancestral meeting house, and as well as that, it sits plonk in the middle of the house. It's the heart of the house, and that's serious. It's also deep and serious in meaning because it depicts fame and ancestry—all round serious.
>
> Some poutokomanawa are adorned with many ancestral figures climbing from floor to apex, but not this one. This one depicts a single figure at the bottom of the pole. She is carved in a much more lifelike style than what carvers often use, and in this she differs from the other carvings lining up along the walls of the house.[3]

The heart of our house is central to our kaupapa, central to showing who we are and welcoming people into our whare. I invite you to think about who might be the appropriate person or persons for that position. Or at least what the origins of those people might be, for we all have multiple origins.

What I want all of us to take away from this imagining,

most of all, is how magnificent our house is. Even in its potential state. This house is different from other wharenui, so maybe it has a bit of fale Pasifika in it, or maybe, like Kōpinga Marae on Rēkohu, it has a different shape and a different look altogether. We might ask our tohunga toi to help us with that. Imagine it. Our wharenui pūrakau is something to behold. People come from all over the world to see it, and to go inside to hear our stories.

But when I first thought about this, I realised, actually, that what our House of New Zealand Literature probably looks like now is more a colonial villa in Mt Eden or Kelburn than a wharenui. Or perhaps a little weatherboard house on a quarter-acre section, although that image might belong fifty years in the past. And then I thought no, what I imagine our current House of Literature looks like, is a new architecturally designed home in a pretty place like Oriental Bay or Devonport. It's a beautiful house, with a beautiful collection on its walls. When you walk the halls you might get a glimpse of some really iconic Māori or Pasifika art. Oh the dinner parties! Oh the wine and cheese evenings! Don't let my tone be misleading. I love some good wine and cheese. It's a beautiful house.

But few people can afford to live in it. Only the select few gain access to its exclusive parties.

Remember that wharenui? People go there in flood and famine and fire. It is home to all comers.

Perhaps we need to begin again. Perhaps radical renovations are needed. Let's build our wharenui on the same ground as our current House of Literature. But let's go back to the drawing board.

Why do we even need to do that? I want to talk about why these radical renovations are necessary. But first, let us ask:

why are we considering creative texts primarily?

Think about what creative texts do that the other texts don't do.

They ask us to imagine. They ask us to dream. They ask us to think about human interaction and motivation and desire. They ask us to consider the paradoxical nature of human beings, cultures and societies. They ask questions that can only be answered by novels or stories or poems. They embody Te Kore, the place of pure potentiality, what Albert Wendt called 'the Void' in his iconic essay 'Towards a New Oceania'.

As he says:

> So vast, so fabulously varied a scatter of islands, nations, cultures, mythologies and myths, so dazzling a creature, Oceania deserves more than an attempt at mundane fact; only the imagination in free flight can hope—if not to contain her—to grasp some of her shape, plumage, and pain.[4]

Without our journeys into the void, how can we know what our potential is? How can we know ourselves, and consider the issues that face us in all their terrible detail, and creatively engage with the possibilities that present themselves?

We can't. But we keep going to economic and political solutions as if they will solve the problems that flung us into the void in the first place. We need creativity. To remember who we are. To imagine who we might be. To create our worlds afresh. To save us.

When I began my PhD research in creative writing, I was shocked by the lack of scholarship on Māori literatures. Despite thinking I was an informed reader, until that point I hadn't really understood that there was such a big problem around lack of Māori representation in New Zealand literature, and this is how I knew that the majority of readers probably weren't aware of it either. So I started to do some counting.

Using the *Journal of Commonwealth Literature*'s yearly census of New Zealand literature, I calculated that in the three years beginning 2007, Māori fiction in English made up 6 per cent, 1.6 per cent and 4 per cent of New Zealand fiction respectively. This, given the Māori population of New Zealand at the time of writing was at least 15 per cent. In some years, Pacific, Asian and other cultures of New Zealand barely feature in our literature at all.[5]

A few years ago, Janis Freegard, a writer whose most recent book is the acclaimed *The Year of Falling*, began looking at these same statistics for later years. Janis started by looking at gender, particularly in poetry, and in doing so noticed that 'only one . . . was written by a Māori poet, two written by Pasifika poets and none by Asian poets'.

She has been collecting the stats each year since, with revealing results. I'm grateful to Janis for doing this work, and for agreeing to my request to discuss it here.

Bear in mind that, according to the 2013 New Zealand census, Pākehā made up 74 per cent of the population, Māori 15 per cent, Asian 12, Pacific 7, and Middle Eastern/Latin American/African 1 per cent.

Fiction titles by gender and ethnicity, 2014
Women: 39 Pākehā, 2 Māori, 3 Asian
Men: 27 Pākehā, 3 Māori, 1 Asian

Poetry titles by ethnicity, 2015
European/Pākehā: 91 percent
Māori: 3 per cent

Pasifika: 3 per cent
European/Jewish: 3 per cent

Fiction titles by ethnicity, 2015
European/Pākehā (68 titles, or 91 percent)
Māori (3 titles; 4 percent)
Asian (3; 4 percent)
Pasifika (1; 1 percent)

Nonfiction titles by ethnicity, 2015
European/Pākehā (18 titles, or 85 percent)
Māori (1; 5 percent)
Pasifika (1; 5 percent)
European/Jewish (1; 5 percent)

Fiction, nonfiction and poetry titles by ethnicity, 2015
European/Pākehā (151 titles, or 90 percent)
Māori (6; 4 percent)
Pasifika (4; 2 percent)
Asian (3; 2 percent)
European/Jewish (3; 2 percent)

Janis, who is a Pākehā New Zealander born overseas, writes: 'Fairness matters. Having a national literature that represents our national population matters. Being able to read a diverse range of voices matters.'

I once discussed these questions with someone who then asked me if there wasn't enough Māori and Pasifika publishing because there wasn't enough talent. You know that's still something people will ask. But in my experience, the opposite is true. In an essay in *The Fuse Box: Essays on Writing from the International Institute of Modern Letters* (2017), I put it this way:

> In a class of young, middle-class+ Pākehā students (i.e. the majority of university classes) there are many clever, witty, talented, politically astute and very pleasant people. Some of them are beautiful writers. Educationally, they have always been surrounded by writers, theorists and educationalists with the same socio-cultural capital as them. Few of them have stories to tell. Yet.
>
> In a class of Māori / Pasifika / immigrant students (not so many middle class, not so many young) there are many clever, witty, talented, politically astute and very pleasant people. Some of them are beautiful writers. Few of them have ever had the opportunity to read writing from their own communities. Few of them have ever had the opportunity to write from or about their own communities. Yet, I struggle to remember a single one that didn't have a compelling story to tell.[6]

In 2014, I convened the first Māori and Pasifika creative writing course at Te Herenga Waka—Victoria University and my undergraduates would tell me, year after year, that they came because the course was designed for them and there was a Māori teacher. Perhaps they felt there was a greater chance that their stories would be safe in that room, that someone would understand where they were coming from without them having to explain. The majority cannot know the fatigue of having to explain your world view over and over, even before you get to do anything productive. Then the fatigue from knowing that your explanations can never quite breach the gap where experience sits. And behind all of that, the deep, intergenerational trauma. Some of us wear it lightly and some of us protect ourselves from the world because of it, even at the cost of our own progression.

Imagine coming into a room where no explanations are needed. Where everyone is grappling with the same questions as you. Where finally you can open the door to that quiet knocking that's been going on in the background of your life for years. That is what a space for Māori and Pacific creative writing and literature does.

One final word about literary representation. You know, we signed a treaty, and that treaty is complex, but I'm going to boil it down to a simple interpretation. Te Tiriti said, you may come and share this place with us, but please keep your people in line and protect that which is precious to us. We'll keep being who we are, and you keep being who you are and we'll share this whenua, okay? But that didn't happen, of course. The protection did not happen, nor the respect, nor even the sharing. That bit about being who we are is called tino rangatiratanga in te Tiriti itself, but how do we get tino rangatiratanga when our stories barely feature in the literature of our nation? How do we know ourselves? How do we show others who we are? If we wanted to honour te Tiriti in any way, we'd be talking about going way past representation to ensure we get things back in balance.

In a bicultural nation, at the very least you would expect to see Māori literature considered as a distinct field alongside New Zealand Pākehā literature. We walk hand in hand towards whatever future awaits us, and I can tell you, and you already know, that we are failing one half of that equation.

One thing people fundamentally misunderstand about biculturalism is whether it includes other cultural groups. Of course it does, but we have to get that first relationship right so that other cultures have a place to stand too. Everyone who ever went to a pōwhiri will understand that the process makes the visitor family. It's all about establishing welcome and connection. In a truly bicultural nation, all other migrant cultures are welcomed into the whānau. Opening our nation to a truly bicultural process allows that to happen, because at the heart of everything Māori do is whakapapa, which is just another way to say relationship and connection, which brings us back to our whare.

Maybe we can't yet build an entirely new house, but let us start by carving a poutokomanawa that will sit at the centre of our imagined wharenui. There is an orphaned poutokomanawa at the British Museum. He is likely from Ngāti Kahungunu, Central Hawke's Bay, early 19th century. The notes at the museum say only that he is a 'Carved Male Figure' made by 'Māori'. This poutokomanawa, to me, represents so much that is lost to us. The heartpost to our house, alienated from us by Empire. Let us reclaim our poutokomanawa, set it strong and tall in the centre of our house to connect earth and sky, to hold up the tāhuhu and rafters, with all our genealogies and ancestors and living people gathered within. Let us honour it and keep it warm so that it might sustain us as we strive to create ourselves anew.

I want you to think about what you would like to see at the heart of your national literature. I know that my literary poutokomanawa begins deep in the lands and seas of Aotearoa, where the stories of this country began, aeons ago, and that even then our whakapapa connected us to the entire Pacific. I know that eventually our stories became inextricably linked with another culture from far away, and then more. I know that what makes us strong is *this* story, not one of an inherited English literature, but one of the extraordinary mix of language and narrative and metaphor that could only take root in this one place on earth. So I ask you: what might happen if we were to place this understanding at the heart of everything we do? That is the wero—the challenge—before us.

First published on *E-Tangata* and
Academy of New Zealand Literature (2017)

Spinner

It is the summer of my 15th birthday when Dad has the party. It's still the start of summer, the end of the school year, and even though it's mostly old people at this party, I'm glad to have free access to the booze. Usually I have a friend with me, but this night I don't, which is a relief really, considering what comes next. I don't know if I have any friends left at this point anyway, given the way the year has gone. There have been a number of poorly judged friendships and relationships from which I emerged as lonely and lost as ever. Too many cigarettes smoked and too many awkward experiments with bogan teenage rebellion. As usual, I don't think I've fooled anyone into thinking I have anything together or am cool in any way, which, embarrassingly, is probably all I want in life. I haven't learnt to embrace my inner weirdo yet. Or her outward manifestations.

I'm in the kitchen leaning against the long Formica bench where all the drinks are lined up. Dad used to take me to the pub and give me 'ladies' drinks' like Pimms and shandy, but I don't think he bothers policing what I'm drinking anymore. I'm in a conversation with Dad's best mate, who is ten or so years younger than him and not as gross as all the other middle-agers in the room. He always has an attractive girlfriend too. This memory is 30-something years old, so I don't know how we get to this exact moment. It's just suspended there, this one conversation and what comes after. We're talking about the nature of women's orgasms, and he has it wrong.

'That's not how it works,' I hear myself saying. I'm searching his face for some sign that he's taking the piss, that he has some ulterior motive. I might not be any good at dealing with kids my own age, but I have impeccable instincts when it comes to adults.

'But I thought when the guy shoots his load, you know, the woman is done too.' He seems genuinely puzzled, if slightly amused.

'Nah—it's different for her.' I've never actually *had* an orgasm, but I've read the collected works of Jean M. Auel and Alice Walker. Those books are *educational*.

'Really? I always thought that when it happens for him, it happens at the same time for her.' He pauses. It's impossible to have this conversation without imagining him banging away at his current girlfriend, and her efforts to look completely satisfied when he finishes. How could it be that none of them have told him?

'How does it happen for the woman then?' he asks.

This is the big question. I'm not sure how to explain. It's one thing to point out how it doesn't happen, quite another to get into the intricacies of how it does. Anatomical words will need to be used. If I'm wrong, and if there is some other motive at play in this conversation, it could all get very uncomfortable very quickly. I'm not entirely sure why it has been comfortable to this point. People seem to be treating me like an adult. I've been told I look like one.

But suddenly I don't have to explain. Suddenly Dad is there, yelling.

'What are you talking to my daughter about? I invite you into my home and you talk to my daughter like this?'

'It's okay. She's not worried about it.'

'I'm worried about it.'

'It's not a big deal.'

At this point, Dad becomes enraged. *Of course it's a big deal.*

I don't understand the fuss. Nobody else understands the fuss. I've spent much of the last year being dragged to pubs and house parties by my father (better than leaving me home alone), surrounded by middle-aged men and their women. I've seen more than a few drunken liaisons that I wish I hadn't been privy to. But this is my dad. Some line, known only to him, has been crossed.

'Mate, I didn't mean anything by it.'

'How dare you talk to my daughter like that! How dare you!'

People try to get Dad to calm down. But this makes things worse. *Everybody get out.* A punch or two is thrown and dodged. There is pushing. People are shaking their heads.

'Mate, you're crazy.'

'Out,' he yells. 'Get out, the lot of you!'

People head towards the door. Some of them are still trying to calm him down. Maybe someone asks if I'm okay. I give them a noncommital affirmative; what are they going to do if I'm not?

Dad goes to see the stragglers off. The party's over. Friendship too.

I retreat to the lounge. On Saturday mornings I come into this lounge and watch reruns of *The Addams Family* and the original *Star Trek*. There's a massive 1970s rock-wall fireplace in here, two old lounge chairs beside it. Other than this, the house is mainly empty of furniture. I sleep on a mattress on the floor. It's our third or fourth place this year, since my big sister left home. Soon it will be my birthday, the day before

New Year's Eve 1988, and the following night, while getting a ride to a party, Dad will be so drunk he'll try to exit the car while it's speeding along the motorway. When we get to the party and discover how dire it is, we will both want to go home and he will insist on taking someone's car to get there. Afraid his drunk driving will kill me, I will refuse to get into the car with him, the first time I've ever done such a thing. It's not the first or the last time I will fear his drunkenness or his driving, but after a screaming row that raises the neighbourhood, we'll walk the two or more hours home just before the first dawn of 1989, exhausted but alive. In a couple of months we'll leave this house. Dad will leave town and I will stay to finish high school, boarding privately. That bleak New Year's will also be the night that saves me, since it will be the moment we both realise that it can't go on, and Dad will eventually give me the gift of his departure and my independence.

But right now I am by the fireplace and the world is spinning. I close my eyes to enjoy the sensation. Things have gone quiet. Dad comes and sits across from me, by the fireplace.

'You okay?' he asks.

'Everything's spinning,' I say.

'Yeah, that happens sometimes,' he says. I can tell from his voice that I'm not in trouble. The fight has gone out of him, and now he sounds gentle. He leans back, mirroring my pose.

'You gonna puke?'

'No—I don't think so.'

And we sit in companionable silence for a long time, the world spinning in bliss or madness, I don't know what.

1988

The Story that Matters

Beautiful writing alone is not enough. Not now.
Look around you.

> Maxine Beneba Clarke, @slamup, 2017, Melbourne

kaupapa

In creative writing classes, we often ask the question: What's at stake? What we are asking is why the reader should invest time and emotional energy in reading a particular piece of writing. Why does it matter? Why should we care? We usually mean what is at stake for the characters in a story or the speaker in a poem emotionally or intellectually, ethically or spiritually, rather than what is at stake for the world in a greater sense.

Kaupapa is a word that can encompass both purpose and the concept of a manifesto. It's worth thinking about. What are you here for? What graces brought you here? What will you leave behind? I'm not suggesting that we must develop a manifesto, but perhaps we should think about the wider purpose of what we write.

Still, we can't force our work to have a greater purpose than finding out what's at stake for this or that character, or figuring out the mechanics of that one story, the kaupapa at the heart of this particular piece of writing. Creativity doesn't work that way. And yet for many, having a greater purpose is the only way to develop creativity. How do I manage to invest time in my creative work when there are so many other (more lucrative or personally important) calls for my creative energy? Perhaps the closest thing I personally have to a kaupapa is the belief that because I have been given a voice (meaning, the genealogical, historical, cultural and creative capital to have stories to tell; the ability to write; the power to publish and speak publicly), I have an obligation to use it. And then, given the great soup of things there are to write about, certain stories will always rise to the top of my pot: the urgent, untold, underrepresented; the stories that make us look again at what we thought we knew about ourselves, our history and our cultures. Stories that shake us. I don't know if I have achieved it yet, but I do agree that the tell-tale sign of a good story is one that stays with us long after we have finished reading—a story that destabilises us at the core just long enough for us to see the world afresh. There's nothing unusual about this.

on beauty

Sometimes I try to write one of those cool kinds of essays in which the writer makes no apparent argument. I always fail. I'm always making arguments. I used to think life was too short and desperate and filled with urgency not to be making passionate arguments. But I also used to think I didn't have time for beauty without purpose. Now I'm not so sure. Take your beauty where you can get it.

Fortunately, the short, desperate urgency of life is beautiful.

show up

I've come to think of writing, most days, as a matter of faith. Show up and stuff will happen. If we're doing it right, most days we're not going to know what's going to happen. The best things happen without our plans. Even though I would like it to be doing something different, something more artful and less bossy, this essay is saying, write with purpose. But it can't be forced. It won't be forced. Ideas and philosophies and politics don't make good stories, they make good research. Then we have to stand back and let story lead us. If there is purpose in our thoughts, our research, our conversations, our general perception of life, story will out us. What really matters to us will come through when we write; it will come through our stories; it will arrive in the imagery of our poems.

on discomfort

It was my lunch break, and I was browsing the New Zealand books table at Unity Books. I noticed her before she noticed me, and I tapped her on the shoulder. We laughed and embraced, caught up a little. I hadn't expected to see her there. It was one of those moments that seems strangely serendipitous: I rarely have time in a lunch break to head to the bookstore, and she is rarely in the city. This was someone I have a great deal of fondness and respect for, but around whom I always feel inadequacy and slight discomfort. She had been a key participant in the research for my book *Where the Rēkohu Bone Sings*, and I therefore feel as if I owe her a debt I can never repay.

After we chatted for a while, that day in Unity Books, my friend invited me upstairs to where an important meeting was being conducted. They were having lunch, and I should come and say hello, she said. The meeting involved leaders of te imi Moriori, and government representatives, researchers and lawyers; imi/iwi–government meetings of this kind happen regularly all over the country, but particularly in Wellington. I was happy to reconnect with other hūnau or wider family, and meet some I didn't know, but as each new person was introduced, and my book and I were introduced to them with much generosity, my discomfort was beside me, like a badly behaved dog who couldn't sit still. To each of these new people, as well as the ones I already knew, I felt such a weight of responsibility. I had written a story that was more theirs than mine. I could only hope that I did it well enough. I had created what I consider to be a lifelong obligation.

But signs were positive. At one point, they described my book to officials and other participants at the meeting as a way of getting closer to their history, and understanding what life had been like for their people, and the kinds of experiences that are very common for them. This was the main reason I had wanted to write it, so it was quite something to see that happen. If my discomfort actually was a dog, he would have rolled on his back at this point, paws in the air, and waited to have his tummy scratched. But he wouldn't have left. Everyone joked that they would go downstairs and immediately purchase the remaining copies at Unity, and wasn't it convenient that the bookshop was down there? *Yes*, I laughed, cringing inwardly and outwardly that this wasn't something I could just give them freely. My discomfort stayed with me to the very end, while people offered me much warmth and lunch, and I said *no-thank-you-I-must-get-back-to-work*, and we embraced and promised to meet again soon.

I don't expect the discomfort to ever go away. And this

dog has at least four legs: the discomfort I've described above, the personal discomfort of any lingering dissatisfaction with the work itself, the perpetual discomfort of having a fairly public occupation, and the slightly different discomfort I feel around my other relations for shining light on dark history.

When the book was published, I had several options. One, commonly employed, is to claim the holy creative right to write *as if no one is watching*, and to publish as if no one is watching too. Writing as if no one is watching is useful, when needed. But the reality is that someone is always watching, and words have consequences, sometimes massive consequences, and maybe you have to be without words, or to know people without access to words, to understand the power that writers wield. So at some stage well before publication, it is best to acknowledge those who might be affected by one's writing, and take responsibility for that.

Which makes me very uncomfortable.

Other options include asking for permission from every person who might conceivably be affected by a work, and developing very complex systems of denial. The first is practically impossible and has the almost certain outcome of preventing publication, and the second is tiresome and dishonest. You can also simply claim it and be proud. *Yes I wrote this, and that's okay.* I know writers often make peace with being somewhere in between. I chose to accept that my discomfort with what I have written, to some extent, will always be with me.

Discomfort is the companion to having a voice, and being given publication. My discomfort sits alongside anything I write that carries risk. Anything worth saying generally has associated risk—it may offend, it may contain errors, it may cause controversy or bring unwanted attention to the writer.

Chiefly, *someone might get hurt*. It might make things worse.

Writers almost always have a pet discomfort. Some people ignore it, lock it in a room, appease it with elaborate feedings or punish it with regular berating and time-outs; perhaps try to lull it into submission with extended Netflix marathons.

The point is, writing will inevitably require us to make a decision. I have chosen to try to live with my discomfort, to notice it when it arrives, say hello, and allow it to shadow me for the day. Often over a meal or a drink it fades, though it has been known to get vociferous at this point, sending me home to a sleepless night, or waking me at three in the morning. But that doesn't happen often, because I've decided to make friends with it, and I know that when it shows up there's a good possibility I'm doing something worthwhile.

tell me I'm wrong

Observation: in a room full of young middle class+ Pākehā students (e.g. the majority of university classes) there are many clever, witty, talented, politically astute and very pleasant people. Some of them are beautiful writers. Educationally, they have always been surrounded by writers, theorists and educationalists with the same socio-cultural capital as them. Few of them have stories to tell. Yet.

In a room full of Māori/Pasifika/immigrant students (not so many middle class, not so many young) there are many clever, witty, talented, politically astute and very pleasant people. Some of them are beautiful writers. Few of them have ever had the opportunity to read writing from their own communities. Few of them have ever had the opportunity to write from or about their own communities. Yet, I struggle to remember a single one that didn't have a compelling story to tell.

128

There is a bias in these generalisations, and for every generalisation there is an exception, but I don't think it invalidates the observation. There is a palpable difference between these different groups. There is *so much more at stake* for the second group. That they are even in that room is a small miracle. Do not let me take away from the small miracles that happen in the lives of Pākehā students. I get it, I do, but this is not meant to be a competition. Sit with these classes and their stories for a while and you soon realise the power that something like being able to read stories from your own communities has. Your voice matters, the Māori and Pasifika and immigrant students learn. This is often shocking for them to internalise.

What is shocking for me is the immense pool of talent that goes unnourished and unnoticed in Aotearoa. Unleash the literary power of these communities and we would have the international literati at our feet. Not that that matters, but it would certainly boost the literary economy. What matters more is that generations of people from certain communities would grow up with enhanced senses of themselves, their abilities and their voices. Publish their stories and ensure they are taught at every level of the education system, then come back and tell me that I'm wrong.

non-required reading

This essay suggests we write something that matters. But what that is is up to you. Patricia Grace writes simply about the lives of ordinary people. Ordinary lives she knows about. She makes no pretence of ever doing anything else. And yet her work is seen as culturally and politically, even spiritually and nationally, important and challenging because these are the lives of ordinary people who were largely invisible to the majority Pākehā population until people like Patricia, Witi and Hone started writing. Sometimes simply writing about your life and the lives of people like you can deeply matter.

Sometimes, though, you are writing in an echo chamber. Sometimes there are lots of writers like you, writing lots of stories like the one you are writing. Go to the edges of the room. Feel along the walls for cracks and crevices, for draughts. Find the windows to other rooms. Dig away at the ingrained dirt in the corner. There are so many stories unwritten. So many lives unnoticed. Be brave. Make yourself uncomfortable. Do the work required.

imagine I am whispering

This one is scary to write down: *I don't like Katherine Mansfield.* I don't mean her work, or her character. More, what she has come to represent. I just want to say there are other writers in New Zealand. Possibly more interesting writers worthy of as much attention. And while we fawn over a great writer of a certain time and place and class and colour, and a certain amount of privilege, who spent most of her career overseas, who are we ignoring in Aotearoa now (or even in her time)?

write only

I would never tell you to write only towards political, social, cultural or spiritual purpose. Write what you are compelled to write, and if you choose to write only for the sake of it, for the sake of art, understand that this, too, is choosing a political, social, cultural and spiritual position.

permission

For the Te Hā hui of Māori writers in 2015, we invited author Nic Low to come and speak about his work. He talked about wanting to imbue his stories with kaupapa. He might have called it something like political purpose. He talked about how unpopular that is, how it's something we're 'not supposed to do'. The response from many in the room was relief and pleasure at encountering this point of view, at being given tacit permission to write about things that concern us directly. Nic's short story collection *Arms Race* is funny, clever, scathing, dark, entertaining and wide-ranging. He could have written about anything.

Nic talked about the thing he is writing now. It's his big story, he said. The story you know you're meant to write, but you don't know if you're ready for. Are you good enough? Do you possess the right skills and background? Have you spoken to the right people? Did you get the permission you need? It was something along these lines, what he said. We nodded. We all knew about those stories. Many of us discussed the ones we had tucked away. Mostly we felt inadequate to do them justice. Nic looked unsure, concerned, determined. You never feel adequate, but if the story is in front of you, he seemed to be saying, you've got to rise to it.

kaupapa

This essay was written in the wake of the Trump campaign and early presidency of 2016 and 2017, the refugee crises of Europe and Australia (not the fact of the refugee populations pouring into those places, but the way they are treated), and Aotearoa's own shame at not alleviating the suffering of just a few more refugee families. Prince Charles is among the many comparing this moment in history to the 1930s; certain factions of society are somehow not even ashamed of Naziism anymore. The news in New Zealand this morning is that we have destroyed our rivers to the extent that they are unlikely to recover, but it's also unlikely the agricultural economy will be held to any real limits.

We live in a time of jeopardy. Some say we are already living our dystopia. When I was very young I understood that progress meant things would only get better for each successive generation, but I have spent the last decade grappling with the realisation that the world my daughters encounter may not be as ethically, emotionally, spiritually or even physically safe as the world of prior generations. We have to stop it, I think. Our children watch us with eyes haunted by their own futures.

And I sit here writing, for that is all I know how to do. It is the only thing I am good at.

Writers are sometimes hesitant to put their opinions forward. 'Who am I to speak?' they ask. 'Who are you not to?' is my question. Now is not the time for passivity or meekness. Write the hard thing. Write the unpopular thing. Write the challenging thing. Open your eyes. Write the thing you are scared of. Now is the time for you to step into the story that matters.

First published in The Fuse Box: Essays on Writing from Victoria University's International Institute of Modern Letters (2017)

Bread

At the end of things it's just me and the girls in a motel room in Victoria, B.C., Canada: one of those rooms you can rent by the month. The room is plain, worn, dated, but basically clean. Two double beds, a TV. It doesn't smell bad. I attune my antennae to the surroundings: don't detect malevolent vibes beyond our door. I've been in worse situations. When we need to leave the room to get some fresh air and walk and play, I see that the other inhabitants are like me: not from around here, keeping to themselves, seeking only a safe and quiet place to wait until more permanent options become available. When I was 14, after my big sister left home, Dad and I lived in a hotel room for a few months, and this is better than that. Not in terms of décor, or location, but certainly in terms of personal liberty. And I have my girls. Even so, I can't believe that I am twice as old and still, somehow, in the same situation.

It's taken a long time to reach this point, to extricate myself from a relationship that hasn't seemed good for any of us for years. I had needed to decant so many self-deceptions and outer illusions, work through so many layers of denial. Looking back I see how fiercely stubborn she was, this 20-something woman who would not let go or go home, even when all signs were pointing to disaster. How thrilled she found herself when she finally said goodbye to all that. She owned nothing to speak of, near the end of her third decade on Earth; she'd fucked some things up, but she had those two smiling girls: all cheeks and giggles, dark eyes and thick, thick hair, bouncing on the motel beds. Relatively unscathed, she hoped. Snuggling in pyjamas and watching cartoons. That's what she had.

After the motel we'd find a basement flat in a different neighbourhood, and after that an actual apartment. I don't remember exactly how those things happened, but it was remarkably easy. I'd read an advertisement and arrange to meet someone at the accommodation, with my 18-month-old and seven-year-old in tow, unless the latter was in school. I'd say I want it. Later, I'd give them money and sign. No real competition, no letting fees, no sideways look at my unemployed single parent status. Victoria could be a lovely place.

But this story is set before all of that happened. When we were first free. We were so free I didn't know where the next meal was coming from. That first night we were so free I wondered what I would need to do if the girls' father didn't come with the food he had promised. I had residency but I was a nobody. I had no money, no friends, no connections, no status. I was as green and invisible as a person could be. All of which was very freeing.

But he was late, and while he was being late I thought about what the next steps would be. The girls would only last so long. I couldn't go to the authorities, not that night. Maybe not ever. Whatever happened, I couldn't put my daughters in any danger. Perhaps I could go to the motel owner and ask for food to be put on a tab. But I didn't even know if they sold food, especially on account. I don't know what I considered then. I still hadn't told my parents, far away and completely uninvolved, about our predicament. There was so much I hadn't told them, so much I didn't want to tell them. But surely, if I needed them, they would help. Begging or sex work would have crossed my mind a couple of times, in a fleeting way, as fantasy solutions rather than realistic options, the logistics alone being too mind-boggling to deal with: how could I keep my girls safe? How could I keep myself safe? Even if I could reassure myself, how does one begin such a transaction? How long would it be before the dial on my safety dashboard moved from 'staying away from strangers with ulterior motives' to 'obtaining food whatever the risk'?

But luckily I was never forced to go there. He arrived, a couple of hours later than expected, and I promised myself I would never wait for him again.

The next day I went to the Mustard Seed Food Bank, the first of many trips that year. They took our details and registered us. I was allowed something like two packages a month. Just enough to tide us over when the money ran out. There were certain days we could go—or maybe that was the women's centre, where I also obtained free food, clothes and toys.

I liked the food bank more than I thought I would. We'd been poor all my life, but I hadn't realised it, because we were the kind of poor who liked to pretend we were middle class. Dad would probably have sold everything we owned rather than set foot in a food bank, which was tantamount to begging. And besides, food banks were likely to attract dirty, drug-addled people. Dirt poor. The drug of choice in our house had been alcohol, but everyone drank alcohol and they weren't all poor. We went without in other ways and then turned our noses up at the idea of asking for help.

But now I didn't have anything to sell. We had no choice but to live day by day, ask for help, and be thankful for it when it showed up. At the food bank we stood in line with other mums and dads and children, and yes, some drunks and druggies too. But no one was better than anyone else. Everyone waited patiently, not just because there was a behaviour code, but because we knew. Gravel-voiced grandmas and thin, lank-haired men in trucker caps engaged in polite conversation with more recent immigrants, refugees, First Nations families, anyone who needed a kai. No one had to explain anything. We knew. And the Mustard Seed provided.

Sometimes I'd detect family tensions: parents and grandparents putting on brave faces or trying to control frazzled children as we proceeded to the next room where the clothes and toys were. Some of us made a day of it, our children playing together while we searched through the piles. Canada, it seemed to me then, was an affluent place. I made a whole life out of the stuff people threw out. Nice stuff. And bread, there was always an abundance of day-old bread: danishes; white, fluffy, nutrient-free loaves; cheese buns; bagels; piles of it. I would eat this white abundance and wish for salad, but we weren't hungry.

The pushchair became an all-terrain vehicle piled high with whatever it could hold: food, toys and clothes packed into the basket, tied to each side in plastic bags and balanced on top, my one-year-old locked safely into the centre of this bag-lady ensemble. My arms grew strong from keeping the whole wobbling tower upright. We'd board buses awkwardly, and I learnt not to look or care what others might see.

There was a modest kitchen off to the side of the motel room where I could cook for us. Food parcels usually contained some beans, rice, pasta, cereal, maybe eggs or dairy or meat, and then a bunch of odd bits and pieces. When the alternative is nothing, you can find ways to make this work. Make it fun even. One night all we had left was flour, an egg and marshmallows, so I made marshmallow pancakes for dinner. The girls thought this was great, but pancakes became such a regular last-resort food I can't stomach them at all anymore.

At the women's centre, I found an advocate who helped me obtain welfare, and we found a school and a great community. The money was never quite enough to cover much more than rent and bills, though. I had to find more. I wanted to be at home with my own toddler, so I posted hand-made flyers around the neighbourhood offering childcare. I'd done this before in New Zealand. I had a few references. It was remarkably easy to find clients. Preschool childcare was strangely scarce and inflexible in this most liberal and prosperous of places. So we did okay, in the end, for money. The food bank trips became less frequent. I don't know how I managed it, but by the time we left that place we had everything we needed.

And we didn't need much, not really. Most days we walked somewhere, a playground or park, the library, the sea, a petting zoo. Built universes out of sand, water, secondhand toys. We made very good friends. Went swimming. Ice-skating. Simple things. In those early years we had nothing but each other and sometimes it was very very hard and sometimes it was very very dark but we were free and I'd never been so happy.

2003

On All Our Different Islands

FESTIVAL

It's shaped like an oblong scone, and the golden-brown colour of something that has been made from flour and fried.

'Festival,' Patrina says, opening her mouth to let the final vowel and consonant sound out like a song, like a sigh.

'Festivaaahhl.' Our poor mimicry, like all our other small ignorances, embarrasses me. I don't quite let the thoughts surface in this moment, but looking back I can see I wanted her to know we aren't just tourists and I'm not really white. At home my ethnicity is usually discernible, despite being mixed, but here I suspect I simply appear white, and on the first day I acquire a sunburn like a brand on my bare shoulders to ensure there can be no mistake.

'Oh, it's like frybread!' Festival is sweeter and more dense, probably not as deep-fried, but I recognise this. She nods and smiles her polite smile, and moves away. We call our inadequate thank yous. I remind myself that this is her job, and it's probably a well-paying job. Jobs, I was told by the first person I met in Jamaica, are scarce here.

As always, I'm excited to find any sort of cultural similarities between the place I come from and the place I have arrived. Festival is a sign of kinship. We make this too! Or a cousin of it anyway. But of course we don't have such a wistful and grand name for it. In Aotearoa we have a habit of giving things obvious titles: frybread, North Island, South Island. Unless we're speaking Māori—then it's all metaphors and gods and goddesses and impossibilities made real. Te reo Māori embodies a world that transcends Western notions of secular positivism. I recognise this same impulse in Jamaican Patois (Patwa)—the way Jamaicans use the English language seems to me an impossibility made real.

We are here for the Calabash Literary Festival, as are half the island, including 'the Jamaican intelligentsia', someone tells me, and more young people than I have ever seen at a literary festival at home. The crowd is excited and attentive and vocal, cheering and laughing and commenting as each writer takes the windswept podium, the sea a living backdrop. From the podium, Kwame Dawes, illustrious organiser and MC, calls us 'bashers', meaning those who attend Calabash.

And everything is colourful—the food, the clothes, the houses, the hair, the words. We ask for ackee and saltfish the next day, because we have heard this is the local breakfast, but ackee is out of season. I have only ever encountered it in books, and in my imagination it is a green leafy vegetable. It is actually, I am told, a fruit. I soon discover the local green has an even more sumptuous name: callaloo. I begin a private campaign to get a taste of callaloo, but every time I arrive at the front of a food stall line, the callaloo has run out. I love flavourful cooked greens, and the taste of this word is so delicious I wonder how the food will live up to it.

I have been reading Marlon James's *The Book of Night Women*, which I began just before I left New Zealand. I carry Lilith and her sisters and their men with me everywhere, through airports in the US, past a prison and abandoned factories and corrugated iron shacks in Jamaica, over pot-holed roads, past groups of shirtless men at fruit stalls and

schoolgirls in bright uniforms. All that time I carry with me
backs cut to shreds and girls forced to breed, brutality beyond
my reckoning and the small everyday indignities perpetuated
on dehumanised people by inhuman people. It is not without
irony that I witness myself writing about being branded by
the sun. Or note that somehow this mark of true whiteness
shames me in this place. Here, I have no history, no claim
to the legitimacy signalled by my Indigeneity in my own
country. Words like 'brand' have a different meaning for me
now, but not for the locals who have always carried the Liliths
of history with them.

EVERYTHING IS EVERYTHING

On our first day, before the festival begins, the other Calabash
Literary Festival organiser, Justine Henzell, comes to pick us
up. We can't get the seats down so we ride in the back of the
vehicle freestyle, and everybody laughs and takes photos. It's
okay, we say, we're Kiwis. We grew up riding in the backs
of vehicles on half-formed roads. It's just like home. At least
there's not a dead sheep in here with us, we should've said,
which sounds like a bad joke, but wouldn't have been unusual
in 1970s or 80s New Zealand.

It is boat trip day, but the boats we wade out to are
different from the comfortable tourist vessels some of us had
envisioned. These are hardy fishing boats, more waka than
yacht. The sea is choppy—the waves tip us from side to side
in a continuous motion, just rough enough to induce anxiety
in the less intrepid. Despite our earlier jokes, none of us have
really lived that old-school Kiwi lifestyle for a long time.
We are used to comfort and seatbelts and Health and Safety
regulations. No one wears lifejackets in our boat. But I find

myself drawing up the fortitude of my childhood as we head out. Hold on. *Itwillbeokayitwillbeokay.* I am not in control of anything, I'm a child again—with no great influence over the moment I find myself in. But the adult inside keeps reminding me that I can't swim and what about those people who lost their lives in New Zealand because they didn't take precautions and the lifejackets are right there. Finally, I slip a conspicuous bright orange item over my head.

I think I must have prayed a lot when I was a kid. Or something akin to prayer. I remember a time when Dad was driving drunk on a windy gravel road with a sheer drop over a cliff on one side and no particular sense of a centre line for any traffic coming the other way. I just held on and tensed up, as if controlling the muscles and breath in my body might exert some control over the world.

The precariousness of girlhood is often with me when I travel. On this trip it is there most of all on that first day, when I am out of my depth, and on the last day when we drive the three hours to the airport during the school run, and I see little girls and young women and grandmothers lined up at bus stops and walking along pathless roads, in bright yellow or green or purple uniforms, their hair done in tight elaborate patterns. I think about the stories of violence I have heard from new friends, who live here or places like it, and think about leaving, but where could they go? The ladies from *The Book of Night Women* are still with me, of course, and my own babies, and my own childhood, closer now than usual. I wonder what it is like for girls here, and I hope that it is mostly innocent and happy, at least for a time.

UPFULL

I can tell you the exact moment I arrive, fully, in Jamaica. Travellers know how the body can be walking around on one part of the planet while the rest of oneself is still in the ether, the speed and bluntness of our physical technology somehow not attending to the pace of our metaphysicality. It can manifest as dizziness, or sudden ineptitude, or the uncontrollable desire to sleep. People call it jetlag, but the regularity of that word doesn't fully encompass the effect. If you travel almost anywhere in the world from New Zealand, you quickly become aware that you are time-travelling. You don't lose or gain hours, but whole days, sometimes more than one. The most eloquent description of this I have heard is from the artist Troy-Anthony Baylis, who called it drag, and described how he liked to work in the drag state, and sometimes dressed in drag while in transit, physically embodying multiple in-between states.

So I can remember the exact moment I arrive, because words bring me back into my body, and I remember thinking, *Oh, I'm home*. It is the second morning of the festival and the crowd has already been lifted and set down by words multiple times, language working on us the way the waves work at the shoreline ahead. At regular intervals pelicans swoop in and out of view, mirroring the aerial feats of stories or songs put together in such a way that to speak them is like hitting the water full-speed, diving, then emerging once more into hot air to fly despite the salt-wet weight.

I can remember the exact moment I arrive, because it is when Kei Miller reads his gold poem. I last heard Kei read in New Zealand, where the rich melody of his voice and the way he put together a line of words earned him an instant following. 'I just want him to read me to sleep at night,' said more than one friend. This time he took us into Buckingham Palace, where he had been asked to write a poem in response to the provocation of the *In the Realms of Gold* exhibition in the Queen's Gallery. He seems puzzled that they gave him this task. Didn't they know what they were asking for?

> Oracabessa—origins disputed but most likely leave over from the Spanish. *Oracabeza, Golden Head*, though what gold was here other than light shining off the bay, other than bananas bursting out from red flowers? But this too is disputed—not the flowers—rather, the origin of bananas; they may have come here with Columbus on a ship that in 1502 slipped into Oracabessa the way grief sometimes slips into a room.[1]

A collective out-breath on that last line, a collective in-breath and cheering, rapturous applause. Because we all get it, get how grief can slip into a room the way colonisation had slipped among our people, but the poem has only just begun, and it keeps giving more, summoning the Taíno language back from its genocide. We cheer at every beat, every line. 'Such language as could summon wind to capsize Columbus's ships,' says Kei, and we are all of us triumphant. It isn't even the collective joy of that moment with all those people suddenly made kin that brings me home. It is the aural shape of the words themselves.

There are some writers we think are great, some we admire, some we know have something special, and then there are those who feel like home. Their writing feels like home, and we trust the writer, we go to them because we know we're safe with them—in their words we will find what we need. Maybe that is what I hear in the voices of people rejoicing as the festival continues. Wherever we are from, we are finding our way home. I realise I can go anywhere in the world and if I find my way to a gathering like this I will be home. Even if it is just one writer out of dozens who takes me there.

By day three of Calabash, I think of Pacific friends often, and begin to imagine I can see them in the crowds. I hear their laughter. There is much English spoken, but the striking women and men of Caribbean literature often speak a patois so thick and musical I cannot net the words as they rise above me like butterflies. These words lift up even those of us who can't grasp their meaning. The Caribbean is such a different sea of islands from my own, marked by such a different history, but it is also familiar. The rhythm of Jamaican (Patwa) gathers me in as time goes on, and I think I can understand more. Patwa expresses the same impulse to mess with language as we have at home. Chur. Poly Swag. Make it niu. Half pai. Chop Suey Hui. Just as the English language has colonised us, so we occupy it, indigenise it. On all our different islands.

On the final day I only just stop short of speaking Māori to the local vendors. Even though it makes no logical sense, I feel like they would understand me if I gave them a 'kia ora' as thanks. Instead I use a new sound of affirmation that I hear all around me: mmmm-hmmm. It is a Caribbean sound, the way the tones rise and fall in a way that says, I been there, I know exactly what you're saying. I start to use it to mean 'yes please', because it is the most Caribbean sound I can make. I imagine it also can mean 'Oh yes I know more about that than I care to know' or 'My aunty knows it and my grandma knows it and all my people for all time have known it' or even 'I know it, but I doubt you know it as well as you think you do'. Perhaps mainly it just means yup. Sometimes in conversation someone makes this sound and I feel very warm, as if they have placed an arm around my shoulders.

I am dismayed that my ability to make this sound fades within 24 hours of leaving the country.

HEARTBLESS

When I get back, my daughter is leaving home for the second time. It is a much more joyful leaving than the first, though this means it is harder to see her go. She smiles a lot these days. There were a hard, dark few years where that didn't happen and I didn't know if it would again.

See: two girls turning somersaults in the ocean, skin brown and glistening like seals as they flip and turn and dive, agile and swift under and over waves. If you listen hard, you can hear the giggling, even over the ocean roar. Only mermaids are this complete in the sea. Watching from shore, bound by the gravity of Earth and the neverending list of small jobs adults always seem to have waiting, a mother may discover an invocation in her thoughts: let their lives, always, be like this. We know it won't be. It can't be. But suspend that one moment, stay in it as long as you can. Make it possible for them to stay there, even as the sun begins to go down.

Later, we'll remember, and that will make other things bearable. Bodies covered up. A folded, inward frown. Sullen-hanging lips. The beach? Okay, if I have to. Earphones in. The memory of freedom is there though, where we left it. The sea will be there when they are ready to return.

Some nights I wake and there is nothing that will take the anxiety away. I listen to the sounds of the house, suspecting my children are not safe in their beds, and if they are, well, will they be safe on the streets tomorrow? At 2 or 3am, there is really nothing that can convince me they will be. I'm not one of those mothers who is interviewed by the papers after some tragedy, saying, 'I never would have imagined . . .' or 'How did this happen in our neighbourhood?' I have imagined everything. I have suspected everyone. There will be no surprise tragedies, for I have lived them all. It's an old habit from too many years parenting alone. If I imagine it, by some trick of magical thinking won't I be able to protect my girls from it?

No. Of course. I understand this too. And I haven't imagined it all anyway, for I haven't the heart or the stomach.

Hinenuitepō fled to the underworld after discovering her own mistreatment, there to wait for her children so that she might embrace them after death. When she saw the cruelty of the world, all she could do was be there, in the darkness, to offer them solace. Men speak of her as a figure of fear. Women know her as a figure of strength. She took her powerlessness and transformed it into power, but to do so she had to shift worlds.

All mothers know what it is to be Hinenuitepō. The hardest thing to do, in the darkness, is to just be there, to stay. Hinenuitepō, the Great Lady of the Night, is there for her children and generations of grandchildren, for all time. Even Māui couldn't change that.

WALK GOOD

Walk Good. The message of joy and farewell that circulates social media as we prepare to leave Jamaica: *Walk Good.* Two simple words placed side by side, just so, a configuration that carries more meaning than those two words in any other sequence I have seen. Something to take home.

Our people are our homes, as much as anything. But when I try to write of my husband, the words don't come. Perhaps this is as it should be. I could paint a picture of domestic bliss, of the expression of devotion in mundane tasks. Perhaps the planning of a life, the making of a physical home. But none of this is where my home in him is. And none of this, once solidified into words, is true.

One morning after I return, alone on a train overlooking the Kāpiti Coast on a clear morning, waves pulling roughly in and out, just wild enough to look inviting and uninviting at the same moment, I see. It is no different for him and me than it is for anyone else. Our home is in our bodies.

I cannot write to you of that.

I look at the waves, the clear horizon, the moon descending the morning sky. The coastal rockpools. The waves. How can I write to you of home? Even this morning; the clear, sacred breath of it. Take a path to the beach and let the sea take you. The sound of water closing over your head, now blood in your veins, in your ears, a pulse, the heartbeat. The fresh alchemy of skin–water–air. Now, the rain. Taste it in the air. The smell as it hits warm concrete. Walk through streets you've known all your life and look as if for the first time. Hear the children next door, or maybe a birdcall that isn't heard anywhere else on the planet. Come inside. See your beloved. Make him laugh. Prepare a simple dish to share: maybe bread, some fruit. Slide into the seat beside her, touching feet / hands / arms the way you two do. Just so. A sigh, an expression of the unspeakable. Yes. You are home. You are home.

KOROWAI

I attend a small gathering of reo Māori learners at a marae in an economically depressed area north of Wellington. At lunch we eat frybread. The women who work with us carry the kind of gentle command and authority that we call mana. We are fortunate this day, because these kōkā, aunties, are tohunga or experts in particular areas of knowledge that are rare even among our elders. We frequently experience awe at their teachings, and despite the part of the city we are in there is nothing in this experience that is impoverished. If we didn't have to eventually exit down the long driveway, we might begin to believe we had found everything we needed in the world.

Sometimes our teachers tell us about the vibrations of certain words or sounds, how to stand, how and when to karakia, how to address each other by recognising the highest within the other person. They demonstrate the truth of their teachings in their own presence. This is not something I can explain on paper, but if you were to meet them, or if you were to hear the songs and words they gift us, you might begin to understand. The words we learn carry meaning that is not simply based on the shape formed by their letters, but also their sound, their aural shape. These sounds of my home are so old they carry the voices of our ancestors, and some aspect of our own voices that we can't access any other way. This story would not be complete without some of them, but all the English in creation will not explain their meaning to you. Maybe it's okay for these words to sit here, even if you cannot understand their full meaning. Maybe they exert an influence by their very existence. My world and my concept of home is not complete without them.

Tino rangatiratanga
Aroha
Mana
Āwhinatanga

Kaitiakitanga
Oranga
Rangimārie
Ora o te iwi
Wairua
Āhurutanga
I raro i te maru o te aroha

Before I leave, I ask one of the kōkā where I might learn some of her skills. She gently asks why I want to know. It's a good question. Later, a friend says she herself doesn't possess the power that is so clearly apparent in our teachers' āhua. I suggest that it is not that we don't possess it, but that we don't know how to embody it. I ask the teacher how I can learn, because I can see she embodies the home I haven't yet reached.

I don't know what gods watch me, or how it came to be that my fate brought me to an island in the Caribbean Sea. It was miraculous, not least because in the novel I am currently writing there is a shipwreck in that same sea. I would not know how to write it if I had not found myself in a Jamaican fishing boat one wet and windy day in June, contemplating the whims of the sea and the alligators up the river. But it is equally miraculous to find myself in a humble neighbourhood in my own country, face to face with women who quietly go about their lives, walking between worlds, singing up salvation by connecting us with our own roots.

Festival is a sign of kinship. Festival is a word that means celebration. Festival is a food that has the same name as a community celebrating.

At the airport, leaving Jamaica, I discover Island Grill,

where you can buy traditional Jamaican foods in takeout boxes at takeout speeds. I ask for escovitch fish, a wonderfully spicy dish that I buy as much for a taste of its name as for the fish itself. I also ask for callaloo, but today they have none. Instead, I purchase three festival in a crisp white bag to eat on the journey home. I feel more colour-full now—more full to the brim. I carry a blessing with me. Walk Good.

First published in *Adda* (2016) and *Home: New Writing* (2017)

Māori Writing: Speaking with Two Mouths

In the beginning was Te Kore, the void or chaos before anything existed—though perhaps we cannot say it was the beginning because there was only the formless double-negative state of potential—no beginning, no time, no before or after. Somehow, the many different and esoteric states of Te Kore proceeded, and eventually Te Pō emerged and manifested aeons of long nights. Finally, Te Ao Mārama came into being and light came upon the world, Earth and Sky, Ranginui and Papatūānuku. The children of Earth and Sky populated the world then, beginning with the atua or gods, reaching down through the ages to us today.

All Māori creation stories follow this whakapapa one way or another—our arrival out of chaos and the many long dark nights of creation into the light. Think of it almost like the Big Bang and the Western scientific version of creation, for there are many parallels there. This is both creation story and karakia, whakapapa and invocation. You will hear this invocation over and over in many different forms almost anywhere you find Māori people gathered. It is the way we connect ourselves to the world and to each other.

Whakapapa means genealogy but also in Māori terms all forms of connection and relationship can be understood as whakapapa: it underpins all Māori knowledge systems. You might say our theoretical understanding of the universe is based in whakapapa. Whether we begin with the first genealogy at the inception of the universe or with whakapapa that is closer to our present time, in any situation we first and foremost recognise where we come from and how we are related. This is what the pōwhiri at the beginning of hui and tangi is about, among other things.

Te Kore may be known in Western terms as 'the Void' or 'the Chaos', but it is also known to us as the place of pure potentiality. From this 'nothingness', everything sprang. It is the place of nothing and not-nothing, the place of pure paradox. This, for me, is where creativity comes from, and so to whakapapa or link myself back to Te Kore is the most powerful thing I can do as a creative person. I try to remember that every time we create we are engaging the same spark of chaos and paradox, and recognising our connection to everything else.

In 2013 I graduated with a PhD in Creative Writing from Victoria University of Wellington, and I attended two graduation ceremonies. For one I went into the city centre and celebrated with the thousands of others who were being capped that week. We were ushered on stage, given a warm greeting and our paper certificates, photographed, and ushered off again. Since I was receiving a doctorate, I had the honour of joining the ranks of the staff on stage, and for the first time in the many different graduations I had attended, I had a real sense of joining the academy.

For the other ceremony, I joined a smaller but no less significant group at the gates of Te Herenga Waka Marae, and was welcomed with a pōwhiri. We then entered the whare and were honoured with speeches, songs, and additional certificates. I had been to Māori graduations before, so all of this was familiar to me, but one thing that happened was unexpected. Each graduand was gifted with a taonga:

pounamu or jade, our most precious stone. Because I had completed my doctoral study, I received an additional gift, this carved bone pendant.

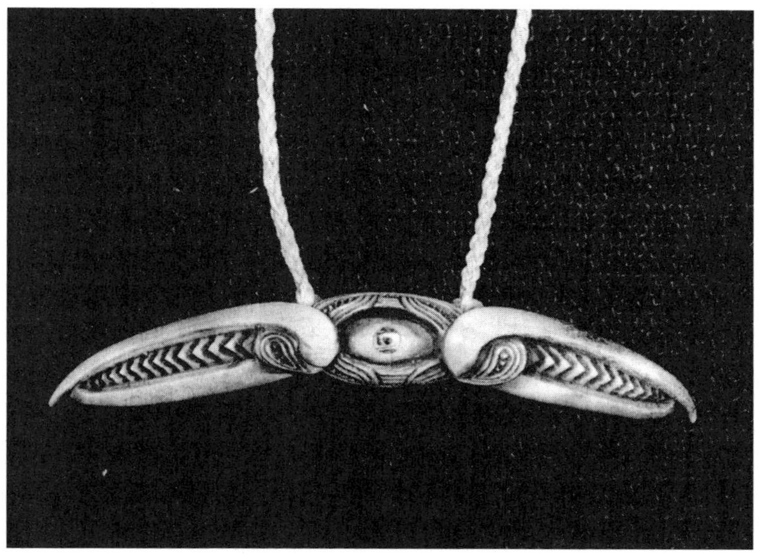

It's very beautiful, but also it held immediate and profound meaning for me as a writer. I'm not sure what was intended by the artist, Gareth McGhie, but I can explain how I read this taonga. This is a manaia form, meaning a profile of the human head. The manaia can be very stylised, and the level of elongation that occurs in the mouth caused some early (non-Māori) theorists to suggest that the manaia is a bird form. My understanding is that it is not bird, though in many cases it might be spirit, moving between the earthly and spirit realms. In this way the manaia is a figure of transformation and communication.

My taonga has a single eye and two mouths. The two

mouths face in opposite directions. On first seeing it I knew that this taonga represented the task of the writer, particularly the Māori writer: to speak with two mouths at once, to communicate two sometimes opposing forces, to exist at the centre of the paradox. In particular, this taonga spoke to me as a Māori-Pākehā individual telling the particular stories I tell, and as a Māori person writing in English. There is a duality in this act for Māori; writing in English is already an act of translation. But there is added complexity in the modernity of the Indigenous writer. We are not performing simple translations into English of traditional ways of being or of pristine cultures. If we try to describe our cultures that way we end up solidifying something that was never solid. Our cultures, like any cultures, are in constant flux, so from the very first contact between Māori tribes and European settlers, our cultures transformed. What this means is that what we now think of as traditional is quite often already post-contact or post-colonisation. So my writing practice is always concerned with duality, contradiction, cultural fluidity and paradox. This taonga with its one eye and two mouths facing in opposite directions symbolises that for me. The two mouths speak:

of the dead and the living

of the earthly and the spiritual

of past and future, and how they are interlinked: we can look in both directions at once

of new things and ancient things

of Māori and Pākehā, or of Indigenous and Settler peoples

of English and te reo Māori

of communication styles that sometimes work in opposite ways

of contradictory tikanga or cultural ways of doing things

of male and female genders, the eye at the centre suggesting a continuum between one direction and another

of those with power and those without

of violence and peace.

What this taonga represents in totality is the necessity to speak in both directions at once in all the work we do as Māori writers. We always have at minimum two audiences, even if we're talking at the simplest level to Māori and Pākehā New Zealanders. We're constantly working with many conflicting dynamics, even if we're starting with the act of writing about Māori concepts with English words. We are in the constant act of bilingualism and biculturalism. At a deeper level, our position at the centre of such long-standing contradictory forces gives us immense power, if we can learn how to harness it. Histories, narratives and lecture plans that start from European assumptions will reproduce stories that centre European perspectives, and Māori writers and writing will end up at the margins of the main story. For example, the Māori Renaissance of the 1970s comes after the cultural nationalism of the 1930s; the short stories and novels of Witi Ihimaera are marginal to the main post-war story of the hunt for the 'Great New Zealand Novel'. But nothing could be further from how I see our work: we are in the centre of the fire, in the belly of the beast, and that's a place of immense creative energy. That is, in fact, Te Kore, the chaos, the origin place of the universe and all creativity—which brings us back to our creation story and our whakapapa.

*

The orthodox syllabus, its division into periods, its tag-names of certain kinds of writing in certain periods—that map is a construction. —Raymond Williams[1]

The previous section describes my understanding, as a Māori writer, of what Māori writing is, but the way academia has taught our writing is somewhat different, and the teaching of our literatures remains widely misunderstood, if given any attention at all. I don't want to undermine the interest and respect that is evident from non-Māori who study Māori literature, because we need that interest to continue. However, historical and contemporary non-Māori approaches seem fundamentally different from the way we as Māori might understand what Māori literature is and how it should be taught. And the points that Raymond Williams makes, particularly about the 'selective tradition', resonate with me.

The teaching of Māori literature in English departments in New Zealand universities *tends* to look something like this:

Imported English Literature: Early, Elizabethan (Shakespeare), Romantics, Victorian, Modernism, Postmodernism . . .

↓

19th / early 20th-century New Zealand literature?

↓

NZ 1930s Cultural Nationalists: Glover, Curnow, Fairburn, Brasch

↓

1950s Neo-Romantics: Baxter, Campbell, Frame, Hyde

↓

1970s: Wedde, Manhire; *Māori Writing: Tuwhare, Ihimaera, Grace*

↓

1990s onwards: Contemporary, postcolonial, global?

A version of this schema is likely to be the kind of thing we use, though typically there are variations according to the perspective of the individual lecturer. The principle is that written literature arrived in the late 18th century along with European settlers, that New Zealand literature emerged sometime in the early 20th century (or maybe late 19th century if you're particularly progressive), and that Māori literature arrived sometime in the 1960s (or 1950s, or even 1930s if you're particularly progressive), with Hone Tuwhare's *No Ordinary Sun* (1964) and Witi Ihimaera's *Pounamu Pounamu* (1972) signalling the 'beginning' of written Māori literature in English.

This approach assumes that Māori were not creating substantial literature before this point. But important recent work challenges this way of imagining the literatures produced in these islands. Arini Loader and Alice Te Punga Somerville's powerful scholarship in the anthology *A History of New Zealand Literature* (2016) shows how much richer and more multifaceted, complex and long-standing Māori writing has been, and how many more places you can find it in the records of the past if you know where to look. But this scholarship needs a wider base of readers, teachers and respondents. The near absence of the teaching of Māori literature as a distinct subject in New Zealand universities[2] makes this almost impossible. Māori literature is invariably placed as a subsection of New Zealand literature, which is still a regional subsection of English literature, and a late-arriving one at that.

My understanding of Māori literature in English, and how it should be taught so that scholars understand where it comes from and what it is saying, looks a little more like this.

A Whakapapa of Māori Literature

Te Kore, Te Pō, Te Ao Mārama, Mātauranga Māori
Creation narratives and Māori knowledge systems

↓

Whakapapa, Ngā Pūrākau, Ngā Kōrero Tuku Iho,
Karanga, Whaikōrero, Waiata, Oriori, Mōteatea
Oral literary traditions

↓

Ngā Toi Wharenui, Ngā Toi Waka:
Whakairo, Raranga, Tā Moko
Visual narrative traditions: Carving, weaving, body arts

↓

Te Ao Hurihuri: Arrival of European settlers, Land Wars,
English language and literature:
Development of newspapers, biography, family history
and written genealogy

↓

Contemporary Māori writing in English and te reo Māori:
Māori theatre and film, contemporary Māori
visual arts and curation

Or, perhaps more accurately, this:

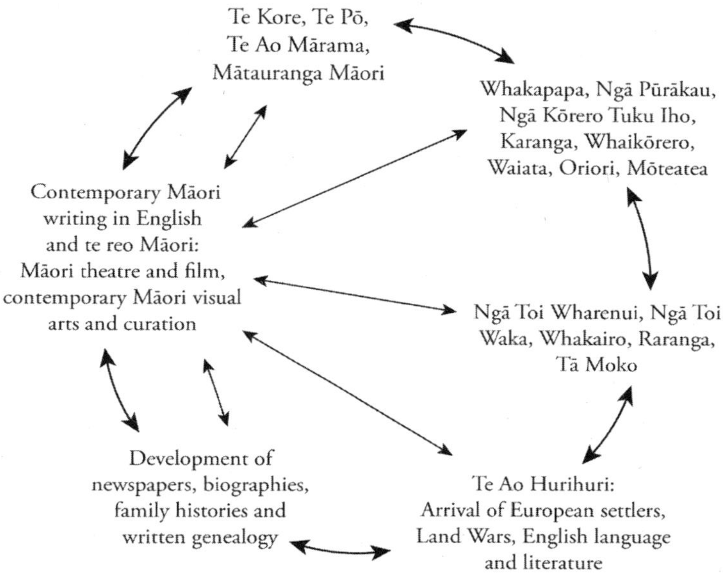

This chart attempts to delineate the exchange of ideas between origins and present manifestations, particularly the sense that while we might envisage whakapapa as something of which we are the product, we must also recognise that our understanding of culture, stories, history and ancestors is transformed by the moment we find ourselves in. The whakapapa of Māori literature does not work in only one direction; culture is always in flux, and colonisation—the ongoing process of colonisation and decolonisation—shapes, limits, distorts and shifts how we know and tell our stories. We are constantly spiralling back to reconnect and re-enact that whakapapa, so imagine all these elements interacting dynamically with one another, a spiral galaxy in motion.

The whakapapa of Māori literature in English, as I envisage it, places writing in English and English literatures as a late but very important addition to a Māori literary heritage that was already incredibly rich in literary forms and already long-established. And yes, this includes visual forms; in other words, 'written' literatures.

The difference between the two systems is as profound as the difference between Māori and English world views. It is hard for me to imagine why you might choose to misunderstand Māori literature so fundamentally by viewing it only through the lens of the first system. What we need, in this bicultural nation, is at the very least the two systems existing side by side, and what we urgently need are more Māori scholars of Māori literature to occupy this as-yet-unrealised field of study. The reasons why this hasn't happened yet are probably too myriad to quantify here, so I will simply say that they are a product of colonisation and institutional bias, but that there are many complexities. Māori literature in English seems to occupy a space that puzzles both English literature departments and Māori studies departments, being essentially a hybrid of both.

I quite like occupying this in-between space, as my taonga that speaks with two mouths testifies, but it can be discomfiting and uncomfortable, and things that don't fit are apparently easy to ignore and dismiss.

Of course, there is a deeper history here of how English literature has been set up to privilege only one kind of seeing. My first encounters with Raymond Williams offered me a history that demonstrates how that selective tradition is built in, and how it leaves other traditions out.

In my own work I have been lucky to encounter few negative responses, though it sometimes worries me that this is somehow due to a lack of comparative work or the ability to engage with Māori literature on its own terms. But one element of feedback about my last novel illustrated for me the difference in world views I attempt to describe. The main

Moriori ancestor character in *Where the Rēkohu Bone Sings* is not physically alive. I dislike calling him a spirit or a ghost, because that is not what he is. I'm not sure he is even a kēhua, the Māori word for such beings. He is simply not alive, but he has lingered around his descendants because of the manner in which he was killed, during the invasion of Rēkohu (Chatham Islands), and eaten. Cannibalism was traditionally used in Māori warfare to desecrate and insult the dead, and steal their mana (personal, ancestral and sovereign power). If you aimed to demoralise and conquer an enemy, there was no stronger tool for doing so. Moriori, the Indigenous people of the Chatham Islands, had outlawed the practice hundreds of years before Europeans and then Māori began to visit their islands. It makes complete sense that this manner of death, as the strongest possible act of desecration, would prevent a person from finding peace in the afterlife, particularly a person whose culture is based on non-violence.

The character I speak of is named Imi, and he speaks to us directly in first person. I made up everything about him: his improvised, non-standard, negotiated English, the manner of his afterlife and the manner of his life before death, but Imi arrived in my imagination very distinctly by waking me up at 4am for many nights, telling me his story. He is a character in a book, but sometimes, if we're lucky, our characters come to us that urgently. My job was to translate his story for the page.

Two things struck me about the response to Imi in reviews of the book. One, few critics knew what to make of him. Many readers told me they loved him, but many commentators didn't 'get' him, either because he wasn't alive or because of his manner of speaking. (This last I accept as a valid criticism of the writing.) Almost without exception, reviews described him as a useful or clever narrative device, using that exact phrase: 'narrative device'. I guess everything in a book is a narrative device, but I wondered why so many critics had trouble reading or describing Imi as a character as real as any of the other characters. It hadn't occurred to me that readers (and I do mean the predominantly non-Māori or non-Moriori reviewers) would have difficulty digesting a character because he's not alive. After all, all characters are figments of our imagination, and for Māori and Moriori people, being dead doesn't necessarily make you less present.

The other thing was that few reviewers engaged with the manner of Imi's death in any depth. This had been so difficult for me to write, and so important to Imi as a character, and to the story. The one exception came from a non-Māori blogger, Morgan Davies, who wrote an eloquent and insightful analysis of the passage that describes Imi's cannibalisation:

> As the spirit becomes attuned to his new afterlife, his relationship to his body changes, and the perspective of the invaders slowly approaches knowability in his eyes. The crucial moment comes as he witnesses part of his body fed to an infant, and through this moment, leaves his body and moves perspective to hers. The description, unflinching in the detail of chewing and swallowing and digestion, is subsumed under the child's innocence, and the spirit becomes able through [the child] to perceive the other oppressors as people driven by their own fears and needs and loves. The sequence becomes, somehow, beautiful.[3]

To which I responded, with gratitude:

> [T]he whole book is about the humanity of the various participants. Imi is the voice of those who aren't usually given

voice: the dead, the victims, history's 'losers'. The story is his, he owns it, he speaks it, and thus the story is somehow given back to him. Rather than using it to put down his enemy, this power gives him the ability to see his attackers in their humanity. And this might be the most important thing about Moriori culture, perhaps this is the heart of pacifism—the decision to see everyone as human and therefore 'just like me' somehow. And to know that you don't have the right to take that away.[4]

It was only when Davies published his blog post that I realised I had been waiting for someone, anyone at all, to engage with this aspect of the book, which was for me the crux of the novel. As I wrote this scene, I thought about how this was a crucial moment for Imi, for me as writer, and hopefully, for the reader. Academic analyses might go deeper than reviews, and it's not unusual for a writer's intentions to go unrecognised by readers, but I suspect the inability of reviewers to engage with Imi as a character and with the intricacies of his death and cannibalism are, at least in part, due to an inability to read the work in its cultural context. None of this means that one must be Māori to understand the work (Davies isn't), but that one needs more than the tools of English literary studies' traditional critical methodologies to get the most from it. This is one small example of why we need a new way, or possibly an old way, to read Māori literature in English, and I will furnish you with one more— one that reminds me of Raymond Williams' approach. This is Patricia Grace in a recent interview:

When *Potiki* first came out there was quite a bit of criticism of it. One of the reasons was because of the use of Māori terms and passages in the book; the other was that some people thought

I was trying to stir up racial unrest. The book was described as political. I suppose it was but I didn't realise it. The land issues and language issues were what Māori people lived with every day and still do. It was just everyday life to us, and the ordinary lives of ordinary people was what I wanted to write about, so I didn't expect the angry reaction from some quarters.[5]

It surprises me how often I've referred to this example, and how often it has been instructive—how it continues to startle in both its simplicity and depth.

As Māori writers, we are all speaking with two mouths, sometimes without being aware of it. Patricia was simply writing the everyday, ordinary stories of her community, which others read as radical and political. And of course they are, but more because of the assumptions that go hand in hand with accusing people of 'trying to stir up racial unrest' simply by describing their lives. In the fiction anthology *Black Marks on the White Page*, Witi Ihimaera and I dubbed this 'radical ordinariness'. It's amazing what you discover when you look in a different direction, speak with a different voice, step into another's shoes. This is what all literature does. The ordinary lives of ordinary people. But then, what is ordinary in one community cannot be assumed to be ordinary in another, and if we select only one way of seeing as our national literature, *and* if we select only one way to *interpret* our literatures, we're all at risk of missing the point. This is what I take Williams to mean when he writes: 'Culture is ordinary: that is the first fact.'[6] Ordinary here does not mean uninteresting or unremarkable. It is to do with community, and with collectively produced difference. 'Every human society,' Williams goes on,

[. . .] has its own shape, its own purposes, its own meanings. Every human society expresses these, in institutions, and in arts and learning. The making of a society is the finding of common meanings and directions, and its growth is an active debate and amendment, under the pressures of experience, contact, and discovery, writing themselves into the land.[7]

If we do not seek out Māori ways of finding common meanings and directions, and if we overlook the connections that Māori writers have made and continue to make in their own shapes, purposes, and meanings, all of us—students and readers, writers, Pākehā scholars as much as Māori—will miss the chance to see the active debate and amendment going on around us.

Many Pākehā readers of *Potiki* discovered that a world existed alongside their own that until then had been invisible to them, and many responded positively. So whether you are from Wales, or Plimmerton, New Zealand, or Japan, telling your own story in your own way can be both ordinary and radical. This is another example of the two mouths with which us writers speak, two mouths that seem to face in opposite directions but emanate from the same source.

First presented at *Selective Tradition in the Pacific: A Conference on Class, Writing, and Culture* (2017)

First published in *Journal of New Zealand Studies* (2018)

Dog Love

The dog has eaten a hole in the carpet. We've been in lockdown just over a week. The humans are doing okay. Stressed, sad, anxious, but mainly chin up. People have started getting up and doing exercise and working towards goals. This is a good sign, when the usual response to boredom or stress, for some of us, is sleeping most of the day and spending the rest of it in front of screens. We're making nutritious food. We're getting out of the house, to walk our allotted block, with the dog. But she doesn't know what's up. Everyone is home, all the time, and she doesn't get to go to doggie daycare, where she ran all day with other dogs, and we don't go in the living room anymore, where she used to have quality time cuddling humans on the one item of furniture she's allowed on, because this side of the house is self-isolating from the other side of the house so the international travel germs don't get us all. She now goes between our bedroom (where I work) and the garage (where my spouse works), up and down the hallway, and occasionally outside but not as much as she used to.

We got her four months ago, and it was weeks before we heard her bark properly. Now, at night, she wanders restlessly from one irritation to the next, chewing, and pacing, and then when the frustration rises above her capacity to chill, she barks at us—a shrill, uncomfortable sound. Barking for her is distress, or overexcitement, which are the same thing for dogs, according to some experts. Our last dog, Nala, barked for the pure joy of sound, a deep and loud woof that expressed all of her emotions—joy, excitement, courage, anger, fear, happiness. She was a huntaway, and her bark was her honour. Piki does not have the breeding for barking. She's a snuffler, a cuddler, a wiry ginger ball of neediness, her Staffie-Vizsla-Whippet genes priming her for play and affection above all else. She wants to be with us at all times but the more attention we give her the more anxious she becomes, and so in the beginning we carefully constructed a weekly timetable that gave her the exercise and independence she needed. But now it's just us and her, and sometimes that unnatural bark, a pre- or post-cursor to naughtiness, acting out, distress. She stares straight into our eyes, and her confusion is clear. *What the hell is going on?* She can't say it in words, what she needs, but she's unsettled by all the changes, by our behaviours and feelings, so many feelings, which are all as clear to her as the thousands of smells that she can detect and we can't. Dogs are all sense, all feeling, body language, smell, sound. She knows exactly how we are, more than we do most likely, but what's she supposed to do with all that? What does it mean to her small, muscular body? Tension without release.

But she's also like any dog, and having people at home all the time has its advantages. There's always a desk to curl up beside, sometimes even a heater. Food prep has been moved to one of the home offices to lessen the need to enter the shared kitchen. In one week she has learnt much more about the joys of human food and scavenging than she knew before too. Sometimes people leave the office for a moment, on some errand that will only take a minute, and so the dog is left there, innocently curled beside the desk, in front of the heater. And sometimes it takes a whole day for the humans to notice the butter is missing, the little bowl of it for toast, at least 50 grams cut from the block and added that morning. Where did it go, they say, in much the same way that yesterday they kept asking, what has the dog eaten? Why is she throwing up so much, and why is it yellow and white, the stuff she's throwing up? And also, why does she look so longingly at it, as we drag her away, as if she would like another go at it, as if it is delicious?

It takes multiple expulsions for a small dog's body to reject a small block of butter, and one of these, just a small one, occurs in the hallway between one home office and another, and even though the humans see it, and clean it, or so they think, that superior nose, those superior senses, know the butter has been there, processed though it has been through a small dog's gullet and multiple chemical cleaning sprays. And the following night, after being kicked out of the bedroom for barking a shrill and demanding bark, a small dog might find the spot where the butter has been and, unwatched by human eyes, consume the entirety of the small patch of carpet, the fibres anyway, so that all that is left is a white plastic underlay gap for the humans to discover later. And it takes until this moment for the humans to put the throwing up and the carpet eating and the new office-food-prep configuration together with the missing butter, and to see where things went wrong.

The small dog's carefully constructed exercise and training programme now enters another phase of vigilance. Yesterday we returned to the living room so she could curl up beside us on her couch, nuzzling under our arms, breathing her contentment in audible huffs. It's what we need too, the calm that descends as we stroke her fur, scritching the soft, soft ears and watching her eyes go sleepy. Perhaps today she will roll to expose her tummy for rubbing, the final sign of complete trust. It's a while since she did that.

First published in *Sunday Star-Times* (May 2020)

Bleeding on the Page:
On Writing, Community and Reviews

In which we don't ask if it's good
By the grace of all that is holy, I teach writing for a living. Excuse the religious overtones; for me it is a blessing to get to do what I do. I know how lucky I am—fortune, luck, privilege—they're all part of the equation. Add to that whakapapa, ngā taonga tuku iho o ngā tūpuna, aptitude and, gasp, training. Also, community with a circulating flow of aroha, generosity and the deep seam of something that runs through all our lives, that it is vital to our existence, something I think of simply as story. We all need our stories. For an Indigenous writer, telling our stories, in all their shapes and manifestations, means survival.

Not all of my students are Indigenous, but story is important to all of them, and in that way, no matter where we come from, we connect. Speaking of good fortune, a couple of years ago fate brought me to a workshop with the writer Joe Stretch at the Manchester Writing School. Joe Stretch is a rock-star name and Joe himself had a bit of the rock star about him: the accent, the looks, the stovepipe jeans, the confidence. He darted about the room bestowing upon us a collection of writerly admonishments. 'Don't ask if it's good,' he exclaimed. 'I can tell you now it's bad. So let's forget about that question.' At one point, he literally leapt onto a desk in one movement. Part of me wanted to dislike all this swagger, but it might have been the most entertaining workshop I've ever been in. And it was also one of those classes you walk away from with a couple of gems you'll never forget. Don't worry about all this other stuff, Joe told us, then he quoted another writer, who said that in the end 'fiction is just one person in pain telling another person in pain a story'. Just focus on that one person, Joe said, instead of worrying about what the masses will think.

I hold that one close and bring it out frequently for students who are struggling. Students at postgraduate level often already have strong technical skills, so what are they doing with us? I guess it's one thing to have a talent for writing and quite another to see a project through from beginning to end. As well as figuring out character, point of view, structure, the nuances of tension and plot, how to end things, how to begin things and what syntactical style to use (my current class has a most pleasing ongoing conversation about the pleasures of the semicolon versus the em-dash), a new writer has to wrangle with their reason for doing what they are doing, and whether it is okay to do it—and this is perhaps the most overwhelming question for many of them. As I once heard a colleague say: 'It's 80 percent perseverance,' so the question is serious business.

This year, across classes and with other teachers, we have spent many hours on this topic. Invariably, students want to be given permission. It's our duty to provide them with a wide range of experiences of other writers: visiting speakers, articles, interviews, challenging provocations; but in the end, the only person who can give them permission is themselves. To do that, they often must work through a series of questions about what they're doing and what effect it will have. For some the equation can be simple, but many will encounter painful or difficult questions. It's careful and crucial work, and it needs to be done in a way that doesn't stall the writing completely. And, after all that, there are no guarantees. The best a writer can do, in my experience, is get comfortable with their discomfort. Find the space they need to write, and keep going, because in the end it's just you, the words on the page, and that person in pain at the other end, and that's more important than whether you feel like it's perfect or not (clue: it absolutely won't be).

Last year I found myself in a room with some very great writers, wishing I could just stop talking because nothing I said could possibly be significant, when an Indigenous writer of much greater experience than me declared, 'Just don't tell anyone that none of us know what we're doing!' Three books in and I'll never know if I got them right, but every time I get lost in that question I think about the importance of stories, the stories I never had as a kid, and I think about my own person in pain. I'm much more confident about the anthology Witi Ihimaera and I made, *Black Marks on the White Page*. It's easier to know something is right when you include as much of your community as you can, when it's expansive rather than individual, when it's not about you. I guess that's one reason Witi's been doing it all these years: bringing people into the fold and nurturing the production of an expansive literature. The more stories there are—the more voices, the more ways of speaking—the less inclined people may be to see your work as representative of a wider something or someone in a way that prevents it being read on its own terms.

But there are things about the writing world that are much harder to talk about or even describe. Tensions that are likely apparent inside writing lives and communities but not so much outside of them. This year, such a strange year, watching my students take their first tentative steps into writing lives, I became aware not of how things are becoming more open and accepting, but of how the writing world might be in danger of somehow contracting. Sometimes, when a movement is growing—and our literature certainly is, being more colourful and multi-faceted now than it's ever been before—a certain fear creeps in. Sometimes people deal with this by trying to make hard and fast rules about how things are done and what is allowed to be said. It's a weird paradox that our efforts to open up our literature can produce a new sort of orthodoxy. As we prise apart older systems and canonical forms, sometimes we disagree about how best to do that work. The force of so many tensions pulling against each other can be scary.

Are we doing it right? Are we using this platform the right way? Are we saying it correctly? Are we worthy? Who is 'we', anyway? What is correct? The fear occurs, I think, when our world suddenly expands and becomes subject to more engagement and thus more scrutiny. The fear comes partly from the way things used to be, the way things have always been, when we weren't allowed to speak. It is also a fear of the unknown, the future, and the ways in which what we say might be used against us. We've seen this before. During the Māori cultural renaissance, reclaimed aspects of Māori culture were solidified in ways they had not been before the arrival of European settlers. The dynamism, fluidity and diversity of everything from haka to wharenui and te reo was codified into straighter lines, more defined boundaries and tighter definitions. In order to survive, cultures become intent on preserving. But as we move beyond survival, we witness an opening out and a willingness to experiment and diverge.

While New Zealand literature has been in hearty good health for a long time, I've written before about how Māori, Pasifika, immigrant, queer and other groups who lack easy access, visibility or privilege have been poorly represented by our literature. While I still think we have big issues, it's clear that collectively we are changing this. Almost every New Zealand publisher and book festival is moving beyond tokenism to real engagement. That's cause for massive celebration. But such things can easily fall away, and have before, so it's no reason for complacency. Depending on the day, any one of us might waver back and forth from surviving to thriving in the literary world, so like all good things, it's complicated and fragile. And that fragility can cause us to feel anxious and over-protective, that we need clear and containing boundaries. I don't know if fear is the right word, but whatever this is, it can lead to a kind of conventionality.

In which we meet the hard wooden floor of our history
I turned to creative writing because it offered ways to explore a world I found lacking in any simplicity, and because hard rules and definitions felt limited in their usefulness. Other disciplines lacked the ability to address that which cannot be defined, and creative writing allows me to work with those fuzzy boundaries. But that's a dangerous place to spend your time. There is never any certainty of correctness.

These days I wonder a lot about what it's like for new writers to emerge into our literary environment. I suspect in some ways it is more difficult now than when I was first published. We see reviews admonishing writers for seemingly incorrect cultural representations of certain characters, as if characters are not specific individuals in specific circumstances; we see pressures placed on writers to represent whole cultural groups, though there is nothing new in this; we see internal tensions about rights and responsibilities, in which misunderstandings are swift and painful. These tensions occur as often within the same sociocultural groups as between different ones, which can be confounding and distressing.

Sometimes I wonder if there's a certain carelessness about the use of language and its impact, and perhaps social media is part of that, but I'm so tired of things being blamed on social media—we're grown-ups and we can configure things positively if we choose to. It's probably less well-known that even positive attention can place a writer in the untenable position of being seen to represent something much more than the specificities of their own work. This in itself can represent a crisis for the new writer, especially for the new non-Pākehā writer. And while the literary scene and its tensions in Aotearoa are vastly different than they are, say, in North America or the United Kingdom, our writing community is very, very small, and very, very valuable, and the effect of these seemingly small tensions can become huge.

Publicly, reviews are the place where such questions and conversations are teased out. The last 'negative' review I received was from someone I know quite well. It took so long to come out that I figured it wasn't going to be great because, knowing the reviewer as I do, I had suspected she might not be enamoured of the book. We're quite different writers, I think, who value quite different aspects of writing, but also she's extraordinarily well-read and famously straight-talking. Much more, on both counts, than me. And she did talk straight, but she didn't weaponise her talents. I could see she had taken care with her review, and with our community. In the first instance, she tried to see what the book was doing;

I don't know if she and I would agree about what that was or the way it was done, but in voicing her opinion she was attentive to the book, impersonal and professional. It was the best I could expect. Critical engagement itself is a good thing. When done well, it strengthens the literary environment (Look at us! We can agree to disagree!) but done badly it can create an environment of distrust and overprotectiveness.

It's not just reviews; books and book events are also discussed widely online, on social media, in online articles and in classes or hui. The way a book is experienced depends very much on the expectations and preconceptions brought to it by readers. But in a review or discussion, it can be unhelpful to read a book only for its sociopolitical ramifications. Perhaps stories are fair game, since my statements about the importance of stories rest on my belief that stories can change things at a societal level. Yet I find myself resisting the reading that sees only the politics of a piece, the representations, the symbolisms. What then happens to enchantment? That magical thing a book does, when it takes you away from the strictures of the contemporary political moment and offers a parallel world? The beguilement of 'what if'? What happens to characters who don't fit the analysis, or to world-building that works inconveniently against the theory? Unless we allow for the untidiness of narrative, the paradoxical nature of good characters and plot, and the unknowability, even to the author (and almost certainly to the reader), of all a story's layers, we may not quite grasp the story at all.

In a field that is all nuance, a poorly constructed review can strip all the subtlety from a work. Fiction and poetry, and creative nonfiction, are thought experiments—we read them not to be told how the world is, but to encounter questions about how it is and how it could be. Or, at least, that's how writers tend to see it. As someone with a social science background, I try to quiet my urge to apply sociopolitical analyses to my own writing. That path leads to rather clunky and tightly controlled stories, whereas I want to draw characters so real they jump off the page and run from me. I don't think I ever quite manage it. I admire writers who allow their characters to be as disconcerting and unsound as real people can be. I admire that bravery.

It's all up for grabs, in the writing of a book—enchantment, politics, social comment. A complicated matrix whose magic owes as much to the writer's efforts to see from the outside as from within. But some reviews and discussions seem to imply that if we are to write about different cultural groups and the interrelationships between them, or even create a made-up world that references those things, it must be done in the correct way. It's never entirely clear what this correct way is. And writers are compelled to do what they do despite this, knowing the way ahead is uncharted. Literature is more mirror than map, and if we are lucky, it can reflect our lives back to us in all their complexity. Literature is messy and fathomless, and of the many thousands of ways there are to enter a conversation about cultural identity, we're lucky to see a couple of New Zealand books a year that do. If one of these books emerges after years of writing and rewriting, self-doubt, first readers and writing groups, lack of time, lack of money, expert readers, the vicissitudes of the publishing world and more self-doubt; if a book finally makes it out the other end of that, thoroughly tested and angsted over, by all means review it, but let's remember how much guts and graft it took to put it out there.

This doesn't mean giving the book a free pass on all the complex questions it raises, but giving it the benefit of the doubt, as a starting point. Let's imagine an author who has done their due diligence. Let's imagine a writer who has worked and worried over the very questions at hand for many years (it will be clear, I think, if the writer hasn't!). Let's begin with compassion, recognise the work that has been done, and then, if the writer appears to have missed a beat, or a few beats, or tripped over and broken their nose on the hard wooden floor of our history, gushing blood everywhere, let's raise some questions. The questions can be raised with sensitivity and aroha. If I ask you this, will it make our stories better? The questions can be raised without inflicting harm or shame on the writer or the wider conversations about writing in Aotearoa. The reviewer can be assured that in most cases the writer has ample shame of their own to mix into the equation, and that such questions weigh heavily even when raised with the lightest of touches.

In which we think about te mea nui
When my first book came out, I had no clue what I was doing. I just wanted to tell stories. I've always been grateful that the literary community was gently welcoming as I stumbled my way through its doors. It meant that I was able to grow in confidence and gain knowledge, just enough to take the next step, and the next. Now I get to pass that on, as best as I am able.

We need more writers who engage with questions around our various identities and in order to have that, we need a literary environment that nurtures them. My hunch has always been that having more writers telling our stories in all their manifestations will lift the weight of representation from the few who make it through. We need a literary environment with open and flowing discourse, not one that feels scary to enter. In our desire to get things right and hold people accountable, we have to be really careful that we don't create an environment that is hostile to creativity, experimentation and different perspectives. We have to be careful that we don't hold each other back. We have to be careful that within our own cultural communities, we don't make the accountabilities so heavy as to inhibit creative work.

We tell our students to do the work, pay attention to the complexities of these issues, research, ask more questions and think about their positionality. Where do you write from? Who do you write for? What should you be aware of? And when you've done all that and you still don't know everything, perhaps it's okay to enter the conversation anyway, recognising your own fallibility, taking tentative steps, always asking questions.

At the beginning of this essay, I described the flow of generosity and good faith that runs through our writing and reading community. Despite a few minor petty crimes, I've always loved this about our writing scene: New Zealand writers, aside from being sensitive creatures, are a friendly bunch, which can be essential for new writers to find their way in the world. A wonderful part of my job is to coax a crop of excellent new writers out into a strange world where people read things that previously existed only inside the writers' minds. Things that, in fact, even they have limited access to. It's incredibly raw and exposing.

But it's easy to become alienated. It's easy to feel shut out. Even those of us that have been around for a while and seem established feel this keenly. And part of me thinks maybe that's okay. Individually, maybe we're not so important. But another part of me knows that if I can feel such estrangement, even with a few books behind me and people in the 'right' places who support my work, what message does that send to fledgling writers who may have none of these advantages? How does that make for a more diverse literary scene? Community matters, even for the solitary art of writing.

There is some controversy over who said it first, but the saying goes that to be a writer all you need to do is 'sit down at the typewriter, open a vein and bleed'. And the longer I stick around, the more I believe that's true. It's not worth anything unless you risk everything. The really good writing is always the stuff you're scared to put out there, the stuff for which you imagine you will pay at some point. That's the stuff that readers come and talk to you about, the stuff that connects to real pain in their lives. Writing is not the most important job in the world, but it takes a fair bit of courage and foolhardiness, and it matters. It's a funny kind of occupation: nobody needs you to do it, not really, not you in particular, and yet sometimes our words on the page mean everything to someone. That connection, that sharing of pain, is it. I start my classes with a brief invocation that embodies much of this and ends with the line 'Ko te mea nui, ko te aroha'. The most important thing is aroha: empathy, compassion, fellow feeling, generosity, even critical engagement. I know that today in the safe space of my classroom I will see aroha in action. I'm grateful for the magic of that experience. When my students graduate into the world of published authorship, I hope the reading and writing community will extend them the same. Tihei mauri ora.

First published in Kete Books, 2020

14 Saint Mary Street, 2014

Our daughter is 11 and she is so angry and sad. We're moving her away from her school and her friends for six months in the final year before high school. How could we be so callous? Last time I moved an 11-year-old away from her school I had a depressed 11-year-old who turned into a depressed teenager, so I'm pretty sure we're the worst parents ever, except this is how we're going to pay the bills. I have no permanent job, and residencies like this are the way I must make my way in the world now. All the PhD in Creative Writing did was make me overqualified for anything other than the most specific and rare positions, such as writer, or teacher of writing, and academia is so precarious, who would go into that?

I am at the beginning of writing a new book set in 1846, which means reading lots and going to the Alexander Turnbull Library and the New Zealand Archives to research old newspapers and books, and finding out as much as I can about a time and place of which I know little. The house at 14 Saint Mary Street, with its Victoriana, its tiny museum in the wall, its attention to historic detail, the old stove and wood and brick paths, is the perfect place to begin this work. The cottage garden is a marvel I want to emulate—the way every flower and plant seems randomly placed, tightly packed, yet harmonious. No rows or bark mulch here. The flow of people is a bit like this too.

Oh, the other thing the PhD did was help me produce a novel, which is a miracle no matter how it comes to be in the world. Every week my publisher sends me the bestseller list if my novel has made an appearance. This happens most weeks for six months, which I now know is more amazing than I realised then. But later I will also discover that it is possible to be number 5 on the bestseller list in New Zealand by selling only 21 books in a week, so it pays to engage an appropriately Kiwi definition of the word 'best' and the word 'seller' in this context. I don't know how anyone in the industry makes any living at all.

The new school is not so bad. Although for a number of weeks I am still the Mother Who Wronged Her, our daughter discovers something new: what you thought mattered the most might not actually be as important as you thought. She meets new friends who live in inner-city apartments, look more like her, and come from all over the world. When she comes and tells us she quite likes it, and that maybe Kāpiti is not the centre of the universe after all, we can finally relax. It is still a bad thing I did, getting this residency and causing us to move house, but maybe I'm not the worst mother in the world.

My husband writes in the shed out in the garden, I write in the front room. We walk up to the botanical gardens frequently, or down the street to the dairy or the local pub. Too often, I am called away to do other things I promised to do before I got the residency—talks or teaching or organising. During the Te Hā Māori Writers Hui in Auckland, which we have resurrected after a latent period of many years, I develop a rash and a few other symptoms. I call Healthline to check whether I should still be at a hui, and talk to a nurse who we quickly realise is a cousin I've never met. Given the symptoms, she suspects shingles, as does the doctor I see on my return. I take to my bed with some heavy-duty medication, but because we've caught it early, it doesn't become much worse. It will not be the last stress-related illness I come down with as a writer, but I enjoy the forced bed rest extravagantly. How very Victorian.

To be a writer is to exist in a little old house of naivety and hope, which we tend daily. We bore our children at the dinner table with endless talk of books and writers, but they constantly find new ways to tease us about that, and it pays to not take ourselves too seriously, despite the earnestness of this metaphor. By the start of the next decade, I will have lost my naivety and a good portion of my hope after encountering a streak of hostility in the community, and I will miss them greatly. It's a simpler thing to create when you believe in the goodness of what you do, and when you believe others are in it with you. All we have, in 2014, is belief, and the evidence that if we keep writing, people will read. I'm trying to get back to a place where that is all I need to know.

At night, a ruru calls from Te Ahumairangi Hill behind the house. Ruru has always been kaitiaki to my whānau, so her call is a comfort and a welcome. For a while this area was known as Tinakori, and later we see a story that this name comes from the lack of meal provision by settler employers to Māori road workers. But while we are there, we don't experience this lack of manaakitanga. We bring our loves and our pains with us into this neighbourhood, and we are welcomed in.

First published in Room to Write: 20 Years of Randell Cottage Writers (2022)

He Whare Taonga

~

Make Way for Them

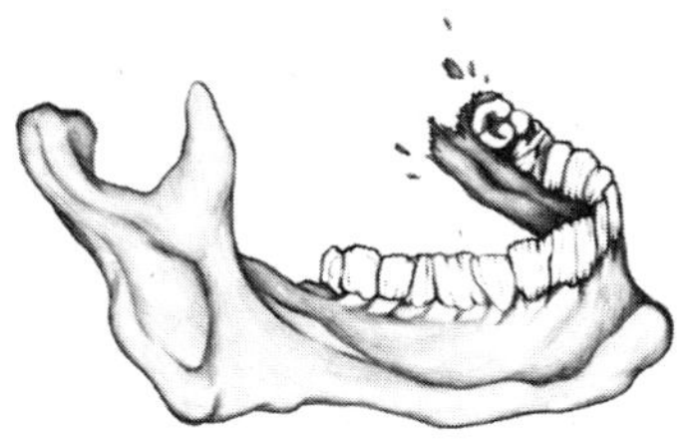

This Compulsion in Us

The year is 1979. I'm five years old, walking into the Wanganui[1] Museum, hand in hand with my father. I wear woollen tights and buckled shoes, and most days there doesn't seem to be much difference between what I can see and what I can imagine. On my fifth birthday I was so disappointed by my playdough kindergarten birthday cake that I tried to eat it, having decided the act of believing would magically transform it into something sweetly edible. Already, real life has proven itself fraught, though I have found solace in storybooks. At home I spend hours drawing Cinderella dresses over and over—tightly cinched waists, crinolines, pannier skirts. In Wanganui Museum, approaching the Edwardian Street, I travel back in time: olden-day shops with toys and sweets, a living room, mannequins with real Cinderella dresses. I have no concept of the era, only that this is as close to the imaginary world of story as I am likely to get.

And there is Dad's hand: dry and warm, large and solid and square-fingered. When he lets go to point out objects from his own childhood, there is his voice, telling stories about how things were done in the old days, how it was different, more pure and innocent it seems, even to a five-year-old. Later we climb the stairs and view the animals and birds that have stitches showing, glass eyes and stuffing that springs out at alarming angles. Somehow this is all part of the crusty magic of the place.

In 1991 I return with my first-year museum studies class. We haven't lived in Wanganui since I was six, and I am excited about going back to the first museum I can remember. I walk in with the newly acquired weight of family and cultural history on my shoulders. I reach the first cabinet in the Māori Court—a glass box filled with countless taonga pounamu—and stop. I feel inexplicably bad. Dizzy, almost as if I have stepped outside of myself. I have learnt enough in my Māori art and culture papers to know that these hei pounamu, hei tiki and hei matau once adorned the physical bodies of ancestors, and were likely separated from those tūpuna by warfare, poverty or sneaky dealings. I know that the creation of taonga pounamu was a long, laborious process that could take generations. I know that the taonga most likely still carry the mana and tapu of their original makers and wearers, and the number of items lined up row upon row tells me that they were acquired carelessly, without reverence for their intrinsic value.

I turn and leave. On my way out I try to express my dismay to a fellow Māori student, but he does not seem to feel as bad as I do. I wonder now whether it was the swiftness of two inner worlds coming together that caused my out-of-body discord. As a child I had not found the Māori Court interesting. I don't remember taking more than a cursory glance at the items there. Back then, Māori culture was taken for granted by mainstream New Zealand, and I had not learnt to see its value. I certainly had not learnt the stories behind any taonga I saw, and a trip to the museum wouldn't have taught me them.

This is no longer the case. When I visit what is now called the Whanganui Regional Museum, I meet staff working with both the history of the objects and the ironies of the history of their institution. These days, there is a self-awareness evident in most museums that was only just beginning to flourish around the time I went there as a first-year student. You won't find a bulk cabinet of pounamu on display today, but you will find curators and conservators and registrars in basements and backrooms, trying to bring the disparate pieces of history back together, making connections between objects and people, looking for the sources of things.

Kanohi ki te Kanohi

When I arrive at the Museum der Weltkulturen in 2012, there is an exhibition installed on the ground floor of Villa 37. On the third floor are the apartments a small group of New Zealand artists and writers will share for the next month. Villa 37, Schaumainkai, overlooks the Main River, Frankfurt, along what is known as Museumsufer or the Museum Embankment, named for the large concentration of museums in that area. The city is old and pretty. The locals are friendly and multilingual and uber-elegant. Even the children and dogs appear languid.

The exhibition is called *Face to Face*, or *Fa'afesaga'i* in Samoan, *Kanohi ki te Kanohi* in Māori. It contains pen and ink drawings by the young Samoan–Kiwi artist Francis Pesamino alongside taonga from the Weltkulturen Polynesian collection. I haven't seen contemporary Polynesian drawings by an emerging artist exhibited alongside tatau instruments and carved taonga before. The mix of ancient and modern is illuminating, creating associations a New Zealander, with all our education and cultural awareness, might not make. How does a portrait of Valerie Adams, her sponsor's name like a tattoo on her collar, resonate with ancient tatau patterns and carvings, for example? How does who we were in the past relate to who we are now?

The resonances of *Face to Face / Kanohi ki te Kanohi / Fa'afesaga'i* increase as the days go by. At a press conference, Tanea Heke, who is director of the New Zealand at Frankfurt programme, speaks of this concept—the relationships we have formed and how we have all come to be in this space at this time. We all bring, she tells the German media, our people with us.

At the exhibition opening there is a bit of celebratory mingling, and Yvette Mutumba, the curator of the African collection, asks about my visits to Weltkulturen's other collections. I tell her my main observation, which is how much everyone loves and cares for their collections. She tells me that in Germany they do not use the word 'curator' for their work, but 'Kustodin'. This word gives a clearer picture of what their work is, she says, opening her arms wide like a bird taking chicks under its wings—they look after the objects. I think of how close the idea of custodianship is to kaitiakitanga. It's not the first time I've found myself thinking that the way they do things here is closer to the way we do things at home than I thought it would be.

The collections of the Weltkulturen are vast, and this is unsettling. The institution's main benefactors were collectors in the days when the objective was to obtain as many different examples of one type of thing as possible in order to swap items with other institutions. Before I left New Zealand, I asked a curator friend if there was anything I should do to prepare for an encounter with taonga that had been taken overseas. She told me that when she was in Berlin she had been taken without warning into a room filled with shelves of skulls. Better to write ahead and tell them I didn't want to see any human remains, she advised. And whakanoa—cleanse with water—whenever possible. The Kustodins are very mindful of my request, though the director, Clémentine Deliss, tells me about the mokomokai that have been repatriated to Te Papa, and assumes I will want to see images of them.

Our 'job' as writers and artists in residence is to respond to the collections at the museum. A fresh eye can bring new ways of relating to and interpreting collections. This idea was introduced by museum staff as a way to approach an old museum problem that had been exacerbated by World War II: all the taonga had been saved because they had been sent out of the city; all the museum records had not. While colonial collection records may still have been inadequate, they would have been better than none at all.

The medieval city of Frankfurt was flattened by the war. Afterwards, it was impossible to recreate the worn beauty of stone structures imbued with history. Clémentine tells me how even now the city plans historical recreations into their rebuilds, striving for a pre–World War II authenticity that no longer exists. The town centre, Römerberg, is disdainfully referred to as Disneyland by locals. Postcards for sale all around Römerberg display Frankfurt at different stages of annihilation, pre-annihilation, and reconstruction. The famous Römer is a facsimile of something Frankfurt lost to successive bombs that ended 5500 lives.

At the exhibiton opening, Clémentine herds us towards a table of food, like a very European marae auntie. 'Eat, eat! Come and sit down! You must eat. Where's Francis?' As the youngest in our crew, and the freshest to overseas travel, Francis is the subject of much concern, which gives us ample opportunity to tease him—'You've got some German aunties now, eh? Bet you weren't expecting that.'

Later, I think about how perfect the title of the exhibition is as a symbol for what is happening at the museum. *Kanohi ki te kanohi* is an oft-repeated Māori proverb that suggests that communication is better served by meeting face-to-face. Māori implicitly trust face-to-face contact as a means of avoiding misunderstandings and misinterpretations. The effort undertaken to meet face to face also suggests a level of respect and keenness to establish effective relationships. It's like shaking hands or sharing food—a communal, physical gesture of relationality. Or the pōwhiri ritual of encounter, which forces visitors and hosts to lay bare their intentions, antagonisms and interconnections. I imagine that someone from the New Zealand at Frankfurt team must have suggested this title, but when I ask Dr Eva Raabe, who curated the exhibition, I find this is not the case.

Eva's idea was that Francis's portraits and the objects from the collection would face each other, and that viewers would face them. Clémentine suggested the name Face to Face, and Eva agreed. Only then were translations into Māori and Samoan made. Because I don't believe in coincidences of this scale, I like to think that the staff involved in putting together the exhibition had developed some sensitivity to the cultural resonances of the objects with which they work. How else could a concept so fundamental to Māori culture have found its way into their lexicon as they worked with objects from Aotearoa? Māori believe that our taonga are living, breathing representations of the ancestors—could this not be one way they show that indeed they are already in dynamic relationship, kanohi ki te kanohi, with their guardians in this institution?

'Taonga are our time travellers,' Paul Tapsell said in his 2011 Gordon Brown Lecture. 'They made real not only the ancestors, but also their surrounding landscapes by burying a sense of ancestral belonging deep into our living core.'[2] Taonga, he explained, collapse time so that descendants can emotionally engage and experience ancestral moments in the now. Perhaps even non-descendants can pick up echoes of meaning from these emissaries of time and place.

Later, during one of the collection visits, Eva admits to one of the Kiwi visitors that at times of stress or conflict she touches the objects and talks to them. This information is eagerly passed among us. Later, when I ask her about it, she speaks of the very oldest stone objects, barely identifiable, which seem to carry a deep feeling of strength and calm. Perhaps her colleagues would disparage her for such actions, she says, but she has risen in our already high esteem.

If I had any preconceptions, it was that I would perceive the containment of Māori taonga in institutions like Weltkulturen in terms of our loss, but instead I discover a sense of exchange and yearning. The older impulse to collect objects, to colonise and contain, I do not understand. But now that the collections are there, custodians and audiences display a curiosity that is more unguarded and receptive than snatching and appropriative. The objects in the collection hold a charge that, as much as possible, is honoured rather than suppressed. This is not without its risks, but the practice recognises that museum collections contain taonga—precious objects that allow us to touch something ancient and deep and much more knowing than we are.

Before we leave, we are to take part in discussions and readings as part of the Frankfurt Book Fair. One quiet afternoon, I take the key we have been given and go downstairs to sit with the taonga and write. On the day I am to leave, I take an audience into the same room and ask them to face the canoe prow, or tauihu, displayed there. I tell them the story the taonga tells me, of history, wars and appropriations, losses and connections; of time passing and two nations brought together, face to face.

In Case You See Yourself

Passing through the main entrance of the Canterbury Museum, visitors are confronted by life-sized dioramas of Māori from the moa hunter period. They are posed in the classical style: a stuffed moa in the foreground, a man with a spear crouched near him, ready to throw; a woman squatted low with her kurī at her side, their faces drawn in anticipation. In one sense, it is a carefully rendered scene. Elsewhere, a woman with a fish in one hand leans over her waka, breasts drooping realistically. Men are making fire and flint, houses and storehouses in the background; a woman cooks small birds on a kind of spit. The scenes are as real as any that can be viewed in the best museum dioramas in the world, the human forms and expressions carefully moulded. I've seen much worse recreations of colonial European figures: loose beards and frightening eyes, arms drooping where elbows and muscle-tone should be.

Faces and voices from all over the world move swiftly past these entrance-way dioramas. When they stop, it is for no more than 30 seconds or so. One or two walk slowly, peer more closely, but none stay as I do. What do they see, I wonder? How do they read these displays? And then, do they see me? I am a later manifestation of the people in the cases. Few would think that. Few would look at the half-naked, brown-skinned, dark-haired figures in the cases and make a connection with the light-skinned, red-haired, clothed figure beside them. But if they looked more closely, they might see the broad nose, thick lips and fuzzy hair. Perhaps even that would not be enough, but what would they conclude if I looked more like my ancestors? What if I looked like my cousins?

A pre-teen girl comes through the gallery, gawping at my still-life friend with her fish and her waka, bare-breasted and bent forwards for all eternity, and exclaims loudly, 'Soooo not appropriate!' like a character from *Mean Girls*. I almost laugh out loud. She's right, of course, in more ways than she's aware of.

The dioramas are a window to a version of the past: 3D fabricated stills of history or 'pre-history' that fit a particular way of viewing the world, evolution, history and technology. The narrative they actually offer is about colonisation and the history of museums, rather than anything about the people they are meant to represent. Move to the next room and quite a different picture emerges. Here objects *made* by people in centuries past can be viewed—adzes, carved pou, ancestral figures, fish hooks. I overhear a mother say to her son, 'Look how they were able to turn that piece of rock into a tool.' Here there is the opportunity to understand how the ancestors lived via the material goods they left behind. Viewers are forced to slow down and engage their imaginations.

Furthermore, the objects are imbued with power. That power might be a kind of archaeological and historical patina, or it might be the inherent power left by the makers of the objects, otherwise known as mana and tapu. These museum artefacts carry the stories of everything that has happened to them and their people. A kind of nexus is therefore possible between the museum visitor, the object, and the people who long ago created and used it. A quiet walk around the gallery might create in the viewer a sense of awe. In this, there is a kind of magic.

These artefacts are presented in a way that suggests they signify a progression from the moa hunter dioramas. If the hypothesis, based primarily on Eurocentric analysis of material goods, is that Māori developed a more cultivation-based, stratified and 'sophisticated' culture as time went on, then something is wrong. The people represented by the dioramas didn't spring from the ground fully formed, nor did they evolve from apes in a land that knew no mammals. They navigated their way here following star maps and sea paths their ancestors had devised over centuries of experience and careful observation. The arrival of wave after wave of mighty sea-voyaging waka was not accidental, nor were their return voyages or other explorations. They brought with them the animals and plants they needed to survive and sent their strongest and cleverest men and women, including tohunga and rangatira. These were people who knew the constellations, winds, currents and their own technologies so well they could confidently sail for months to settle an uninhabited land. They held a level of knowledge and sophistication that few of us can claim. The dioramas show none of this.

In contrast, most contemporary museums are moving toward interactive, story-based exhibitions that contextualise historical experiences. This is essential, since representing human groups without giving them space to tell their own stories continues a line of thinking that takes us, if we follow it to its natural conclusion, to dark and inhumane territory.

Looking at the diorama figures, I can't help wondering how far they are from other parts of the natural history collection. All other living things were collected and stuffed by naturalists in vast quantities to be shared with other museums all over the world. Brian Gill's *The Owl that Fell from the Sky: Stories of a Museum Curator* explains the world of taxidermy and categorisation, collection and taxonomy. Gill is passionate about the need for such collection and preservation. 'Fully documented natural history specimens are called "voucher specimens",' he writes.

> Each provides a documentary record of biological occurrence and distribution that is superior to a mere literature record [. . .] As natural history collections grow they become massive directories of the animals and plants that have lived in different areas at different times, and may hold the key to how the characteristics and distributions of species have varied with place and changed with time.[3]

Gill goes on to give examples of how natural history collections have been useful for conservation and scientific discovery. More important for research than the mounted specimens we can view in museums are 'study-skins', which 'require the same skilled taxidermy but for easy storage and examination they are set out straight, like a human body laid in a coffin'.[4] Sets of loose bones are also essential for identification work, as are the 'bones of an individual joined together as an articulated skeleton', and animals preserved in alcohol.

Even as I nod along with Gill's naturalist enthusiasm, uncertainty marks my reading. I have enjoyed museums and their collections all my life. I have come close to (admittedly dead) animals I never would have seen alive, and learnt much from the experience. But something about this is inherently uncomfortable. It is not a far leap to wonder, while viewing Canterbury Museum's moa hunter dioramas, whether museums would have taxidermied humans if it had been ethically possible.

This might seem an extreme position until one considers that naturalists did once collect human bones, especially skulls, to categorise ethnic groups and genders according to cranial size; that living humans were displayed in museums and zoos until at least a third of the way into the 20th century; that in the Canterbury Museum itself, a fully intact Egyptian mummy is displayed, her wrappings intact but her body X-rayed, researched and scanned for all that she can reveal about her people; and that in our national museum, Te Papa, human remains were an element of the recent Aztec exhibition. If there were some acceptable way to preserve the human form posed in action, just like the birds and mammals of the Antarctic exhibition, wouldn't they have done it? What if there were Neanderthal remains that could be resurrected to look natural? Would that be more acceptable, like stuffed mammoths or orangutans? *Imagine the benefits to science and the potential audience.* How human is too human?

How naive of me. A little more research reveals that the study-skins and bones of humans *were* collected. I've known for some time about Khoikhoi woman Sarah Baartman, who was exhibited in Britain and Europe while alive, and whose bones and body cast were exhibited in France for decades after her death, until she was finally repatriated to South Africa and given the dignity of proper burial. But I am unprepared for where a little more research takes me:

In the nineteenth century [. . .] many Khoikhoi women were treated as taxidermic material, their skins stripped and stuffed to preserve them as specimens of the anomalous. Sir John Herschel, during his visit to the Cape in the mid-1830s, noted that he had seen a 'Hottentot woman's skin—stuffed . . . with all the extraordinary peculiarities attributed to these nymphs by travellers'.[5]

We are not so far from our animal cousins. Some of us more than others, according to pre-21st-century museography.

The Museum in the Living Room

Here is the paradox of the museum: it preserves and contains treasures, but also captures and immobilises things that make sense only in motion, things that should breathe and transform. The uncontainable. The living. Somewhere in the centre of that paradox is the niggling discomfort that accompanies each visit. In Frankfurt, it was on visiting a friend that I encountered a place that was like a museum without the more worrying aspects of museology. Barbara is a filmmaker who had come to Aotearoa to make a documentary about New Zealand writers, and then invited two of her subjects for dinner during our time in her home city. We followed her around the aromatic and colourful Kleinmarkthalle, where fresh and handcrafted deli foods of all kinds could be bought. Then she took us to her small apartment on a narrow street that I remember as cobbled (Barbara assures me that it is not). In a walled garden we ate and drank and talked, then went inside where she fed us delicate pasta parcels with the ubiquitous, sharp rucola salad. We talked about books and filmmaking and stopped open-mouthed when Barbara told us stories about her other film projects—the time she filmed 'Marty' (Scorsese) talking to film students, and her decision to concentrate her documentary skills on the quieter arts like writing.

Barbara's place was tiny and warren-like, shelves filled yjr wall space with records and books to the ceiling. The upper floors included her office space, kitchen, and living areas, but the bottom floor was full of paintings and older wooden furniture. When I asked her permission to write about this, she sent me a document with photos of the building just after World War II, when it was a bakery. I recognised the outer walls of the garden courtyard we had sat in. In 1976 she moved in, her father taking the downstairs in 1980 as his studio. Almost 40 years later, she hopes to go on renting her home despite rapidly rising rents.

Barbara's father would have turned 100 last year, so she staged an exhibition of his work at Frankfurt's oldest half-timber house, which dates from the 12th century. As she notes, Georg Dickenberger was a brilliant man, his paintings vivid and soulful, sometimes abstract. 'As they were rather poor he did not have extensive schooling, but he acquired an enormous knowledge by reading. He was my Google and Wikipedia long before the internet—about history or art you could ask him anything.' After they died, she restored her parents' nice old and half-broken furniture and took it with their books over to the studio. 'And now it feels like home.'

More than a museum, then. We were only there one evening, but I think of it as often as the Weltkulturen. We had been welcomed and fed and shown a piece of the history of a city, kept alive and warm by a descendant, and her stories.

Going to the Zoo

For six months in 2014, we are residents at Randell Cottage, Thorndon, built in 1867. The day after we move in, I discover the purpose of the small cabinet beside the bookshelf—Randell Cottage also has a museum in the living room. It houses items that were excavated from under and within the house during renovation: 19th-century bottles and toys and crockery. The house is a mix of the original and the reconstructed or re-envisioned. Despite the care given to the reconstructed, it is the original elements that hold an extra charge: floorboards made from ship's timbers, original brick around a fireplace, glass windows over walls that show layers of original wallpaper. Outside there is a plaque under the ngaio tree, and another on the gate. We live in a house with signage denoting its age and cultural value.

My project for this residency is to write a novel based on the story of a boy who was taken to London to be exhibited alongside George French Angas's drawings and paintings in the mid-19th century. Very little is known about the real boy and his life. The first book I pick up inside the cottage is *The Fox Boy* by Peter Walker, which is about a different 'orphaned' Māori boy in the 19th century. I have always wanted to read it, and it seems perfectly apt that I never have until this moment. The abduction of children of one culture by people of another traverses a gap, says Walker, and is 'part of a very old theme, of removal and transformation . . . This is worth examining for a moment. The child wanders into the gap, but the gap is not a real place, it exists only in the mind. In other words it is not so much that the child is in the gap, as that the gap is in the child.' The project of transplanting a child fulfils some need within the coloniser to understand the other, but only to such an extent that the gap can be filled with the colonising culture.

Imaginatively, writing this story will take me to Piccadilly Circus, where Indigenous peoples were exhibited alongside exotic animals, material culture, 'freaks' and curiosities. It may also take me back to Frankfurt, where two years ago, on one of our research forays into the Weltkulturen's vast photography, film and document archive, I discovered a folder filled with posters advertising the exhibition of human groups at the Zoologischen Garten. From around 1878 to 1931, in a circus tent on zoo grounds, European audiences were invited to observe such phenomena as the 1885 Ceylon Expedition, featuring 51 Singhalesen and 12 Elephanten; the Ofrikaner-Karawane exhibition, featuring 16 men, four women and seven children; Das Amazonencorps; Australian Cannibal Boomerang Throwers; Krao the Missing Link Half Monkey Half Woman; and Schaustellung der Samoaner-Truppe (Flaunt the Samoan Troup, according to Google).

Later exhibition posters for Samoan groups are somewhat in keeping with one Weltkulturen Kustodin's comment that Samoan groups were treated better than the African or Asian groups that came. 'Our new compatriots,' crows one poster above the title 'Ausstellung Samoa'. The S for Sāmoa is formed by a snake wrapped around the top half of a heavy-lidded temptress dressed only in a tooth necklace and a flower tucked above one ear.

The truth is, I am captivated by these posters not only for the historical story they tell, but for the exotic whiff they exude. They are odd, and old, romanticised and beautiful. Whatever horrifying tale they tell, I am just as voyeuristic about it as the audiences that would have flocked to the zoo for entertainment. Would that I could watch those audiences as they watched the people forced to parade or perform for their pleasure. How did we reach the moment in history that made such an activity acceptable? Desirable? Shouldn't I be more repelled by this story? I am strangely attracted to it, understanding the dehumanisation in intellectual terms, but unable to instinctually reject a story that tells me something about what human beings are, what we are capable of.

The old and odd. I want to understand this compulsion in us. The freak show. The talk show. Reality TV. The world's biggest, smallest, grossest, oldest. A moment on the internet is enough to show we haven't moved far from putting people in zoos, making assumptions and feeling superior. The modern museum may have an uncomfortable relationship with this, removing itself through changes in focus and display and interpretation. And so it should. But inside me still is the child who was fascinated by the old and dusty exhibits in Wanganui—the (forgive me) *weirdness* of it all, and it's she who sometimes drives the writing.

And maybe it's she who turns to history as a place of refuge and solace, as a place I can pick apart and puzzle back together, a place that despite all its tragedies and travesties is infinitely more comfortable than the harsh realities and uncertainties of the heaving, polluted, terrifying world as it is now. She seeks comfort, and the museum is like a book: full of adventure, mystery, the vastness of time and travel, but contained and manageable and seemingly safe. Sometimes the museum is where we encounter the 'other' and if we look closely enough, understand that we are looking at some fantastic version of ourselves.

Going Home

Why is Wanganui Museum the one I remember best, of them all? Why, after living in at least eight places between the ages of three and thirteen, do I think of the town I lived in for barely two years as closest to my hometown? Looking back from over here, from this different place, this different time, I see the footsteps my family left all over town. My grandparents took up residence there in the mid-20th century and stayed until they took leave of their terrestrial lives. There was the bike shop, the schools, the yearly routines. My father, aunts and uncles grew up there. With their families they made homes and careers, and left, and came back. I barely knew most of them, but perhaps that is all it takes for a place to become a cornerstone of a life. I see now the ghosts of significant places and events: first school, first best friend, first memories, not-quite-first trauma. Whanganui has a resonance that other places we lived never carried. They don't carry the same draw, the same vibration as a town that bears a familial stamp.

Sometimes, the museum is where we go to find parts of ourselves we thought we'd left behind. On the day we return to Whanganui so I can research this essay, we also visit my father, who has found his way back to one of his hometowns. I haven't seen him for nearly three years. As we pull into the driveway I glimpse him in the kitchen, the still-solid hand unsteady now, square finger and thumb pinched around his cigarette as he inhales. He turns, and at first I am not sure he has registered our presence because he doesn't move towards us, and his expression doesn't change. I can already see this will not be a good day. I steel myself to get out of the van. As we approach the house, he comes out and blocks our way. I try to draw him in, promising a lunch he shows no interest in. He makes a couple of jokes about our van and how hard it must be to live with me.

For the next hour, he reminds me of a scratched 33 LP record being played too slow, the needle jumping back to the same point and repeating the same out-of-tune warble.

He doesn't drink, but his half-full glass waits for him in the fridge. My daughter watches warily. My partner laughs politely. I make food.

An hour later, before I have figured out how we can make a graceful exit, my father says, *Well, it was nice to see ya.* He has gained some lucidity, with the food and the talk. But neither of us seems to have the stamina or forbearance for this kind of encounter.

This last memory is not really about a museum. I don't know if it is really about my father either. Last time we talked he was positive, almost wise. *Most people are basically decent, you know*, he said. I hadn't even told him I had been struggling to live with the world I heard about every day in the news. That world was not of my making, or my choice. That was a world that had begun to look increasingly ugly and threatening. It was a private pain, but fathers know things.

Sometimes we have to excavate the good from things we have always viewed as bad. Appropriations, lost families, colonised and hidden histories; these are all part of our family stories, not just our national ones. There are always things that are hard to take, things for which we seek solace. But this my father gave me: afternoons at the museum.

First published in *Landfall* 229 (2015)

Address to the Tauihu
in the *Face to Face* Exhibition

E te Rangatira,

When I look at you I see ocean voyages, men at your back working in hard rhythm with hoe, thrust and sweep, salt ocean flicking foam over you, the slick of it pushed down and off by the wind. I see you at the front of your waka, parting the way—the bringer of life, the bringer of death, cutting a fine line between worlds. Opening the way to the tapu realm of war. You work like the haka, all pūkana face and flashing eyes, bringing up the ihi and the wehi for these men who you protect with your widespread arms.

I see the tohunga whakairo with his chisel, carving deep lines and notches, his strong eye and arm for symmetry—the prayers that roll through his mind as he works. He cannot afford to make mistakes. There can be no wastage. The tree was taken from te wao nui a Tāne with great ceremony and effort. There are no plans, no sketches, no pencil lines. Each cut is deep and permanent. What stories he has to carve, what teachings to pass on.

I see Papatūānuku and Ranginui, Tangaroa, Tūmatauenga, Tāwhirimātea—stories reaching back into the past until we find ourselves at the dawn of time, just as light filters into the world, and further, to Te Pō—the many long dark nights of creation—and back again, to Te Kore—the place where time did not yet exist, where both the nothing and the everything had not yet come to be. I see the eternal moment before the Big Bang, the chaos in all its beauty, the moment of ignition where all the matter of the Universe began to coalesce, spread, oscillate ever outwards. This is the takarangi spiral. Darkness and light come into being. Atoms find each other and create matter. Eventually there are worlds, planets and stars, the sky and Earth. Day and night. The duality and perfect symmetry of the universe. The Sky, Ranginui, and Earth, Papatūānuku, have children, the Gods, who create all living things, including human beings, to clothe their mother. This is whakapapa.

Genealogy that links humanity to the universe. All this I see in your design.

But I see the fire gone from your eyes now. No pāua shell discs for the sun to ignite and reflect the ocean. Your arm is broken and lost, your tongue made blunt, your decorations and harakeke lashings long gone, along with the body of your waka. You sustained injuries on your way here, or maybe over those long years in basements and on shelves, moved from one place of storage to another. You have seen wars, at home and in this walled city far from the sea.

I see blood spilt. Tribe against tribe, tribe against newcomers. Confusion. Instability. Fierceness and desperation and taonga taken apart and hidden. Were you lost? Stolen? Swapped to feed the tribe? Given in exchange for safety, allegiance or money? Perhaps you were gifted, though what a gift you must have been. It must have been a big promise made, whatever it was, or a great sadness when they took you away. I see many of you, piled up, taken to new homes, symbols of a dying race.

I see you come here, e Koro, packed and processed and put in storage. Spoken about but never spoken to, not anymore. A strange object in a strange land. I do not know what value is placed on your dark brown skin. I see you waiting. All that time, in the darkness. Displayed. Studied. But mostly, darkness. Two wars come, bigger and noisier and more deadly than even the ones you witnessed in the flesh. Sounds like thunder and the city falling about you. They move you for protection. You are a treasure to them, but not in the same way you are a treasure to us.

At home, your people did not die out after all. But what do you know of this, as the long 20th century marches on. The people you live among rebuild after the war. They create the city and the cultural world anew. This is part of your story now. And strangely, it is not so different from the story of your people at home.

E Koro, some of us have come to see you now. We bring with us the sounds and flavours of Aotearoa as it is today. You bring the hā of Aotearoa as it was then—te ao hurihuri—the tumultuous times. But you bring them to us, too, and us to them—the tangata whenua of this place: their history, their culture—the hā of this place. Your being here creates a relationship between us. Your presence is not what I thought it would be. You are not lost.

Weltkulturen Museum, Frankfurt, 2012
First published in *Five Dials* 32 (2014)

Bugger

It's November when I tell Lorry my writer's instinct has finally gotten the best of my relationship with my father. Dad and I have started a relationship again: it goes like this, every five or so years a new cycle. We're speaking again. But every single conversation we have now concerns his death and what he wants me to do as soon as it happens.

'You've got to come right away. Grab the keys, the car, anything you want from the house. Otherwise those buggers'll get it. Possession is nine-tenths of the law. You gotta be here fast. It's for your sake, eh? Not mine. I'll be ashes. Gonna cremate me as soon as I kick the bucket. Before you even get here. I'll be gone.'

It's literally the same conversation every week or two. The exact same words.

'Are you gonna be ready? Possession is nine-tenths of the law. I'm telling you. They told me—they're just gonna come in and sell everything to the Sallies for 50 cents. You gotta come straight away. Grab everything you want. Get the keys for the car. You'll both have to come so you can drive both the cars home. It's for your benefit.'

He lives three or four hours away. Sometimes we start on other subjects: how we are, my children, my sister who remains estranged from him, but always we land here.

'Now this other business. It's for your benefit to get here quick, eh? If they get their hands on it there'll be nothing. I've paid for the cremation. Nobody can believe I got it for that price. They wanted me to buy a coffin but I said nah. Just to burn it? I'm not buying a flash coffin just to burn it. I found out they can just put me on a board. So they're just gonna put me on a board.'

I've given up trying to reassure him that I'm not particularly worried about what happens to his stuff. Neither of us has been very good at this father–daughter business, even though there has always been just enough caring to carry on. And I don't expect to get some boon from his death. But he seems offended by the suggestion that I don't care about his material possessions, and he's obsessed with the idea that what little he has should get into the right hands after his death. It's become necessary to play along.

I understand it. His partner of 25 years died recently after a long, long illness. He has no one to take care of now, and only his own death to plan. Because that's how Dad sees the world. He's been talking about his imminent demise since I was about eight, which means since his mid-30s, when he was diagnosed with high cholesterol and high blood pressure and maybe a touch of sclerosis. I think the emphysema diagnosis came later, and there's been a bunch of other stuff since then: skin cancer, a burst appendix that turned to gangrene, bad knees, a few punch-ups. Lately there's been a bunch of stuff he doesn't bother to tell me anymore. He just hit 70. But also, he's been a heavy daily drinker ever since I can remember. The alcohol has messed with his brain and alienated most people he knows and loves. That his body keeps going through long-term alcohol and cigarette consumption is testament to bloody hardy genes. Genes I sometimes hope will triumph over my sensitive Māori genes from the other side: Dad's folks died in their 90s; Mum's in their 40s and 60s. But Mum always says they died of broken hearts, so maybe that's different. Dad has been avoiding the kind of softheaded emotions that can kill you all his life, though I'm not sure it's helped him to live.

It was always a difficult relationship, so despite the morbid repetition of death instructions, talking to Dad these days is peaceful. There's only one focus. I know what to expect. It's tiresome and troubling, but predictability is a gift for any child of an alcoholic. I continue to be prepared for him to say something so nasty I won't be able to talk to him again. He has a gift for it, and you'd go a long way to meet any human who gives fewer flying fucks what anyone thinks of him. Until suddenly he does.

So one day after one of these conversations I say to Lorry: I kind of wish he would actually get on with it. And Lorry looks mortified but also unsurprised, because he's met my dad and there's not an odder or more overtly offensive man you could meet, and he kind of gets it, I think. But I know it's an awful thing to say. So I say something like:

'Yeah I know, but he's been building up to it for so long, and I want to write about him but I can't while he's still alive.'

It's the ugly side of this profession: the compulsion to write *everything*. And the longer I do it, the less I resist. It's just necessary, like eating and exercise and taking the rubbish out. Essential to some sort of balance in life.

I do have loyalty to him. I still censor what I tell him. I still censor what I write down. There are some truths I just won't get into, repeat, go over—the many things in his life I shouldn't have been party to and wasn't protected from. Partly it's the lengthy build-up and my own frequent, childish wish that he would disappear from my life that make it difficult to really be concerned about this demise he's so intent on planning to the last detail. Maybe there is a little chunk of

Dad in my heart, obstinate and cynical, who doesn't give any flying fucks what anyone thinks. He's my dad, and if he wants to die then that's his business, and I'll get some peace.

But the problem is, I don't believe he actually wants to die. Despite what we do or don't tell each other, we know how things are, Dad and me. And when I hear his tired old voice over the phone there is some aspect of it that is so familiar and so very much a part of the world. Part of my world. Alive. So I say to Lorry:

'I love him but he's such a stupid old bugger.' And he says that's true, and we laugh because sometimes that's all you can do.

And later, in a small space where I pretend it will not be read, I write this story.

2017

Make Way for Them

You're just a person with lots of needs and anxieties and opinions about the world, and this one big yearning that drowns everything else out. And there's a relationship, which may or may not be a relationship that is conducive to the nurturing of children, but you think it is. You're 22 and you think lots of things that you will revise in future years, but of some things you are very sure, and you should enjoy this confidence while it lasts. So even though other people your age aren't doing it, at least none you know, there is a whole other miraculous human in your arms, who you gave birth to in a studio flat in Palmerston North. Just you and the midwives, because by now you know the relationship *isn't* conducive to the nurturing of children, though for years you'll keep trying, because you're stubborn and you don't believe you could possibly have chosen wrong. And your mum is there, but rather than staying with you and rubbing your back like you imagined she would, like all the homebirth books showed the husband doing, she runs around collecting and washing towels and generally cleaning up and you learn something about your mother you didn't previously know.

And the baby is the most beautiful person you have ever laid eyes on. You maintain for the rest of both your lives that she was unusually well-formed and beautiful on the day she was born, with a thick mop of black hair and limitless, searching dark eyes, and a quiet, serious way about her that makes your first days together contemplative and a little bit scary, because she seems to know things, to look right inside you, and you understand what people mean when they say a baby is an old soul.

But also like all babies she is completely helpless, and so your days take on the rhythm of caring for her: feeding, changing, feeding, cleaning, feeding. And when she begins to laugh, long and loud, you both sit on a blanket in the warm light that comes through the ranch slider, and you find ways to make her laugh again and again.

It is spring.

Five years later in a different spring, on the other side of the world, everything outside is under dirty snow. And you've been told, many times, how bad you are at this parenting thing, how you make poor decisions every day, how you are incompetent and emotionally damaged. Deep down, the part of you that you've kept hidden all your life doesn't believe this, not for a moment, but you've let your other selves, the unsure, surface parts, the parts that certainly have been emotionally damaged, take it on, and now you don't know which way is up or what to do. You've been depressed for months. This was your last try at making things work, but you are not good enough, nothing you ever do is good enough, and you're finally ready to admit that maybe your heart doesn't know what it's doing. You're ready to admit you've been wrong all this time, but you haven't taken yourself home yet, because you're still stubborn and full of pride, and you don't want everyone to know what a failure you are.

And besides, by the time you finally, finally work it all out, there's a new pregnancy, which makes you happy at the same time as you feel deeply hopeless.

Early on in the pregnancy, you worry about these feelings hurting the baby and hurting your five-year-old. It is the first time in your life you have seriously contemplated suicide. You think about this obsessively: which way would be most painless, how you might get access to the tools, whether it would be best to simply disappear, whether you know of any cliffs high enough or traffic fast enough to have the desired instant effect. Maybe you could access the requisite drugs. But you still love your daughter, who is still the most beautiful person you have ever known, and this new baby is likely to be pretty spectacular too.

One day when you are out walking hand in hand with your daughter and working through the logistics of one particular suicidal act in your mind, she looks up at you and says, 'I don't want you to die.' That's when you know that you will never do it, that you were never going to do it, but somehow it has given you some relief to imagine you have some control over *something*. Maybe you still think about it from time to time after that, but as your puku grows bigger the fantasies grow smaller.

You're having a snow fight with your daughter when you feel a twinge, and then later another twinge, but not until close to midnight do the twinges become pains that can no longer be ignored. On the way to the phone to call the midwife, you collapse to your knees with a great pop and gush. The rest is very fast. Another homebirth, this time so swift the midwife barely has time to set up her equipment before your second daughter is born, an extraordinary hue of red-brown, gasping lungs full of air to scream with. This

216

one has plenty to say. And you are happy, so happy you can't believe you were ever so sad. Joyful, in fact, and you know the baby brought this with her, this feeling, and that she has saved you just as her sister did, and that everything will be okay, one way or another.

You are so happy for this miracle, this beautiful bundle, this look-at-me-change-in-perspective-in-human-form that you decide from now on you will always choose to be happy. So when the hard times do come, you remember this decision and what came before it and how everything can change in an instant, and you're okay; even through the hardest, hardest things, you figure out how to hang in there.

And the hardest things are when your children are hurting in ways you can't help. When they become old enough to see the world we have made and they react as any sane person would: with anguish and anxiety, with deep, deep sadness. They see so clearly that you think the rest of us should step aside and let them lead, but you also think we should clean up our own messes, just as we have taught them to do. Watching them grapple with the pain hurts so bad you don't know how to walk through it yourself, and so sometimes you fail them, and sometimes you react badly, and sometimes you just tell yourself over and over to just be there for them, and to shut up, for goodness' sake, until they're ready to talk. Just hang in there.

Because your children are becoming who you hoped they would be. Artists and social activists and politically engaged critics and loving family members, courageous and engaged with the world and *kind*. And you're beginning to realise there is more than this, too. You see you lacked imagination, even though you thought your dreams were too big. Your children speak languages you haven't learnt, go places you haven't been, have conversations you can't conceive of.

And you couldn't be more surprised that you got here, all of you, whole and imperfect.

1996 / 2002

Tea

In Toronto it's the middle of the night, and I am wide awake. I need a shower, of course, and a cup of tea. I'm also stupidly tired. The room is dated in the way that flash North American hotels sometimes are, as if you're stepping onto the set of *The Love Boat*. Also, my view is of the high-rise building adjacent, rather than the lake which much of the hotel faces. This does not correspond with the vision I have carried in my head, taken solely from images I've seen online, all the way here. But I am lucky! I remind myself. In a new city after so many, many hours on so many planes! I will lie flat in a big comfy bed tonight! I attempt to recalibrate my expectations. I'm just tired, from all the travel. And disorientated. And there's something else in the air here, something reminiscent of other journeys in other lifetimes, something I'm not ready to look at yet. This discontent will disappear in the morning, I decide, once I get the chance to explore the city and listen to people talk about books. And after I get a good cup of tea.

But there is no decent tea to be had. There is no kettle. There's a coffee machine and two prepackaged Starbucks coffee filters of the kind that carry the coffee within them. There are two disposable Starbucks cups with plastic stirrers, not even a teaspoon. There are plastic lids for the cups, and a plastic bag full of various types of sweetener and sugar and UHT pottles of a foul milk-like substance. There are precisely two teabags. There is more sweetener than I can be bothered counting, but little to sweeten. I quickly transform the coffee-maker into a hot-water maker by filtering the water through, straight into a Starbucks cup with teabag. While the tea is steeping I jump in the shower and wash off the 24-hour travel grime. After my shower, the hotel room smells like coffee. The Starbucks cup that is now full of hot water and a steeping teabag smells like coffee. It will have to do. I dump in barely half a pottle of UHT—just enough to take the bitter edge off, but hopefully not enough to taste (it is enough to taste), down it, and leave the room.

The hospitality of the festival is lush, and on the top floor of the hotel they provide complimentary drinks and food until three in the morning. Normally, I would shy away from something like this, but I am Wide Awake and Hungry, and I can't stay in the hotel room because the thing I'm trying to ignore is waiting patiently for me to notice it. And since I am wide awake, it makes sense to accept the hospitality provided. I see two New Zealand friends immediately, and throw myself into it, grateful and excited at last.

At some point we go to bed. Sleep doesn't come. The TV stations available are very, very bad, but this is expected. I read and watch Netflix and read. The bed is so comfortable it is uncomfortable and hot. I'm a petulant child. Travel, I think, it's just the travel. Somehow I snatch a few hours and wake excited again—Toronto! I head outside at dawn. There is the tiniest sprinkle of snow. There is the lake, though it is somehow hard to get to, so many buildings lined up at its edge. I will find a nice breakfast place, I think. I walk for half an hour or more, see many small dogs in small jackets. Do not find a café. Walk back. There is a small Starbucks, and I decide what the hell, for old time's sake, and go in.

On the way back into the hotel, I notice there is a Starbucks counter on the ground floor. It has a long line. I have no intention of buying my wake-up hot drink every morning, but my supply will soon run out. I'm already reusing the non-reusable cups. I will be here five days, so it's clear this situation will necessitate talking to hotel staff, a problem which is, in my opinion, barely conscionable. Whatever I inherited from my English forebears, this might be foremost: the unwillingness to engage with strangers to ask for anything personal. That, and the daily need for a calming cup of tea. Suddenly, tea seems like the most personal thing in the world, and the lack of it some kind of personal insult.

mamae
1. (stative) be painful, sore, hurt.
2. (noun) ache, pain, injury, wound.

It only takes a day or so for me to find the thing that has been patiently waiting. It is in my room, out on the street, in the voices that pass by. This is the first time I've been back to Canada in more than 12 years. And it's a big country and I'm at the other end of it. But this is the way trauma sits in us, triggered not by the obvious things but by the minutiae of life.

The pain of my own Canadas past comes to me in the smell of carpet and cleaning products, the colour scheme of the ceilings and walls, the word *toque*, backyards that seem all dirt and no green, condos at the shore of every waterway, the word *condo*, red fluttering maple leaves everywhere, but only fabric ones. I want to enjoy this visit and those who people it wholeheartedly, but my body locates my personal historical tensions instead and forces me to carry those through sleepless nights and cold days, running to our Kiwi posse near the close of each day for respite. I thought I had left it long enough. I thought I had gotten over it. But our bodies are memory photocopiers, and even if we no longer have any interest in the narrative they reproduce, they continue—the image distorting, paper jamming, ink smudged and running.

Collectively, we had been excited about this trip, and now we are relieved to have each other; four writers together representing multiple communities of New Zealand writing: Witi, Brannavan, Kirsten, me. We share our collective dismay at our inability to decipher this place and its pleasures. Kirsten says, *I think it's sometimes easier to go to countries where people don't speak your language and you don't expect to be comfortable.* It's true—we keep expecting to feel like we fit in here because we speak the same words, but there are worlds between our meanings. I can't read the expressions of the polite young women who run the festival. I can't gauge how they might see me. It is only when I talk to local immigrants—an Australian who says *Kia ora* in welcome, or descendants of immigrants, Korean mostly—that I feel some baseline kinship.

Why did I think I could leave past tensions in the past? They're always there, in the smell or temperature of a new yet familiar city, in the way someone pronounces the word *house*, in the growing twist of pain in my levator scapulae muscle, the one that will leave my neck immobilised by the time I get off the plane in Auckland. I should know by now, as our tūpuna keep telling us: you walk towards your past, not away from it.

I am not the only one carrying wounds through this trip, and as the days pass we begin to share them with each other. Some are much more immediate and painful than mine. I don't think any of us would have predicted that this would be the tenor of our journey.

I decide that art is what I need to elevate myself above the closed-in anxiety that is making me too myopic to really *be* in this place, so I head to the Art Gallery of Ontario, where the Anthropocene exhibition is making headlines—the Anthropocene is the proposed name for a geological epoch defined by the permanent impact of human activities on Earth, such as terraforming through mining, urbanisation and agriculture, human-caused extinction and biodiversity loss. At the exhibition, I learn too much perspective can be a bad thing. It is startling, visually stunning and awful. What humans do to the Earth is a kind of nightmare from which there is no waking. A glimpse of the exhibition can be found in this description of the Anthropocene Project:

We have reached an unprecedented moment in planetary history. Humans now arguably change the Earth and its processes more than all other natural forces combined. Climate change, extinctions, invasive species, technofossils, anthroturbation, terraforming of land, and redirection of water are all part of the indelible human signature.[1]

What did I actually think I was going to see? In one installation, a man walks through his workplace, the Dandora dumpsite in Nairobi, Kenya. The looped video runs for 4 minutes 42 seconds. On each side of the man, hills of indestructible garbage—plastics, in particular—are scavenged and sold to recyclers each day. There are 30 acres of this urban landfill, the label says, and even though it was officially declared closed in 2001, two thousand tonnes of waste are dumped there every day. 'For many of the one million people living in and around Dandora, the site is a primary source of income.' The cumulative effect of watching this man walk through the megadump is both awe-inspiring and horrifying.

As is the aerial view of sawmills, coal mines, salt pans—their tidy destruction. The tainted promise of solar panels filling a desertscape and tetrapods protecting a coastline from the encroaching tide. Standing in front of a wall-sized mural of Mushin market intersection, Lagos, I am reminded of the terrible human weight I usually feel only when moving through airports. Where do we all come from? Where do we all go? What about all the waste? The waste. Elsewhere, thousands of elephant tusks are stacked and burnt to prevent poaching, an act which cannot retrospectively prevent destruction of the animals who once bore them.

At the end of it, I am not uplifted in the way that sometimes I am after a bleak film or artwork. The sharing of a troubled world can be a beautiful act. Instead, I'm simply overwhelmed. I recognise the black hilarity of coming to see this exhibition when, down at our waterfront hotel in a flash part of town, the impact of human commerce has made the area inhospitable to all natural beauty. When I have been flown here at enormous economic and environmental expense, and will stay less than a week. What am I doing here?

And so I return to the hotel room for a fortifying cup of tea before the next thing on the schedule I've been given. Of course, in the hotel room there is no easy access to tea, or a non-disposable cup, so I ring room service and they bring me one teabag in a real cup and also another plastic bag full of the ubiquitous pottles of UHT milk and sachets of sugar and sugar substitutes, but not until after I've gone to Kirsten's room in desperation, looking for teabags. She takes one look at me and tries to give me the whole box she purchased after her own search for tea, and some fancy chocolate too. I must look as haunted as I feel.

The wound is the place where light enters you
Rumi

On my final night in town I find relief in the company of creative writing academics—my people, I think. Word nerds are the same the world over. Our hosts are a very small creative writing school, and this is their big event of the year, they tell me, and I am both extremely humbled and a little worried that I am half of the bill for this big event. Luckily, Ins Choi, the creator of Netflix's *Kim's Convenience*, is the other half. I expect he will attract an enthusiastic crowd. I'm trying to shake off dizzy spells and the soporific effects of five days of alienation and lack of sleep, so instead of beer or wine with dinner, I ask for tea. My hosts seem to think this a delightfully quaint Kiwi thing to do, alongside my sudden inability to form coherent sentences. We're at a nice restaurant in Scarborough, Ontario, so the insipid packaged teabag and cup that arrives with water on the side is actually unexpected. It's accompanied by a now-familiar clear plastic bag containing UHT milk pottles and sugar substitute sachets. Sometimes a postcolonial subject of the British Empire just needs a decent cup of tea, dammit! I'm concerned about fully losing it by the time we get to our event at the university, so I determinedly brew my tea as strong as I can, not without spilling water everywhere, and drink it as if it is the waters of life.

Ins and I are a strange combination, but the randomness of this billing introduces an element of chaos that can often be very fruitful in a literary conversation. With no obvious connections between our creative output, our host Andrew plans to simply ask us to talk about our writing lives: how we came to writing, how we sustain it, why we do what we do. Listening to Andrew, I relax a bit. These are the questions that concern writing teachers and their students everywhere.

And so the event is a good one: the room is full of keen young writers and this in itself is a rare pleasure at any literary event. Ins is an absolute fricken delight: hilarious, irreverent, and somehow completely familiar. Even though I am earnest and serious and academic, the conversation itself roars along: we agree where it matters but diverge just enough to make it interesting. And we talk about our pain: of not being enough, of being alone, of being alienated from our own cultures or by the dominant cultures, of doing work that no one quite knows is going to be successful or worthwhile. And then being some version of successful, and looking around, and still being somewhat alone, and needing them, our young audience, to come through. I'm appreciative of Andrew's final question, which is about hope. We've been talking about diversity and representation and whatever has just happened that week in Trump's America, so we are able to say to the wonderfully diverse group in front of us: you are the hope, because the monolith across the border is a lie, and your lives, your stories, are real.

Afterwards people line up to talk to Ins, and I find my way to the complimentary tea and coffee set-up at the back of the room. As we brew our tea (not bad, comparatively—I'm acclimatising), a nervous young woman comes up to me and tells me about her writing, and how, because I have mentioned Alice Walker, she thinks it's cool how women of colour can inspire each other across time and place, and how she wasn't going to come out tonight but then she forced herself to and she's happy she did because she's motivated to continue her writing now. She doesn't tell me about her pain, but I recognise it in some of her words—the way it is clear that it would have been easier to stay in her room. I only recognise this because it is almost a collective pain among people of her generation. And because I have children of her generation, it is now a source of my own pain too. I'm so grateful she found the courage to speak to me, but I have no words to make it all okay, so I try my best to encourage her, and I hope it will find her, the thing she needs to pull her through the all of it, the mamae. Perhaps, for her, it will be writing, as it is for me. Sometimes, like today as I write this, leaving behind the discomfort and worry and ineffable sadness of things beyond my control and making time to place words on a page is still the thing that saves me. The beautiful page, and its struggles; beautiful words, and their inconsistencies; the urgent pursuit of story because it is the thing that takes me beyond myself, the thing that connects me to people like her; a room on the other side of the world, a young woman getting outside of her own pain.

Yes, every limb,
every bend
every bone
is a recollection of
who has been before.

A memory
of all the bodies that have been
the making of me.
Karlo Mila, 'Inside Us the Dead (The NZ-born Version)'[2]

In London, there is a coffee machine on the ground floor and proper cups with many and varied teabags, and an actual kitchen in the room. It's gratitude with every step in London, every sight and experience. Lucky, lucky, lucky. I am having a movie-fucking-montage of a time. The Thames and Trafalgar Square on our actual doorstep. Fleet Street and Piccadilly over there. One evening we have dinner in a huge apartment overlooking the city in a wide panorama, windows instead of walls all along the waterfront. We are dumbfounded by what that kind of real estate must be worth. The next night, we give a reading on the top floor of New Zealand House, again with astonishing views. I get up most mornings to walk the 100 metres to Golden Jubilee Bridges, breathing in the city coming to life. At night I go to see the lights from the same spot. One morning I meet a man selling *The Big Issue* on the bridge, and we have an exceedingly pleasant conversation. What a beautiful morning, he says. Yes, it is, I say, and I mean it more than I have ever meant it. I give him my coins for a copy. It's a magazine that unhoused people sell, 'a hand up, not a handout', it says on the cover. I hope he has a nice place to sleep now, if he's still unhoused, the man selling the magazines. I'm David fucking Copperfield. I am my own novel's protagonist: Hemi, seduced by the glory of London town and her panoramas, her exceedingly interesting people, her monuments, the way it's okay to swear and drink a lot of beer.

But it's only a week or so since Toronto, and I have been in sustained pain since. American airports and airlines are torturous in their own special way, and my neck is susceptible to misalignment at the best of times, but in recent months I've learnt I may have early onset arthritis, most likely have had it for years. Pain is often easier to brush off, fix up quick, treat like an isolated incident. Until it's so deep and chronic one episode is barely distinguishable from the next. In London I can almost ignore the pain. Almost. I can barely move. My friend Suzi suggests deep tissue massage. I have tried many treatments before, but not massage. So in London, I locate the closest and cheapest massage therapist, down a little lane that runs along one side of the National Gallery. The building is poky and run-down, and to get to the massage room we have to descend a steep staircase with closed-in walls and a ceiling I can run my fingers along even though I am only of average height. Maybe it was a pub back in the 18th century. In Wellington a building like this would be demolished for the likelihood of collapse should Rūaumoko so much as sneeze.

The Chinese therapist is tiny but wiry. I'm so sore I'm a bit scared she'll hurt me, but she manages to find exactly the right balance of intensity and gentleness. *Ooohhh you're so stiff!* she exclaims as soon as she touches the muscles at the base of my neck. Unusually so, her voice says. It's usually only men who get this tightly wound, she tells me. She offers me her special massage ointment, one that usually costs more, for free, obviously moved by my predicament. Her hands are sure and efficient. She knows the business of people's muscles. I marvel at the worlds of tension the massage reveals. It is not that I have an emotional response to it, other than relief, but that as the massage goes on, more and more areas and levels of pain are exposed. By the time she is done, I have more movement and less pain. In fact, for the blissful following hour, I feel no pain. It comes back that evening, but she has healed me enough to carry on.

Earlier, I texted Suzi: *I think my body is full of historical tension.* And then: *what a line.* It only strikes me in that moment that the historical tension that my body carries, that any body carries, goes all the way back to childhood and beyond. I had known this intellectually, but not fully understood it before. What Indigenous people have long known, what all oppressed peoples know, is that we carry ancestral memory within us. *I think my body is full of historical tension.* I marvel at the worlds that sentence contains. It was only when I got a stranger to lay her hands on me in an underground room in Trafalgar Square that I could feel the lifetimes of strain and anxiety and stress that have infused my muscles with rigidity. Everything I've survived. Everything my parents and their parents and their parents survived. And so on. I thought I was fine. But the massage told me that I have been holding everything up by the strength of my own muscles all these years. My muscles have been doing the work my mind told them to. It's just us against the terrors of the world, my body told itself. Our minds and our bodies are such powerful things. But I can finally see what the health practitioners feel every time they touch me. The pressure has been so intense that my bones are deteriorating. Fusing. Misaligning. The muscles are hard where they should be flexible. The muscles have been holding everything together for so long they don't know how to relax.

I don't want to overstate the ancestral thing. If I was carrying all their pain, I would long ago have been obliterated. We are not the victims of unrestrained ancestral pain. By which I mean, our parents stand between us and the violences of the past. It's like a blast at their backs, a storm they keep at bay by leaning their whole weight against a door as it threatens to slam open. Sometimes a window smashes, sometimes the door whips open before they can push it back again. Sometimes it takes more than one of them to keep the door closed. Generations holding it at bay. There might be a tohunga who can speak to the storm and calm it. The storm might tire itself out or be appeased by gifts of remorse. Whatever the case, all of us have ancestral storms of varying strengths and violence. All of us must be vigilant. Adding locks and sandbags and scaffolding.

Muscles working hard. If you are alone, those muscles can petrify against the storm. But that's better than the alternative. If no one holds it back, the storm gets inside you. How it hurts you and yours differs from person to person. There is no inevitability to this. We still get to choose.

But every choice has a price. My vigilance has my neck in a vice grip that reliably gives a little twist now and then.

We don't know, when we look at images of Frida, whether we're looking at her, or ourselves.
—Claire Wilcox, co-curator *Frida Kahlo: Making Herself Up* (V&A Museum, 2018)[3]

The body braces give us a sense of the shape of her, her size, the depth of her pain. Polio; a bus crash that speared her diagonally through the centre, damaging spine and collarbone, pelvis and legs; over 30 operations; miscarriages; gangrene. Pfft, what do I know about pain? The exhibition makes hers almost tangible, close enough to touch, more than one person should have to bear. But it's what she does with it. She makes all the things of her life beautiful. I don't mean that in some abstract, romantic way. She actively transforms each thing she touches, surrounding herself with vibrant colour and contour. Frida doesn't hold the storm back; she becomes the storm, and in doing so she makes it hers.

The plaster corsets are astonishing: there is nothing quite like clothing for giving a visceral sense of the shape of a person, but these are so intimate: moulded exactly to her dimensions, embodiments of her pain and imprisonment and hope, painted by the artist while she wore them. Each is a slightly different shape, signalling the different approaches that were taken to holding Frida together. The paintings on them, like all her paintings, her way of transcending her caged body. Beauty tied so intimately, so inextricably to pain. In the end, she watched her body failing, piece by piece removed or adjusted until the operations didn't work anymore. Even then, a bright red prosthetic leg with green detail, a dragon dancing along the foot.

We have only gained access to the exhibition as guests of the V&A—tickets have been sold out for months. It's easy to see why: the final room contains an abundance of Fridas, Kahlo-shaped mannequins in recognisable poses, wearing her splendid wardrobe. Cotton huipil / embroidered tops, satins and silks and smooth, cool cotton skirts, ruffled and adorned with stitch and fabric, rebozo shawls festooned with the brightest colours. I am fascinated by the voluminous skirts I had thought were simply her impeccable Mexican style. She wore them, at least sometimes, to hide her beleaguered legs. Extravagant, storied jewellery. Nail polish, make-up, seduction. Life lived in full colour.

And here, in this final room, her paintings too, at last. It is extraordinarily moving, after we have gained a sense of the pain of her life, to see the beauty she made of it. Paintings beside mannequins that mimic them in posture and dress, the artist herself in the room with us. Our group has already moved through. I'm the last here. I don't know what it means, any of this or the writing of it. Women of colour can inspire each other across time and place, the young woman in Toronto told me. Maybe that's it. What does Frida say? Perhaps, the pain is inevitable. Be a storm. Make beauty.

2018

Driving on a Highway at the End of the World

We love the sea like glass this morning. Through valleys we've cut into hills, the smooth road takes us down, then up, around the curve, then breathe in—the clean sweep of light on the harbour, thick cloak of green a close border, far hills sparsely brown, steel silvering the high rises. Maybe it's worth the crush and cost of parking when we get into town, for this. Maybe it's worth all the other cars, the slow crawl. It's been a good drive. We like to see the country this way, though we rarely drive the eight hours to the other end of the island, and that used to be routine. No, it's all planes now. Fast and cheap, the way we like it. So this slow dawning of place is almost a luxury, and we look and look as if the intensity of our gaze might preserve the seeing. The kids hold up their phones and click.

There's two ways to do it: old New Zealand and new New Zealand. The old is cruising in a gas guzzler, sticky and hot enough to need all the windows down, wind buffeting, elbow crooked on the door, fingers splaying out occasionally to catch the cool, the dog's ears flapping. Salt drying on skin, wet togs under jean shorts, damp patch on the seat and something blaring; take your pick, it's a free country. The new is sealed in an air-tight, air-conditioned, air-bagged capsule, the world a series of landscapes and skyscapes and beautiful coastlines framed in tinted glass, so comfy we can't feel the speed, everything passing by serenely, untouched, no buffeting wind, no hard times just now, and something blaring; take your pick, it's a free country. We love it, this bliss, the kilometres passing under us, our countryside, our rivers and seas, the world's envy. And speed? And winding roads? And mountains? We've got it all, mate. God's own country, not that we believe in that God stuff.

*

The job starts in February, and so does the commute. Neither of us are car people, my spouse or me, so the biggest obstacle and challenge to harmonious work–life balance, for us, is the one-hour-ten-minute commute I must take to Palmerston North from our home on the Kāpiti Coast, and the one-hour-ten-minute commute home again. There is no way around it: the job is better paid than any job I've ever had in my life, doing something I love, and the home is near somewhere I love, the sea, and with the people I love, who all have their own lives in places that are not Palmerston North. My spouse works in Wellington, an almost one-hour commute, but there are trains. Glorious trains. The mark of a civilised society, I announce pompously, is a reliable, modern, regular rail service. Think Germany. Think Japan. By this reckoning, Waikanae to Wellington is the only civilised place in all of New Zealand. Palmerston North is like the wilderness, only less interesting. John Cleese was exaggerating horribly when he called it the suicide capital of the world, but there can be something dispiriting about the town. It's landlocked, for instance. Are you moving to Palmy? people ask innocently. I laugh, pompously. No. I've lived there on and off for years.

There's no way. I feel an uncomfortable stirring in my gut. It's not that bad, people remark innocently, that's not very nice. I know, I say, but, I *know*. There's only so many times you can move away from Palmy and then move back. Besides, the sea.

We don't even own a car when I get the job. We've been trialling a car-free lifestyle since our Toyota Masterace 1991 van died, and it's remarkably easy. There are buses and bikes, and on the weekend the guy around the corner rents us one of his old rental cars for cheap so we can do errands. Most weekends we hire it for one day and he tells us to keep it for the rest of the weekend, we're just up the road if he needs it. This is the Old New Zealand we're both old enough to remember, a marked contrast to the other rental companies we've dealt with, and a delight. With the new job, it's a shame to have to give this system away—it has been liberating to be mostly car-free, we're financially better off without car bills, and we're supporting this local old-school economy. It aligns with our values too—our deep desire for a way of life that might seem like hippy virtuousness but is in fact based in deep pragmatism: if we carry on the way we are, collectively, we're screwed.

I buy a gold Toyota Funcargo from a dealer in Palmy, the only Funcargo I can find but the third in my husband's extended family. When we visit my father the following summer he laughs uproariously. Unbeknownst to us, he also has a Funcargo, the most versatile of small vehicles. But I'm dreading the work commute. I know there will be a physical cost. I can't drive all the curves and bends of the winding roads without slowing down to the recommended speed. This is not the common approach in Aotearoa. Vehicles behind me come up close and pass at the first opportunity, and I tense as I hold the steering wheel, causing my shoulders and neck to seize painfully. By the end of the year my fears are proven well-founded. The stress and tension in my neck and shoulders is so bad it takes three months of chiropractic treatment and yoga to gain back any movement. I have been walking less because I am driving more, and eating more to stave off the tiredness from driving. My new lifestyle has added 8 kilograms to my frame, and it is unlikely I will ever gain full flexibility, things have seized up so badly. Multiple health practitioners make the same noises when they ask me to look over this or that shoulder.

Hmmm, very limited movement here.

It's like a whiplash injury.

I'm surprised you can move at all.

It's not just the driving. There has been a stack of work and life and historical stresses that have caused the crooked stack of my neck vertebrae, though certain driver postures exacerbate my particular tensions. I fervently wish for commuter trains that go north.

There is another drawback to the commute: filling up with petrol every week and driving on that new expressway. The one that cost $649 million so far, and is still being built, and that was supposed to make things faster and smoother but didn't at first, then did for a short period, until they realised it needed $25 million of repairs. The roadworks on the 'finished' road have slowed the commute another 10 or 20 minutes, removing any perceived speed benefit. They *could* have spent the money on a modern public transport system, to bring us up to international standards and, you know, postpone the end of the world as we know it. Just as any forward-thinking nation would, knowing there's no future in individually owned, petrol-run cars.

Some mornings, the light is so clear and crisp it's like all the mornings of our childhood, all the hopeful and bright beginnings, the air fresh and cool, the promise of warmth to come. It's gonna be a beauty, our parents would've said to the neighbours back in the days when such things were said daily. Maybe we say it still, but we don't see neighbours often. It's 20 steps to the car, unlocking as we walk, throw in the backpack, the satchel, the drink bottle, the jacket. Go back to the house for the keep cup, the umbrella, to check the lights and doors and dog. On time this morning, but not for long if we keep this up. Warm the engine, find the music, all the while the echo of childhood mornings in those steps between house and car, the dewy grass, the sense of possibility. It's easy to feel positive, here, at the beginning of things.

Getting to the highway is slow and suburban, then slow and traffic-lit. Three sets of lights before we make the turn, then accelerate smoothly and merge. Decide who to pass and who to let pass before finding a pace, the clean sweep of road and the industrial sights quickly giving way to the hills and wetlands. The road itself is no beauty, but keep our eyes on the horizon, those hills rolling ahead, bush-clad and dense, every shade of green, brimming up into us something we can't name, some filling of a gap. We seek them out each time, those hills, the balm of them. Hemi Matenga Reserve, 514 metres above sea level, not impressive heights by our standards, but the most extensive kohekohe woodland left in the country. Truth is, we'd never heard of kohekohe before we moved here, nearly 10 years ago. There will be nothing else like it the whole 90 kilometres to work, except in the far mountains, the Tararua ranges, which reach up to 1500 metres in continuous peaks.

They appear and recede, depending on the sky and cloud and atmosphere, as the mountains of Aotearoa are wont to do, and some days they are breathtaking. But Hemi Matenga is the whānau range, close in and watching, a warm and reliable embrace against the road ahead.

*

It's hard to capture the all-pervasive sense of hopelessness that has held me for years by the time I first drive on that highway. I have carefully cultivated a good life, a happy life, as close to the beach as I can manage. We live on one of the most beautiful coastlines on the planet. To walk the soft curve of a tideline and look at the sea reminds me always how miraculous and beautiful the world is, how small I am, and I want to say how inconsequential my petty woes and worries, but this is not the case, for I am a child of the nuclear 80s, and the end of the world haunts my every step. Who knew we would face worse threats than the nuclear one? Each time I walk the beach I wonder how much longer it will be there, how soon before it becomes too dangerous, before weather or pollution overpowers our ability to live close by. Most days we pick up plastic washed in from other places. It's particularly bad at our local beach, not quite so noticeable up the road, but there's no such thing as a pristine coastline anymore. The storms have become so frequent and major that one or two days a year we can't drive to work or even catch the train. If we do get there, we might not be able to get home again. Trees fall. Roads get flooded.

And so, a few years ago, in the midst of the physical and undeniable presence of climate insecurity, the National government pushed ahead with their project, 'Roads of

National Significance'. Something did need to be done about parts of the road: the sections that would cut off hundreds of thousands of people in Wellington if there were an earthquake, but even so. The first manifestation of the new expressway took place in our community, despite all the protests, despite the people who didn't want to lose their homes and the ones who didn't want to see the value of theirs disappear; despite the possibility, never seriously considered, that there were other, less invasive, less expensive, less blind-to-the-actual-world-we-live-in options.

Despite reassurances to the contrary, after the road was built, a whole section of the community was left completely exposed. They complained that the truck noise was so loud that at night their windows rattled. Wetlands were kept, protected supposedly, but some of these are between the rattling windows of suburban homes and the road itself. Dead pūkeko litter the roadside. This area of the rattling windows is where we walk our dog, and what was once a pleasant stroll with a view of Kāpiti Island is now simply a walk beside a motorway. We live far enough away that our windows do not rattle, but this is our neighbourhood. It is no surprise when someone suggests this side of the expressway has been left unprotected because it is the less affluent. At night, when we open our windows, the road noise is loud enough to disturb our sleep, so we close them again. We used to hear ruru calling through the still air.

So those first months driving the expressway? It's like scoping out enemy territory. *This* is what it has all been about, I think. I hope it was worth it. I notice that, yes, it is a bit smoother, possibly even safer. I allow myself to be seduced somewhat by the ease and quickness, as long as it lasts, which is not long. The views can be beautiful. There's a certain inevitability to it, this thing. In their final three years of office, National were never going to be forward-thinking; they were never going to acknowledge the extent of the environmental threat. So what they gave us was this nice comfortable road.

*

We feel it now, every day, this pressure behind everything, this other thing that wants our attention, even though it's easy enough to keep our gaze steady on the road ahead. The mountains haven't changed, have they? There they are, after we turn right onto State Highway 57, snow-capped despite the bright blue of the morning sky, so immense we can't contain the sight of them. We can still breathe in. The colour of the sky hasn't changed. And how else would we get around anyway, if there wasn't this?

But it's harder now, to distance ourselves from the news—it comes at us constantly, and so we feel the tension, low and deep, no matter how hard we nod and bounce to the music pumping just a bit too loud for our health. We are not in control of anything, so why try? Why worry about it if you can't change it? Sometimes it feels like we are flying towards oblivion, in our cars, on our planes, in our hearts, but hey, isn't that just the hedonistic nihilism of youth? Maybe we can be teenagers forever, all of us, all searing, careless joy and no responsibilities. Everybody wants to be young and free.

Sometimes, we flick on the news anyway. Choose one particular day, say 30 August 2017. Hurricane floods break the banks of a dam in Houston; 1200 people die from Monsoon floods in Bangladesh, Nepal, India; 14 million are affected; a woman describes sea snakes coming into her house, making her children scream; North Korea sends missiles over Japan, a whole nation crouched and waiting. We pull up to the intersection and think, *That's the line, we're crossing the line now.* All hell is finally, fully breaking loose. We turn towards Palmerston North, cross the rarely used railway lines, see those hills, the ranges, such a beautiful morning, a mist sitting low on the ground. Feel it, we tell ourselves, really feel it and see it. The mountains ahead are as solid as they ever were, the forests a far-off green, the tarmac beneath us grey and solid. Our wheels spin.

*

It's on one of those mountainous crisp mornings when it happens. Two weeks after their surprise 2017 rise to power, Jacinda Ardern's Labour–Green–NZ First coalition government announce their goal of Zero Carbon by 2050. Like everything else, at first it's chatter in the background, but it slowly seeps into the parched earth of my cynicism over the coming days. A week or so later I drive the expressway, as I do most mornings, and suddenly, inside me where there wasn't anything before, there it is: *hope.* It's as if I am being gently released from a cage. I had an inkling I was inside this cage and yet I had no idea what it was like to be outside of it. I didn't know how much the cage had constricted my view. I notice my thinking change: for the first time in decades, I feel like there could be a future. My children, my grandchildren— they might be okay. We might sort it out yet, this mess. This was not something I had considered possible anymore. I have grown so used to travelling the expressway and feeling the terrible inevitability of our effect on the world beneath us every day. And then this most unexpected, glorious, tiny glimmer of news that says *we can change it, just like that.*

But of course it's not that simple. 2050 is too late, for starters. We have a decade at most, they tell us. As I write this, Australia is on fire and no one knows when that will end. This is the essay that will not be finished. Every time I think I have a handle on it there's a new news story, a new extinction, a new set of figures to grapple with, and amidst it all are the Trumps of the world, who seem to want to bring us all to our own extinction.

And also, quite suddenly, there is Greta Thunberg. In August 2019, pictures circulate on social media of Greta at her first climate action, the previous August, sitting alone outside the Swedish Riksdag. Contrasted alongside are pictures from a year later: climate marches of millions, following her lead. Greta takes inspiration from the activist X González and their Marjory Stoneman Douglas High School classmates leading the fight against gun violence in America. In Aotearoa, Pania Newton walks in the footsteps of her ancestors, leading her people in guardianship of their land at Ihumātao. Everything changes, everything changes, and it's young women who've had enough, and young men who are ready to walk alongside them, and it is beautiful.

I want to say to our daughters and to our sons, hold on to your anger, but don't let it consume you. Don't let it burn away beauty and nuance and compassion. Find the thing that gives you peace in the gaps between the highways and the news stories and the hurricanes and the meltings and the shootings and the men with bad hair and no hearts and the wealth and the poverty and the towers crumbling and the Earth on fire and the hurting, hurting hearts. There are always gaps, slivers, cracks. Slip into them. Slip between. Look into the everything but stay in the spaces between. And from that quiet, dark space, speak. Witness the power of your voice unfurling into the world, a tendril, a wavering shoot. See it touch other shoots and dance with them, up into the light. Moving together those tendrils will become a vine.

The old men of the old ways aren't going to let go easily, so this essay won't be finished. Still, life can surprise us. We can set out to write an essay about driving at the end of the world, and three years later realise we no longer need that highway. We catch trains to work, choose land travel over air. Plastic supermarket bags have mostly disappeared and everyone seems to have survived unscathed. Sometimes we walk down to the beach, everything passing by serenely, not untouched, a bit of wind, hard times just now behind us, but also ahead, earphones in or out, take your pick, it's a free country. We smell the sea, our view the thick green of an island bird sanctuary, hear the laughter of family as we bend and collect the small but constant remnants of a toxic life. It used to be shells we collected on the shore. We feel it here, on the tideline, the end of the world. But also the beginning.

2017–2019

This Broken Jaw of Our Lost Kingdoms

It strikes me that the father I have constructed in this text is an illusion—someone who consists of all the parts I can stand to put on the page. There is so much I can't stand to put down, sometimes because I can't face it, sometimes because I have no interest in it, sometimes because I am not up to it. It should be understood that I have not written down the worst of it, and have no desire to. Equally, it is clear I haven't been able to give exact measurements to the length and breadth of this real person's humanity either. Such things sit side by side: good man, bad man, and even though I brought out the scales I find myself unable to make them settle. I think I have begun to understand the saying that we are all better than the worst things we've done. A life is a shining, holy thing, no matter how we try to run from the terrifying beauty and horrifying requirements of being alive.

Sometimes in memoirs, writers are able to say: These are the people and things that made me. I want to say something like: These are the people and things that unmade me, but even from chaos you can construct a life. I'm about 50–50 on whether I should say any of this at all, but since I am evangelical about how stories can change lives, the 50 percent that says *Keep writing* wins.

Whatever the impetus, in the end, there is no real way to understand it all. Writers have long talked about how writing is simply a way to figure out what one is thinking, to meditate on some question. The more I write, the more I wonder if I am moving away from even knowing what the question is. Sometimes things just happen, and we are witness to them, and no amount of writing will tell us what they mean.

The first time it happens I am heading to a café with Ingrid. We've had an afternoon of meetings and now we get to catch up on her months overseas, and my time doing whatever I was doing, which was sometimes overseas too. It's a rare pleasure, this break in schedule which we have actually carefully scheduled. Since we became full-time colleagues as well as friends, we recognise that making time just to be friends is important. Sometimes it's hard to separate the rest of our lives from our work—writing seeps its way into our family homes, our leisure time, our dreams. It is a vocation more than a career, I suppose.

Before we settle, I check my phone and see there are missed calls and messages. I rarely get calls, and it might be my daughter, so I check, but the number comes from Dad's area. It's not his number, I see, so I immediately think this might be *it*. This doesn't feel like *it*, but it could be. It is Highly Likely that something is up. Since he put me on alert that he could die at any moment and that when he does I must rush to collect his things (not say goodbye or have a funeral, just collect his things), I have been expecting a call at some point.

But this is not *it*. This is a care worker explaining that my father has fallen on the concrete and hit his head, more than once perhaps, and is bleeding heavily. He is very drunk, she says, and refusing care, and can I come and help him, please? He needs someone to watch him. They have managed to get him to his flat and have tried to help, but he is yelling abuse. The care worker's accent is so thick I have to listen to the poorly recorded message a couple of times. I can imagine the kinds of things my father will have said to her. *What? Can't understand a word of it. Can't you get someone who speaks English?* Or maybe the other kind of racism, if she's pretty and petite, and especially because she's Asian: ribald jokes, unwelcome gropes, suggestions that she perform other services. I know with terrible certainty that there's no way she will have escaped that kind of attention. I have seen it too often. He shouldn't be alone, she repeats a number of times, he doesn't look good. He won't let them take him to hospital. He won't listen. He is being verbally abusive.

Ingrid asks me what's happened. It can't be good, she says, by the look on my face. It's my dad, I say, he's fallen over or something. Drunk. *Oh*. Ingrid always seems unflappable in the presence of my flailing. In my family, flapping about, internally or externally, is standard practice. We're a bit louder than most, a bit more in tune with our proximity to chaos and the abyss. But Ingrid is clearly concerned. In fact, she seems more concerned than I am. She is, I suspect, imagining how I must feel by imagining how she would feel if this were her father. But I don't have those feelings. I feel nothing. Do you need to go? Ingrid asks. I don't know, I say. I actually don't know. There's nothing I can do. There is nothing he will let me do. Ha ha, ha ha ha. I am horrified by my laughter, but there it is, the most hollow and meaningless laugh of my life. What must Ingrid think of me, I wonder, laughing about this. It's not even the manic laugh of grief either, the laugh that happens when you don't know how to deal with overwhelming emotion. Nor is it an embarrassed laugh. I don't feel embarrassed. I feel nothing, and then I laugh at that. I'm sorry, I say, I don't know why I'm laughing.

What I do feel is a businesslike sense that I am in some way responsible for this human being, my dad, but only so far as to minimise pain for him and me and everyone else involved. Which means my ability to help is greatly limited. It has long been impossible for me to help my father or be close to him in any real way. He will not allow it. And I don't have the fortitude to give him the things he does want from me, which from a lifetime of being his daughter I know are as elusive as the feelings I think I should be feeling at this moment. The hole of addiction is deep and wide and hungry, and if you ever reach the bottom of that hole you will only find more starvation, of a proportion that consumes anyone who tries to appease it. I've been lucky. My instinct for self-preservation, and my dedication to parenting my children first, has given me the strength to turn my back many times. It makes me sad, but walking away from Dad means walking towards life.

So, as this is happening, I make the calculations. Check the inner metrics—input, output, emotional stamina. I can afford this. I ring the carer back.

'Thank you for helping my dad,' I begin. 'I'm really sorry that he was abusive. I'm so sorry.' I can see him, struggling to make words, struggling to see straight, looking up at them from the ground, blood everywhere. Naturally they would be concerned, try to offer him the help they would offer anyone who had fallen down and badly hurt himself. But I know what his response would have been. *Leave me alone. Look at my bracelet. It says leave me alone. Do not resuscitate. I don't want any help. Get away from me.* And then, when they kept trying, he would have found purchase on some choice insults, looked for ways to make them feel bad or lesser or victimised. Because by then the shame would have started to creep in, and in that kind of situation the only way out is to bring others down with you.

'I'm sorry,' I say again. 'I'd like to help but I'm not much use right now. I'm in Wellington.'

'Oh,' she says.

She obviously didn't know I was that far away. I can come, but it would take me several hours. And where would I sleep, I wonder? Not at his place. And by the time I get there he will have sobered somewhat, or the opposite, but either way he will not want to see me. He will not allow me to do anything for him. He will ask me why I came. He will worry about me coming all that way. He will feel worse. I will feel worse, and exhausted, and worried about my family and work.

'I don't know if I can help even if I leave Wellington now,' I say. 'He won't listen to me either.'

'He just needs someone to watch him,' she says. 'He won't let us take him to hospital.'

'Is he okay now?'

'I think so—we just took his blood pressure. We'll go and check on him again soon.'

I reassure her that I will talk to him and see if there is anyone closer who can check in. 'Please call me if you need to,' I say. 'Thank you for looking after my father. I know he can be hard to deal with.'

'It's okay, it's okay,' she says, and I imagine her hand waving me away. I understand from the way she says this that she will go back to him and tend his wounds, no matter how he insults her. She is a saint, I think, nurses are saints. This is the kind of thing nurses do all the time, dealing with belligerent customers who don't appreciate what is being done for them.

Dad takes a long time to pick up, and when he does his words are even slower and more muddled than usual, but I can tell he is already sobering up, or at least pretending to.

'What's happened, Dad—you had a fall?'

'Who told you that?'

'The nurse—she rang—she said you fell on the concrete and hurt your head. Are you okay? Do you need me to come? Can I get someone to help you?'

'Why'd they ring you?'

'I don't know. You must've given them my number.'

'No I didn't!'

'Well, they've got it. Must be next of kin or something.'

'Eh? They should mind their own business!'

'They're worried about you, Dad. They said you hurt yourself badly. Are you okay?'

'No. They should mind their own bloody business. Why are they calling you? They shouldn't have called you.'

'It's fine, Dad. Are you okay?'

'Never mind that. Hit me head. Blood everywhere. They want to take me to hospital. I'm not going to hospital. I've got a bracelet that tells them to just leave me alone. I don't want any help.'

'Are you all right, Dad?'

'Eh?'

'Are you all right?'

'It's a bloody mess. Blood everywhere.'

'Oh Dad. Let them help you.'

'Nah. They just need to leave me alone.'

'Be nice, Dad.'

'What?'

'Be nice to them. They're just doing their job, looking after you.'

'I don't want to be looked after. They're bloody foreigners anyway. I live in New Zealand.'

His voice has started to deteriorate. He is tiring. He's probably weak. He must be in terrible pain. Then I hear the nurses arrive again, and he starts having a go at them, but he's letting them in, letting them come, and this is reassuring.

I go back to Ingrid. We order a pitcher of a cool fizzy drink with ice and look at the lagoon, or each other, and talk. It's a nice day. We haven't talked for ages. I need to decompress. I live worlds away from my parents and their pain, worlds away from my childhood and its pain. I can't decide if it makes me a bad person or not that I don't go. I know that it would make literally no difference to the state my father is in, though it would probably make a huge difference to my own world, and equilibrium is something I fight hard for. And so I talk with my friend almost as if nothing dramatic has happened.

On the way to the train, I discover that Dad has tried to call me while I was talking. I call him back. And there in the grand hall of the Wellington Railway Station, Dad cries his shame and embarrassment that any of this has happened, and that I was called, and he apologises and apologises, and I tell him it's okay, really. It's okay to call people for help. But his feelings are like the noise of the train station around me, an overwhelming hum, making it hard for us to hear each other, hard to reach each other. It's okay, Dad, I say, really, it doesn't matter. They shouldn't have called you, he says, and I can't get him to stop. We talk through the pain until he's out the other side and we're making dark jokes, and there it is, oh yes, I do love you, Dad. And I think I told him that, though it's hard to remember because the Dad I love is not always the same Dad as the one I'm speaking to.

A month or so later I get another call. A different care worker, an almost identical message. Your father has fallen on the road and hit his head. On the road? He was going to the library bus. He couldn't get up. He was very drunk and abusive. He wouldn't let us help him, but he couldn't walk. He's okay now, she says, we just thought you should know. We're going to visit him again soon with the doctor. I'm so sorry, I say, and I explain to this new person why I am of little use. Thank you so much for the work you do, I also say. I'm not going to tell him you called because last time that made him worse, and I don't want to give him another excuse to be rude to you.

We discuss what will happen now and I explain there is a person who will check in on him. While I'm considering what to do next, Dad calls and tells me what's happened.

'I can't move,' he says. 'Can't get out of me chair.'

'What are you doing?' I ask. 'You've got to let them help you.'

'Why?' he says. 'They can just leave me alone.'

'No they can't—not if you're bleeding all over the road.'

'Yes they can—they can just drive around me.'

And we laugh.

Before Christmas, I see an uncle from the other side of the family, and I mention something about Dad.

'How is the old man?' he asks.

'Oh, you know, falling down drunk, literally.' What else am I supposed to say?

'Did he ever tell you about his life?' This is an unusual question.

'Yeah. He told me his version. Other people have told me other versions.'

'Hey, T. Whatever he told you, it's true. And it's worse than that. I've seen it.'

I look to him to try and ascertain the truth of this. He can't have seen my father for 40 years or more. There are so many versions, so many stories. In another corner, my mother tells my daughter her version of other events involving my father. I have my own tales. So much of this has fallen into legend and hearsay. So much of it says more about the teller than the subject of the tale. But I look at my uncle and I know there is a seam of truth to his words.

My father is a lost kingdom. My father is a broken jaw, a broken femur, a broken heart. Sometime a few months ago, the line 'It will end the way it began, not with a bang but a whimper' came into my head and stayed there for weeks. When I look it up, I learn that it's a misquote from T.S. Eliot's 1925 poem 'The Hollow Men'. I have no classical education, so while I'm familiar with that line, I don't know the poem. I'm struck, therefore, by how it has arrived in my head, and how there are whole stanzas that seem completely apt even though the original intent and meaning of the poem is far from the life of which I write. Words, even in their ambiguity, seem the only way to make some sense of things that are nonsensical. I am watching my father die, not the way I had hoped, not out of sight and comfortable, but the way he lived, messy and hurt and trying not to impose but imposing on everyone. Lifting a massive two fingers to the world. Fuck off. I'll bleed all over your road if I want to.

Between the conception
And the creation
Between the emotion
And the response
Falls the Shadow
Life is very long.

2019

Lumpectomy

For a while, I call her Frankenboob. After surgery she has three gnarly scars, if you count the one in the armpit where the sentinel lymph nodes were removed, which I do, plus another lighter mystery wound where something else happened, who knows what. She is bright blue in one big patch, from the radioactive substance they injected to find the sentinel nodes—a sentence I can't write without thinking of *The Matrix*. Much later, when I begin radiotherapy, they explain there are titanium clips throughout Frankenboob too, placed there by the surgeon to indicate where cancer has been, or is likely to develop, so they can boost the area with extra beams of targeted radiation if they deem necessary, which they do, since I am young. One of the surprise benefits of cancer is how often people tell me I'm young. The oncologist and the registrar share an affectionate giggle when they note how blue my breast remains a couple of months after surgery. They are both immigrant women, and I'm pleased to be in their company. This is what women can do, no matter where we're from, laughing about a blue boob—with no men to concern us.

It started, as it always does, with a lump. And then a mammogram, which showed nothing untoward, according to the attending doctor. It was the technician doing the follow-up ultrasound who identified some problematic masses, which meant she had to consult with the mammogram doctor and he had to have a feel. Having started the day thinking the appointment was going to be routine, I hadn't shored myself up for some invasive touching, so it was deeply alarming, but at subsequent visits, I got used to it. The appointments always went like this: could I feel it? Did a mammogram find it? Did you find it? No, I always replied, the mammogram didn't find it. Yes, it was me. No, I wasn't doing a routine check. Maybe I was showering, or tweezing or something, I can't remember. One day it was just there.

'We always do a biopsy when we find masses like this,' the mammogram doctor said, in such a reassuring way that I assumed everything was fine. By this point I was pretending very hard that nothing was happening anyway, so I chose to quietly ignore the technician's expression.

At the time, it seemed unlikely. I thought no one in my family had had breast cancer. I breastfed two children for nearly two years each, smug in the knowledge that this would decrease the likelihood of getting it. In 2020, I spent a large amount of money on an integrative medical doctor who conducted a barrage of tests to try to pinpoint the cause of my chronic stress and ongoing fatigue (aside from, you know, work). We tested my blood and my breath and my poop, re-engineered my diet, and took inventory of my life from birth. There were some red flags in that, to be sure, but no cancer.

For a few days after the follow-up ultrasound, I went on with my life. I was too busy to worry. Then my GP called and left a message in a sad voice, saying she was there if I wanted to discuss anything. She ended the call with, 'I hope you're okay.' I was suddenly, alarmingly, *not* okay. I called her back, and she patiently answered my questions, both of us somewhat concerned that the mammogram doctor hadn't made it clear that there were definitely Things to Worry About. A day or so later I received the first report of many via the Manage My Health patient portal. 'Findings here are probably malignant,' it said for one lesion. 'This is also suspicious for malignancy,' it said for the other. Despite my propensity for optimism and my disbelief that this could possibly be happening, I knew it was unlikely to be wrong.

'I love my breasts,' women with breast cancer often say when explaining their decision to seek breast-conserving surgery or have reconstructive surgery. One of the reasons I found it hard to imagine that I had breast cancer, one of the reasons I wasn't entirely sure I believed it even when I was having treatment for it, is that my breasts have been, on the whole, benevolent: forces for good, not evil, nurturing not only children but relationships and body image and identity. Long before I ever contemplated the possibility of losing my own breast/s, I found that Tig Notaro joke hilarious, the one she made after her double mastectomy, about how her breasts must've got sick of her making jokes about their size, and decided to kill her. How else do we come to terms with murderous breasts, but to laugh?

*

At the biopsy appointment, the specialist pulled up the imaging of my breast from the previous appointment, and was helpfully definitive. 'This is a very clear cancer,' he said, circling an area on the screen, 'and it looks like there's a smaller one here you wouldn't have been able to feel.'

Well, that's it, I thought. Tears came then, just a few, rolling quietly down my face. I reached for my husband's hand. The specialist and specialist nurse waited patiently. They must see this every single day, I thought.

'You did well catching it—it's very early,' the specialist said. I would be told this often, and I certainly felt the truth of it. Nothing else would be conclusive until more tests and surgery and tests of what they removed during surgery, but people who found this kind of cancer early usually had high chances of survival—85 to 95 percent over five to ten years. I hadn't yet contemplated the possibility of non-survival.

The rest of the appointment was somewhat jolly. The surgeon made fun of my profession and my parenting decisions as he used ultrasound to pinpoint my malignancies and inserted massive needles with scissory tips to snip a bit of flesh for the biopsies. I was up for the teasing, tried to give as good as I got. Anything but pity. My husband focused on breathing and not looking. 'Sympathetic nervous response,' the surgeon said, nodding towards him. 'It's often the husbands who have stronger reactions.' We both averted our eyes, but the needles were long enough to flash into my peripheral vision anyway, and despite the blissful numbness brought on by the local, there was a lot of prodding and shoving.

'There's quite extreme variation in the density of women's breasts,' the specialist nurse told us. She was very good at explaining everything that happened. 'Some are like butter and some are like rubber car mats.' The implication was that mine fell towards the rubber mat end of the spectrum.

The test results were 'good', by which I mean non-surprising, by which I mean that it was definitely the big C, but it wasn't nastier than we had anticipated. I had the most common form of breast cancer, hormone-positive, 'easy' to treat. The thing to do was cut it out, and once they cut it out, the cancer would be gone, even though the conditions that had caused the cancer would still be there. Most of the time, they dealt with that by 'sanitising the area' with radiation, or by taking a systemic approach using drugs. It was likely that I wouldn't need chemotherapy, thank all the gods. And then the medical intervention would be done, even though the conditions that caused the cancer might *still* be there.

*

Life is paradoxical—grittily, hungrily, wonderfully and painfully so—and an utter mystery. The mystery that found me in February 2021 said, so, cancer huh? What's that about? Within weeks of my diagnosis, I discovered Dr Gabor Maté's *When the Body Says No: The Cost of Hidden Stress*, and was relieved to find that my gut feeling about what was going on had some scientific backing. Maté writes:

> [W]omen with a history of breast cancer were asked what they thought had caused their malignancy. Forty-two per cent cited stress—much more than other factors such as diet, environment, genetics and lifestyle [. . .] No other cancer has been as minutely studied for the potential biological connections between psychological influences and the onset of the disease. A rich body of evidence, drawn from animal studies and human experience, supports the impression of cancer patients that emotional stress is a major contributing cause of breast malignancy.[1]

Maté notes that women undergoing cancer treatment are rarely asked about this aspect of their lives. This was my experience; in fact that first specialist had a good old laugh when I tried to explain how overwhelmed I was by work. I teach at a university, and my work is in arts and creativity, which in my opinion is essential for life but must be quantifiably less stressful than, say, medicine or law, so even I am a bit confused about why it gets so stressful. Compulsive overwork is a habit in academia, almost a requirement, and few of us say no. Although there is more to it. Says Maté:

> Research has suggested for decades that women are more prone to develop breast cancer if their childhoods were characterized by emotional disconnection from their parents or other disturbances in their upbringing; if they tend to repress emotions, particularly anger; if they lack nurturing social relationships in adulthood; and if they are the altruistic, compulsively caregiving types.[2]

All of which I had experienced at different times, and 2020 had been a particularly toxic year at work. In the three years leading up to 2020, it wasn't unusual for me to go months without a weekend. Sometimes I would plan how we were going to manage at least one day off a week, but it rarely happened. I was burning out every year or so. I underslept and overate to keep myself moving, I drank regularly to relax, I was always wired. If my chronic stress was an underlying cause of cancer, then the way I dealt with that stress only exacerbated things, for sleep and food and alcohol have an effect on hormones too, and:

> [O]ne of the chief ways that emotions act biologically in cancer causation is through the effect of hormones. Some hormones—estrogen, for example—encourage tumour growth. Others enhance cancer development by reducing the immune system's capacity to destroy malignant cells. Hormone production is intimately affected by psychological stress.[3]

Arline T. Geronimus, a professor of Health Behavior and Health Education at the University of Michigan, describes how '[o]n a physiologicals level, persistent, high-effort coping with acute and chronic stressors can have a profound effect on health'[4] through a process called 'weathering'. Weathering is based on 'the concept of allostatic load, or the cumulative wear and tear on [the] body's systems owing to repeated adaptation to stressors'.

> Because the stress response disrupts regulation of various systems throughout the body—for example, the cardiovascular, metabolic, and immune systems—the concept of weathering encompasses multiple systems and includes impacts on them that might not yet register clinically.[5]

I always wonder, if I had known this, really known how toxic stress can be to the body, would I have let it get as bad as it got? Because my work is personally rewarding and satisfying, and because I feel privileged to have it, I found it almost impossible to limit my commitments. Even when I had been diagnosed with cancer, I found it incredibly difficult to let go of work until my colleagues told me to leave it, that it wasn't my problem anymore.

But this is where the story of my sickness becomes about more than just me and my personal chronic stress, because there are some stressors over which some of us have no control—and the more I read about it, the more I understand that my relative privilege offered no protection. I think sometimes there is an assumption that Māori have worse health outcomes because, as a group, we are poorer and have less access to good food, education and healthy housing and more exposure to risk factors. And it is true, those things have an effect on our wellbeing. I bought into this way of thinking myself: our younger whānau members are more educated, have better access to good food and more income than the generations before us. But that hasn't changed things for us the way I thought it would. It hasn't changed things for my peers. We are still more susceptible to early and chronic illnesses than our Pākehā counterparts, no matter what level of 'privilege' we attain. As a Māori woman, the story of my (lack of) wellness is irrefutably tied to the ongoing impacts of racial capitalism and settler colonialism.

It is only after the physical danger has passed that I am able to analyse my over-work compulsion at a deeper level: I am a Māori woman at the top level of her field, and what I feel about this, a lot of the time, is shame. Who am I to do well when so many do not? It takes cancer to show me my shame. It takes cancer to show me that the way I have been dealing with that shame is to work myself into the ground. It is never enough to work for myself or my family—I must carry the responsibility for the profound absence of others like me in my field at my level. The shame says I am not worthy. The shame says I am not 'Māori enough', even though I tell others, constantly, that the only thing that defines us as Māori is whakapapa. I am whakamā, all the time. It is suddenly clear that this deep whakamā is one of the conditions that caused my cancer.

It was not until I was wheeled into recovery from my own cancer surgery that I saw government minister Kiri Allan's announcement that she had stage three cervical cancer. I was heartbroken and shocked for her in a way I hadn't been for myself. At stage one, my condition was barely comparable to hers. As Allan revealed in the *New Zealand Herald*, her predicted rate of survival was 13 percent, because she is wahine Māori.[6] The predicted survival rate for non-Māori with the

same cancer is 40 percent. According to Manatū Hauora—
the Ministry of Health, 'The total-cancer mortality rate
among Māori adults was more than 1.5 times as high as that
among non-Māori adults',[7] and at times it is much higher. A
couple of months after surgery, on my regular appointments
for three weeks of radiation therapy, I would often catch a
glimpse of Kiri, or her visitors, and I understood from this
how difficult her treatment must've been. I was able to walk
in and out within an hour. I had no visitors and I needed
no assistance. Still, by the end of the therapy, it was the only
thing I could do in a day. I got slower and slower, as they told
me I would. It was scarier than the surgery, being lasered by
those beams of radiation. Scarier still was the knowledge that
it could be so much worse.

When I think about Kiri Allan, academic and writer
Teresia Teaiwa, who died of cancer in 2017 and is sorely
missed, and Marama Davidson, who announced her breast
cancer in June of 2024, as well as other brown women
who have been sick while working in high-level, high-
stress environments, I wonder if we should talk about the
cost of success for Māori and Pasifika women, even though
I can't tell anyone else's story but my own. In a session
called 'Fast Burning Women' at the literary festival WORD
Christchurch in 2018, Selina Tusitala Marsh and Tusiata
Avia talked about how to manage the demands of success on
our time and wellbeing, the strategies we must use to place
limits on what others ask of us. It's a frequent conversation
among Indigenous Pasifika and Māori women: how to keep
success from swallowing us up with its demands on our
energy and our voices. The cancers that grow in our bodies,
and the other illnesses we manifest, tell us that it is a life and
death conversation.

Associate Professor at University of Auckland Donna Cormack, who has researched inequities in cancer outcomes and access to cancer services for Māori, is clear:

From a Māori health research point of view, the idea that our bodies take on/reflect our contexts and that living under racial capitalism and settler colonialism is deadly for Brown and Black women is not controversial [. . .] One of the most examined pathways in terms of how racism impacts on health is through it operating as a chronic stressor, that has cumulative negative impacts on our bodies, our health in the broadest sense, our relationships and connections.[8]

Cormack points to Geronimus and her 'weathering' hypothesis, which accounts for early health deterioration among Black populations in the United States as 'a consequence of the cumulative impact of repeated experience with social or economic adversity and political marginalization. On a physiological level, persistent, high-effort coping with acute and chronic stressors can have a profound effect on health.'

It is not until I have cancer that I realise how faulty my thinking has been. I had thought that achieving 'success', meaning higher education, higher income and better circumstances for my family, would act as some sort of prophylactic against the disease that statistics tell us Māori and Pasifika people get in greater numbers than other populations. In fact, as Geronimus demonstrates, relating to allostatic load or weathering:

Among nonpoor respondents, Black women of all ages had at least twice the relative odds of high scores compared with White women. Nonpoor Black women aged between 55 and 64 years had 5 times the odds of high scores compared with their White counterparts [. . .] The finding of larger racial disparities among the nonpoor than the poor, and among women than men, suggests that persistent racial differences in health may be influenced by the stress of living in a race conscious society.[9]

Māori women's health outcomes can be seen as comparable to Black women's outcomes in the United States. The above analysis suggests that doing well, and moving beyond poverty, will not improve morbidity for Māori women, though it may still improve mortality.[10] The reasons for this include that Māori women bear similar responsibilities in their own communities as Black women, who:

> [. . .] bear much of the responsibility for the social and economic survival of Black families, kinship networks, and communities. In fulfilling these responsibilities, Black women may face greater exposure than Black men to stressors that require sustained and high-effort coping, along with the wear and tear on biological systems such repeated adaptation implies.[11]

It isn't seemly to complain about 'success', but in my experience, and the anecdotal experience of friends, the weight of expectation, work, and complex responsibilities to multiple communities, only increases when a brown woman does well. All of this is carried against baseline racial capitalist conditions that don't change and health vulnerabilities that don't improve.

*

An Adverse Childhood Experiences (ACE) score is a screening tool, and one that doesn't tell us everything, but is known to be fairly consistently associated with a person's risk of developing health problems later in life: a high score means a higher likelihood of addiction, cancers and other diseases, and mental health disorders. My ACE score is 8 out of 10 if you include things I can't remember but which I know to be true. By this or any sociological measure, I shouldn't be where I am today, although ACE scores also shouldn't be seen as deterministic. Sometimes a high ACE score can be mitigated by a caring grandparent or other caregiver, but I didn't have those as a child either. It was creativity that saved me, and some sort of fierce mentality; I refused to believe what I was told about life from a young age. But there's only so much you can endure, and while I kept my mind intact, I seem to have absorbed a whole lot into my body. We can call this trauma, or traumatic stress or chronic stress, but it's more complex than a single label. I was relieved to escape from that childhood, though I immediately walked into a relationship that replicated those conditions, and then I became a single parent.

For a long time I thought I could absorb it all, everything that came at us, me and my daughters. If I could just hold everything together with my mind, all the shattered pieces, and just keep everything at bay with my body—the ancestral body, the Hinenuitepō body, the thickset, fast-twitch-genes body, the stressed-out, sleep-deprived, overfed body—then I could keep us safe. If I could just stay awake long enough, be hyper-vigilant enough, persistent enough, strong enough, clever enough, healthy enough, good enough, present enough, available enough, both soft and hard enough, if I could just be enough, I would come between my daughters and all the hard things and all the hard people—the ones we know and the ones we don't know, the systemic violence, the lateral violence, and even, sometimes, the raw, old-fashioned emotional and physical violence. But I was kidding myself. I couldn't stop the world from getting through. Heck, some of the time I was the one who brought it in.

And then, quite far into adulthood, things came right. Life got good. I started writing, seriously. I found community. I put down my weapons, disassembled my imaginary walls. Writing requires an openness and vulnerability that I wouldn't have if I stayed in survival mode. But the thing about healing is, the further along you go, the better equipped you become to deal with the stuff that was left undone in childhood or even adulthood. Sometimes I believe if I can just get it together enough, I won't have to deal with it all circling back around again and again. And again. Trauma is exhausting this way: put full stops against it all you like but it will come back when it is least expected.

Nancy Krieger of the Department of Social and Behavioral Sciences, Harvard University, describes this as embodied harm in her 'Ecosocial Analysis':[12] 'Embodiment refers to how we literally incorporate, biologically, the material (biophysical) and social world in which we live.'[13] To understand how racism and colonialism continue to affect our physical health no matter what forms of privilege we have attained, we must understand that 'we live embodied—and our bodies each and every day biologically integrate each and every type of unjust, and also beneficial, exposure encountered, at each and every level.'[14] The passage of time, even of generations, doesn't lessen the impacts of embodied harm:

An especially important consideration concerns the long-term life course and intergenerational realities of embodied harm.

What may seem 'long ago,' from a legal or policy standpoint, can be but an instant in terms of biological generations.[15]

Krieger's research even makes explicit links between historical forms of racial violence and breast cancer: 'The handful of health equity studies on Jim Crow and its abolition demonstrate its relevance to rates of infant mortality, premature mortality, and *current* risk of more lethal types of breast cancer'[16] (my emphasis). Māori research is similarly unequivocal about the intergenerational effect of trauma, as Leonie Pihama and Linda Tuhiwai Smith articulate:

> For Māori, trauma experienced across generations is connected to colonisation (Mead, 1994; Wirihana & Smith 2014; Pihama et al., 2014), and is perpetuated by systemic, institutional and interpersonal racism that has been linked to the incidence and prevalence of ill health [. . .] Studies related to the interface between culture, trauma and wellness show that Native/ Indigenous Peoples experience higher rates of personal trauma than non-Native/Indigenous People [. . .] The concept of a 'damaged communal self' presents a challenge to Western scientific constructs that reify the individual [. . .][17]

With regard to the onset of disease, Maté describes how in most cases, there is a clear precursor—some acute stress or fracture in social relationships. Against the backdrop of the conditions I was already primed to develop, the thing that tipped the scales for me was an incident of lateral violence. Lateral violence is displaced violence; it is what happens when people within a marginalised or oppressed community direct their anger and rage towards their peers rather than towards the community's oppressors.[18] Our judgements of each other can be harsher and more painful than anything the coloniser can dish out (or maybe I just don't care about the coloniser's opinions). When we take each other down for our mahi, our creativity, our intellect, or for taking a risk and amplifying our voices, we act out the worst of what colonisation has done to us. This experience is not unusual, yet we fear to talk about it openly because it detracts from the real fight. It's powerfully insidious: the wounded feel isolated, alienated and undermined.

In the 1980s my uncle Sir Mason Durie introduced Te Whare Tapa Whā, which demonstrates the four aspects of health for Māori: tinana, wairua, hinengaro, whānau; or physical, spiritual, mental and emotional, family and social. Some models add whenua or land/roots to this structure. The whare needs all walls of the house, and its foundation, so that it can stand. When hurtful action comes from within the marginalised community, it causes deep fracture for the marginalised psyche: it's like taking a wrecking ball to the walls of our whare tapa whā. And what we are left with is an intensification of whakamā.

*

While I was sick, I had two good friends in other parts of the country who had much worse cancers than me, one Māori and one Pākehā, one male and one female. They were both kind and concerned about my diagnosis, but I shared it with them mainly in solidarity with their own, because connecting with them was always an exercise in helplessness and inadequacy. I feel very sure about what my cancer meant to me, but when I see it in other people, it makes no sense. It seems extremely unfair. Making meaning from this disease is something that works for me. But my conviction shouldn't be mistaken for arrogance about what cancer is or why anyone else has it: I didn't think I'd ever be there, and I don't understand why my friends were.

By the time my diagnosis came, despite everything that preceded it, and despite the societal context that Cormack, Geronimus and Krieger so clearly delineate, I was better off than I had ever been, and that made it easy to see my particular diagnosis as a gift: a nudge, a quiet talking-to, a sharply focusing lens.

'It's okay,' I told my sister, when she fretted for me from overseas. 'I'm so lucky. It'd be different if I was alone.' For a long time I *was* alone, or with people who were the opposite of my spouse. 'Moea he tangata ringa raupā,' the whakataukī says: 'Marry someone with calloused hands.' The implication: they'll look after you. Somehow, eventually, I did, and he does. Being married to an emotionally healthy individual is, on the scale of things I expected to see in my life, a miracle. He is simply willing to do the work, whatever that work is, even when the work is on himself. Recovery is much harder without a crew like this.

'Reparations!' my eldest exclaims when she sees her Pākehā matua whāngai / parent doing this work. Nothing gets past anyone in this house. It's true—his efforts are making up for transgressions that go beyond either of us. There is a clear understanding in our home that much of the damage we still carry is directly attributable to a family history that microcosmically replicates the colonial process. Colonial violence has fed into the lives of my children through both sides of their heritage. Like Krieger, Resmaa Menakem, author of *My Grandmother's Hands: Racialized Trauma and the Pathway to Mending Our Hearts and Bodies*, recognises that trauma exists in the body rather than the emotions, and is routinely passed on from person to person, generation to generation. Whatever we're dealing with has been there for a long time, and likely began long before us.

*

On my second day at radiation therapy, the older man before me in line is almost in tears as he loudly gives thanks to the radiation therapists. It's his last day. Prostate cancer. I hope I can be as exuberant when it's my time, though that seems unlikely. But I know how he feels. Every practitioner I meet at the hospital is incredibly kind, gentle, and hard-working. I couldn't be more grateful for their care, their generosity and expertise. The hospital and its people can literally save our lives.

Frankenboob changes everything. The way I eat, the way I sleep, the way I drink. How I think, how I speak, what I give my attention to. But despite the beauty I encounter every time I visit the hospital, of people going out of their way to help other people, none of this is because of treatment or what I have been prescribed. At each hospital visit, they ask me how I am, but they mean how my body is, particularly the areas affected by treatment. I can access counselling, if I wish, through the Breast Cancer Society. Though access to Māori counsellors is notoriously difficult. It's been 40 years since we've known about Te Whare Tapa Whā, but in several months of treatment, no one asks me about my whānau. No one asks about my wairua or hinengaro. I wouldn't have minded if they'd done this the Pākehā way: they could have talked to me about my diet, coping mechanisms, exercise, support systems. I'm fine because I have good access to information, and I'm a researcher, but I think a lot about people who only do what the doctor prescribes. People who don't have the time or energy or easy access to research, people for whom English is not their first language, or who have a big family waiting for them to get home with the kai. It's the only thing that worries me—that our treatment is limited to the body parts in which the cancer has grown. And it would make a difference to have someone ask about our lives as a whole. The evidence is clear that the way we feed and exercise and relax ourselves can make a huge difference to our outcomes. The evidence is clear that we should pray or meditate, deal with our chronic stress, make amends and decide how to respond to those who have harmed us. The evidence is clear that we should forgive ourselves, most of all, and live in good community with others.

During the three weeks of radiotherapy, my breast becomes uncomfortable and itchy and sore. It loses some skin and receives a radiation tan. Mostly it's the fatigue people talk about, and that's the hard part. Still, there's nothing quite like cancer as a legitimate excuse to *not* work. By the time my convalescence is over, I've got used to something called rest, and I've become unwilling to forget that it means life.

I'm still figuring out how to deal with the conditions that caused the cancer. It's all of the above and then some, with added chaos and free radicals and the way the fucking world is right now. At my one-year check-up I am given the all-clear—the name Frankenboob faded long ago with her scars, though there might still be a tinge of blue. The oncologist says it takes one year to recover from surgery, two to recover from radiation. I wonder how long it takes to recover from the conditions that caused the cancer. It could be generations, but there's no reason it can't start now.

First published in *Landfall* 244 (2022)
Winner Landfall Essay Competition 2022

funny little ugly baby

she wants the world to be beautiful. she wants that angle of sunlight falling through trees just so on the dog. she wants all future dogs to be warmed by it. she wants mediocre men to discontinue their mediocre policies, lie down under trees and dream their infant selves back into the world. she wants to ask, how will you keep them sheltered? how will you feed them? oh but she wants to lie down too. she wants to never again be told how to be|how not to be|how to think|how not to think. she wants to never again be told how to *Māori* by pākehā women who think they know. they don't know. she wants to go away and sit in temples that remind her that time is tall and her portion of it is short. she wants to catch trains catch trains catch trains and never smell petrol fumes again. she wants the toxic aunties to soften because there is nothing to be hard about anymore. she wants the aunties and her daughters and her sisters to be able to whāngai themselves back into existence as newborn babies, soft and gurgling, mouths wide open, spitting up the universe.

First published in *Flash Frontier:*
An Adventure in Short Fiction (2023)

PAO PAO PAO

An object tells a story, and the story it tells changes person to person, place to place. Ripples move out from it, resonances, arcs of meaning. This object is a poi made from blanket fabric and fine golden embroidery. The image embroidered on the poi is of two hands shackled, open-palmed, one face-on and the other in profile. The hands are finely rendered and detailed; the braided rope of the poi is slightly frayed from use. The hands look strong: articulate, graceful, expressive. The poi reads as a feminine thing, though poi have not always been so. I cannot view this apparently still object without seeing movement and rhythm: the pao-pao-pao of the swinging poi beat, multiple hands and hips and feet moving in unison.

One thing to love about this particular poi is that it belonged to a young girl who used it in kapa haka. It is art object and artefact, political statement and taonga, but it is first of all a poi and has been used as such. The object is alive with all the ways it has been used in the world, and all the hands that have touched it.

This is the story that the poi tells me. It will tell someone else a different story.

The hands that brought the poi into being were Ngahina Hohaia's. She made hundreds from secondhand blankets, their loose fibres playing havoc with her sinuses.[1] I remember how compelling those poi were the first time I saw them in formation for her artwork *Roimata Toroa* (2006). When art speaks that clearly, it can be difficult to form sentences that fully express the encounter. Each poi held a different symbol or fragment of a sentence; each was as elegant as the poi that is the subject of this essay, and together they spoke of multitudes: generations, collective identity, peace, war, resilience, spirit. All of this was apparent in an instant—myriad stories held in the nexus of those many objects and their relationships with each other, and with their maker.

> Hohaia's show features over 500 embroidered woollen poi made from secondhand blankets. The blanket is a metaphor for the land. She says, 'Te Whiti o Rongomai and Tohu Kaakahi stated to the crown that they were willing to share their "blanket", but that sovereign independence must remain with Māori.' Her poi are based on the Parihaka tradition of poi-manu, the use of poi in ritual recitation of genealogy. 'The poi is the manu, the messenger,' says Hohaia. The images embroidered on the poi are derived from Parihaka oral tradition.[2]

As a single parent at the time of the exhibition, I remember asking Ngahina if I could buy a single poi and, even though the cost wasn't substantial, I knew that when the work became available I wouldn't have enough to spare. There was also the problem of how to choose one, when each was so exquisite.

274

In a way, now I have been given one. I don't know if it is what I would have chosen back then. I would probably have gone for a poi with something more obviously positive embroidered on it: Taranaki maunga, the raukura three feathers of peace. But I look at these hands in shackles now, and I see only empowerment, embodiment, triumph. Whatever was meant by this image, the poi requires me to think about power. I, too, am from Parihaka, though unlike Ngahina I didn't grow up there. I have been there only once, to an artists' hui, when I was a young student. It wasn't a homecoming, because I was a stranger there and I didn't have the cultural wherewithal to make any claims or connections. My family left Taranaki in successive waves of migration beginning in the early 19th century, and I'm only tentatively finding my way back. It is a long homecoming.

This then, is a story about power.

In my origin stories, a Pākehā man and a Māori woman get married due to a pregnancy. From the beginning the signs are not good, but there is a tumultuous kind of love there; anyone can see that. At some point the violence between the pair escalates to the point where something must happen. The thing that happens is the Pākehā man takes the children to a place where the Māori woman cannot find them. The youngest child is two. The man keeps the children hidden by moving from one place to another. The mother does not see the children again until they are fully grown.

I was the youngest child. I carried with me no memories of the mother, but I was given a handful of stories about her, some factual and some fictional. By the time I was 16, I once again had some contact with my mother, and found that her stories did not match my father's and that she was not who he said she was. Many of the stories I had carried all my life were false. I began to understand that I had been given a mythology that explained my existence as a motherless Pākehā child with some trace of a redundant culture in my blood, one part of me cleanly sliced away by a narrative that made sense of our anchorless lives. My fair skin was only further evidence of the veracity of my father's stories.

In my first year of university, I took papers in Māori studies and immediately began to see my origin story as a perfect metaphor for the process of colonisation. Perhaps we can all of us, the colonised, make this metaphor out of our origins, but mine was so clear and immediate it seemed like a gift of understanding. This new interpretation of the stories helped with the anger. My belief in the power of mythology is informed by real-life events that have never ceased to seem mythical.

For all that the above tale seems like one of subjugation, on the occasions when my mother said that she was the sole victim in this story, I found it hard to believe her. It is not that I don't believe that unjust things were done to her. They certainly were. It is that I find it difficult to believe that my mother could be a victim of anything. I want to see her as indomitable. Even though I have been in abusive situations, I don't believe I'm a victim of anything either. This may be an unrealistic and obdurate position, but the only reason I write is because I *am* those things. Naive, also. I refuse our victimhood: nobody can make us; nobody has ever made us.

It is the stories we believe about ourselves that matter. The stories we give light to. But also the stories we refuse. The stories I choose to believe are the ones that make us strong. Especially when it is clear that no single story contains the whole truth.

This story could have shackled my own hands, but I would not have my origins any other way, for the mess of them has given me more, creatively, than an easy beginning might have. And just as there aren't single victims in this story, I don't want to suggest there is a single perpetrator. If anything, we are sometimes victims of our own actions. Everyone has paid a price.

*

Let me try to explain it another way. Us mixed-bloods often talk about walking between worlds, existing in the in-between spaces, as if Māori culture is on one side and Pākehā culture is on the other. I don't think it actually works that way. There is no such even-handedness. I am planted, primarily, on Māori earth. I grow out of those goddesses you've heard about: Papatūānuku, Hinenuitepō; goddesses who were grandmothers to my grandmothers. When everything is whakapapa, those women become more than archetypes. I can look at my own flesh and see their DNA, listen to the laughter of my daughters and hear their voices. The real world exists at this level. Any understanding of women's power, for me, is derived from this deep soil. Women run families and nations and always have. Men work alongside them in these tasks, because they always have. At the centre, the children. To disregard the unique abilities of any one group in this community would jeopardise survival. Everyone according to their strengths.

Superimposed over this is something that came later. Visualise it like I do, if you like, as transparent: layered over the top of everything, drawing lines over the real, like borders on a map between countries that are separate only because some white man drew a line there. In this superimposed world, there are a lot of ownership rules. There are a lot of entrenched ideas about how much things are worth, and how they must be used. Things include people, apparently, especially women and children. Men occupy some higher rung in this strange hierarchy, but even they must subjugate themselves to the requirements of their system. In this world, it helps to have evidence of status: legal documents, ownership papers, money. It is important to have rights to citizenship, to vote, to make noise about equality, to participate in the many, buzzing systems superimposed over everything, for there really are many. And yet they seem as if they don't quite have the density of the real.

I understand it thus: we who find our feet planted on Indigenous soil walk upright. We are always grounded in the real Aotearoa underneath the superimposed world, but we must move through those superimposed worlds layered above it. We must operate on all levels at all times. For example, the vote is important to me on one level, very important. All those superimposed worlds have become very important to me. But that is not where my power is derived from. 'Man'-given rights mean little when you know you are descended from the goddesses of life and death.

This is not simply rhetoric. On good days, I remember who I am, and I remember that all the superimposed worlds aren't real. On those days, it seems a waste of energy to get agitated about the political and economic systems that screw us over, Indigenous and non-Indigenous alike, women and, yes, men too, for what woman has ever looked at her son and thought: yay, he belongs to the patriarchy so none of this will touch him? On these days it is not so much that I live in denial, though that is certainly part of it; it's that I find peace of mind, my centre. Simply, peace. Something eternal. Something beyond what anyone can reach. We all do this. If you've ever spent an entire day at the beach with your babies, making sandcastles and swimming; if you've ever gone bush for a day or six. You know this place.

It is from this place that I create. It is from this place that I respond to the creative work that others produce. It is from this place that I can look at history, and the stories of our young people, my stories or stories of people like me, people with stories that are harder and more painful than mine, and not be crushed. At times like that, I need to be able to look, unafraid, at our thin, superimposed worlds and flip them the bird, look down on them and consider them redundant. In the great scheme of things, they are.

But all it takes is a slow blink. And then we are tripping over plastic on the beach. Avoiding home rivers that are clogged with sludge. Watching people lose their basic human rights in Australia or the United States. Finding change for a person with no home at the train station in Wellington. The superimposed worlds soon flip the bird back, harsher and more brutal. Yeah, they say, you think we ain't real? Look at what we can do to the world. Sure, I reply, but this is what I've got. I don't believe in you; I believe in *this*.

In *Paopao ki Tua o Rangi* (2008), Ngahina Hohaia's poi transform into a bird's-eye view of Taranaki maunga. Circles of poi spread outward from a central circle within which images of tūpuna, whānau and the land are projected. Images appear and recede, light plays on the poi cloaked in sound, some ancient, some contemporary, the pao-pao-pao a spiral dance of time and whakapapa and whenua.

My first encounter with this piece held me in thrall, taking me in and down, or maybe up, to a place beyond the abstract, superimposed world. I felt an intense state of wellbeing, of connection, of transformation. Somehow, I was part of that experience, as close to the mountain and my ancestors as I had ever been. Not separated, not alienated. In a gallery talk about the work, Ngahina described her sense that there is no linear time, that all things that exist in the past still exist. This is the same world view that informs my writing.

I am alienated from the place Parihaka. I have whanaunga there, but our particular family have not kept the ahi kā— home fires burning. Those shackled hands represent a long history of being pushed out by successive impositions: muskets, invasions, confiscations, farming, racism, family dysfunction, sadness, shame. Pōuri. Whakamā. It is not that such things are unmendable, but what took lifetimes to tear apart may take lifetimes to bring back together.

In 2017 the Crown apologised to the people of Parihaka for the atrocities perpetuated there in 1881, when 1400 armed troops invaded a peaceful village and destroyed everything. It was the first time the Crown had acknowledged and accepted responsibility for the rape of women in a historical grievance. The people of Parihaka celebrated a new feeling of hope and reconciliation. It would be wonderful if the words of Te Whiti or Tohu appeared here, or of the women who responded with such grace and courage to the apology, so forgive me that the words that arrive as I'm writing this are from Malcolm X (1964):

If you stick a knife in my back nine inches and pull it out six inches, there's no progress. If you pull it all the way out, that's not progress. The progress is healing the wound that the blow made. And they haven't even begun to pull the knife out, much less healed the wound. They won't even admit the knife is there.[3]

The Crown has recognised its knife and pulled it out. Progress is possible.

It's important to end, I think, where we began. A taonga in a museum. Contemporary, 21st century. Poi. Gentle, articulate hands, shackled. The wide-open palms: alarm? A cry for justice? An embrace? I have told you the story the poi told me, of power and grace—the wielding of it, the claiming of it, how it works in this particular life. A rather abstract foray into the nature of existence. The way art can connect and transform and bring you back in touch with that which you think you have lost.

The image on this poi doesn't read as negative to me, because the act of art-making has imbued it with power. If someone shackles your hands and does their best to eliminate your people, and you are able to turn around and make that beautiful, make it soft and musical, golden and feminine, imbue it with strength, then the violence has been transformed. We take the things that have been done to us and we look at them from different angles until we find a way to enter them and turn them into something else. We put ourselves back into the things that have been done to us so that the power returns to us. The story of a Pākehā man and a Māori woman and their children is the story of colonial imposition on a peaceful people is the story of women's loss and pain is the story of our nation is the story of our liberty. Take the things that have been done to you and listen for the pao-pao-pao of the single poi alongside her sisters. Listen to the story she tells you. It is the story of what came before and what is possible now.

First published in *Women Now: The Legacy of Female Suffrage* (2018)

Postscript
2024

You only have to go through this once

In late 2019, I thought this essay collection was finished. I had gathered a decade's work in creative nonfiction and added some memoir pieces to give the collection what I thought of as more texture and shape. It had been accepted by a publisher. I was happy with it. Unfortunately, I also knew there was no way I could publish it. In writing some of the more recent pieces, I had learnt to love my father again, despite his and my own best efforts, and more importantly I had taken the time to really look at him, and really listen to him, even though most of the time it was difficult to do. Here was a person who was in deep pain. Who had been in deep pain as long as I had known him. It didn't matter what he had done to hurt me or others. It didn't matter that I owed him nothing. He didn't understand my world and he certainly wouldn't have understood why I would want to write any of this down and let others read it. This would have been the greatest of betrayals. This would have caused him—a dying man who was, according to his death certificate, a recluse— even more pain and shame than he had to live with already.

My sister and I have a running joke about how Dad's genes have instilled in us an inability to be around other humans for too long. Call it socialisation, trauma or genetics, I have to be careful about how much time I spend in the company of others. Social settings are exhausting. But what I have long known is that I *need* people, something that Dad would never admit. I *love* people. Writing allows me to connect with people even when my body or brain doesn't want to be around them. Writing allows me to be human in the fullest sense of the word. As I have continued to do it, I have lost any sense of shame about who the person that does the writing is. She writes because that is where she meets herself and others. Because it is necessary.

But I couldn't expose him to this. I couldn't make his last days any more painful than they already were.

It's a truly awful sentence to write, but there were many times I wished for my father's death. It was a childish wish, but I hope you can see where it came from. No more ugliness. No more shame, embarrassment or guilt. No more pain, for either of us. I also don't wish to cause pain to other members of his family, who would tell this story differently, or, more likely, not tell it at all. I have written this postscript, in part, to explain myself and to ask forgiveness. But there are some things for which no amount of explanation will suffice. If I have transgressed in these pages, it is the last breath in a long conversation with my father in which I have not been able to let his damage be the final thing.

When I first heard the missing stair theory, I was, to be honest, pretty relieved to have finally found an apt analogy for Dad. The theory meant other people had lived with or around people like him, and had lived to make up theories about it. I think I first saw the phrase in an article by Emma Hart on the website Public Address. 'It's a person with whom you have to socialise who damages other people . . . The Missing Stair is someone you can't just avoid,' she said, among many other useful things. 'That's the thing about the Missing Stair: everyone knows what they're like . . . Everyone knows the stair is missing. Nobody fixes it. Everyone is expected to work around the Missing Stair.' I first understood that something was very wrong with my father when I was seven years old. From that time until adulthood and on, my sister and I worked around him. We made excuses for him, trying to cover up who he really was. For a long time, he worked with us on that. It was like an unspoken pact we had with each other: things could be dysfunctional and scary and painful at home, but when we went out into the world, we all pretended everything was okay. Given a word was never spoken about it, I don't know how the need to defend the family unit was driven so deeply into my psyche, but I would have chosen my unstable and frightening father over any other adult in the world, so protect him I did.

My sister and I were never under any illusion that we could fix him or even ask for that, so he simply became the dark gap we traversed as best we could. It's not that it didn't hurt. It's not that getting around the missing stair wasn't difficult or even, at times, treacherous. Even when we wanted to include him, he made it impossible. We couldn't invite him to life events because everything would have become about him: managing him, creating some sort of barrier or distraction between him and others. There was just no room around Dad for anyone else. He had a dark talent for destroying relationships.

As we got older, and especially after my sister left home, the façade dropped. Dad seemed to make an active decision not to conform to social norms in any way. He became unrestrained and extravagant in his rage, racism and misogyny. But he could be charming too, especially if he wanted something. He knew how to play the game. It's just that most of the time, he didn't want to. I have to admit, there's something I admire in that.

Relating to a parent primarily through an association with broken joinery is pitiful, but it became a useful way to understand why I distanced myself from real feeling about my father. For much of my late childhood, I hated to be around him. Maybe I even hated him. He scared me, with his rage and his alcoholism, and in more existential ways, when he drove drunk, for example, and I was forced to be in the car with him. He used to pull a bottle or can from under the driver's seat with pride, demonstrating what he could get away with. I don't think he ever got caught drunk-driving when I was a kid. But he was always drinking.

Even when I began to like him again, in the process of writing this book, in his final years he was still an impossible human. We would have reasonable, even sage, conversations on the phone, but then if I ever visited him in person he would use me as a kind of verbal punching bag. I would make excuses, for his age, his mental health, his alcoholism, 70+ years of undealt-with dysfunction, but it was so tiring. It was as if he couldn't stand to be around me in real life.

By this time, my older sister, who had always been his right-hand number one when we were growing up, hadn't spoken to him in nearly two decades. She'd always been his ally, and always far more forgiving than me, until suddenly he took it too far and she wasn't anymore. What was too far in my dad's world? Threats, breaking into our homes, ringing up in-laws, showing up unannounced and making a scene at workplaces, were all normal. The word 'No' was a direct incitement for him to break whatever boundary had been set up, whether it was law, social contract, or basic manners. My sister had endured that kind of thing all her life. You can imagine, then, how far he must've taken things for someone like my sister, who has made a profession out of caring for others, to say: Enough, never again.

If it wasn't so invasive, I would have admired his propensity to give zero shits about authority, but his lack of respect for personal boundaries was impossible to live with. Since my pre-teens, I had told him as little about my life as I could get away with. He was my primary and only caregiver, so this meant I was very much on my own. By the time he was an old man and I was the only close relative he still saw regularly, I meted out my presence in a miserly way, visiting him once a year or so. This was the limit of my compassion. That's how I saw it. I thought, *I can do this for him*, but I knew it was paltry. One visit didn't cost me too much by this stage because I had a partner who was good to me and everyone in my life. He was good to Dad. And I wasn't hurt by Dad's insults anymore. I really couldn't care less about anything he had to say. Even so, it was wearying, not least because it was extremely boring (the tedious repetitiveness of the drunk will be familiar to anyone who has grown up with it) and frustrating. We could have been talking to each other as human beings, like we did sometimes, on good days, on the phone.

He was sick and miserable, refusing healthcare, letting his teeth rot, literally, from his mouth. My childish wish never accounted for the messiness of dying, nor the possibility that my compassion for the old man would take me to him in his last days to 'help' him die, insomuch as he would allow any help. I felt no happiness at his death. It was a sad and painful experience. It was no way to die, just as his life had been no way to live.

Dad had spent many years obsessing over every detail of what should happen when he died, but the thing he hadn't considered was the process of death itself. We had been given our instructions, as had everyone else, for how things should proceed once he went. Everything was pre-arranged, pre-paid, pre-allocated. There would be no funeral. It was a surprise to both of us, then, that death itself couldn't be tidily packaged. Death can be slow and untidy, robbing a man of his ability to walk and talk and control bodily functions before it robs him of his mind. Dad was shockingly lucid right up to the moment he lost consciousness, which meant he remained bossy and frustrated by his inability to communicate or control his environment to the last. He banished hospice staff, who he had called in the day before. 'I think he's scared,' one of them said to me. But his fear of hospital was so great that he wouldn't let them stay with him, and he wouldn't allow them to make him comfortable in a hospice facility. Despite having limited speech, he managed to make these wishes known, and despite having an extremely limited ability to actually do anything, he remained in command. The day before I arrived, he was obviously in need of company. He wouldn't ask me to come but he didn't argue when I suggested I should. 'You won't be angry at me if I come though, will you, Dad?' He said he'd try not to, but when I arrived it was bad. It was the worst. Later, I told my sister, 'He couldn't go without traumatising me one last time!' and we laughed the way only sisters can, in our case a somewhat hysterical cackle that has been known to scare passersby.

I went up for that first day and night alone, and Lorry followed as quickly as we could make arrangements. There were two light moments amongst all of it, when I was alone with Dad on that first day. I'd been wheeling him around on an office chair all day, I didn't know how to change him, and despite him not having eaten for weeks and having no flesh on his bones, I couldn't lift him, and any physical touch pained him anyway. He was still refusing proper hospice care. At one point, in the afternoon, he looked at me carefully, just once, and I could *see* him in there, trying to connect with *me*. He said something like, 'Well, this is it. Is there anything you need to talk about?' No, I said, except how I was going to look after him. 'Like this,' he said, waving a hand at both of us. I shook my head. 'At least you only have to go through this once,' he said. Clear as. I was touched by his empathy. I thought he could see how hard it was. How much he was asking of me. Moments later, I realised he wasn't talking about me at all. He had meant death. You only have to go through death once.

Later I escaped into the night, explaining that I needed dinner. 'Oh yeah, I forgot normal people need to eat,' he said. He wanted me to stay, but I was all out of fuel. The hospice people came while I was out, to give him pain and sleeping meds, the angels, not that it helped me sleep that night. Even though everything about being near him was unrelentingly painful, watching him die was strangely akin to bringing my own babies into the world. I kept vigil over him, even in his sleep, even from my room in the Airbnb I had booked. I was wakeful all through the night, worrying about him, feeling as if we were attached by some invisible cord. After each of my daughter's births, it was joy and excitement that kept me awake, and perhaps a hard kick of oxytocin and endorphins. With Dad, perhaps it was adrenaline or the stress hormones he'd raised me on. I needed to be in a different house for my own sanity, but it was no use: until he passed over, or into someone else's hands, I was his guardian in the space between life and death.

The next morning I went to him before dawn, hoping to slip in before he woke. But he was already awake and struggling with the box they'd attached to his arm to deliver painkillers and medicine the day before. He was fighting to make any words at all now. He grunted sounds as he had previously, but they no longer made any sense to me. I tried to make him comfortable. It was clear he wanted to get up. It was clear he was frustrated. It was clear I couldn't help him move at all anymore. After ten minutes or so, he fell back to sleep. I sat on a chair by his bed, watching the sun come up through his window, while he slept deeply, his chest rising and falling in great slow breaths. His kidneys were failing, possibly his liver too, but he had the lungs and heart of an ox, even after all those years of smoking. It was the most peaceful time I had had with him since I was a very small child.

In the following days, as he lay unconscious and Lorry and I nursed him and began packing up his life, we were struck by the lengths he had gone to in order to control all aspects of his existence, and the way that life, and death, will humble us, one way or another. Dad was so defiant, so belligerent about the possibility that anyone might ever have sway over him. To the end, he couldn't admit that we don't get to be in control. But maybe he was just scared, like the hospice worker said. So much of this must've come from fear.

Hospice staff could now come freely to help us care for him, but we tried to stick to his wish not to be moved to a facility. While they taught us how to give him his meds and keep him comfortable, the hospice staff also told us no family should have to do what we were doing. It was easy to see how highly they valued the work they did—how they considered it a privilege to help people die peacefully. I didn't even really cry until a hospice nurse looked deeply into my eyes and told me we were doing a good job. Goddammit, lady, I thought, don't make me *feel* things right now! Lorry nursed him with the dignity and care that only someone who is not directly family can offer, protecting Dad and me in the process. We kept telling him: you won, Dad, you got what you wanted; now you can go. But he refused to surrender, even to death, lasting days longer than is usual in a case like his. Each evening we would take our food outside, confused by how to manage tapu and noa in a house where there was no separation between the dying and the food consumption areas. Eating made us more aware of how alone we were, how alone he was, how unnatural it is to die in isolation. There should have been family around us, aunties and uncles bringing kai, mokopuna running around. This is your precious way of life, Dad? This is what you wanted for us?

I am finishing this book for the second time, now in Waitohi. I don't think about Dad every day, but when I got off the train at lunchtime and looked out to the Sounds, one of my favourite views in the world, Dad was there to greet me. My mother's people are from here, but Dad lived here once too, and the first time I came to this place was to visit him. When I arrived today, I stood on the foreshore and thought about all the different ways this is home, which I always do when I plant my feet on this whenua. I thought about my tūpuna who were as comfortable on the water as I am on land, how they were always out there, at Arapaoa and Tōtaranui and Kura Te Au. Then Dad was there with me, a friendly presence, reminding me of the times we were here together. On the train I'd seen a large pod of dolphins close in to the coast south of Kaikōura, doing 360-degree flips, leaps and dives, playing joyfully. I thought I'd never seen anything like it, but Dad's presence reminded me of my first trip here, how he took me fishing and for the whole day a few dolphins followed the boat, leaping at the bow. Don't ask me why but I knew his presence meant he is ready to rest now, or maybe it meant I was ready to let him rest. If we're lucky, death has this miraculous power to enliven the good memories about a person, and diminish their sins.

After Dad's death, my uncle reminded me of how close we used to be. The idea seems preposterous to me now, but it's true, I do remember being a little girl who loved her dad and thought he was the world. I've become so unaccustomed to thinking of him that way. It wasn't until the last couple of years that I really understood how hard he tried. He didn't stand a chance, a postwar baby who left school at 15 and found himself parenting two girls alone by the age of 28 in the 1970s. He certainly brought that on himself, but still, what was he gonna do? He fed us, kept a roof over our heads, took us to A&P shows and libraries and museums. Told us about the world as he saw it, instilling in us fierce independence, a deep distrust of authority, and a cynicism towards accepted societal proprieties. He made us anti-establishment and socialist while also failing to make us misogynists and racists, despite his best efforts. He said things that made no sense— 'Grow up to be a lady, not a woman. *Women* are terrible'— while also teaching us to live completely without men.

I sometimes wonder, but not very often because it seems an impossibility on his timeline, what his life would have been like, what our lives would have been like, with better mental health care. It is easiest to be compassionate when I think of him this way: trying so very hard to be everything he thought he was supposed to be, self-medicating debilitating mental illness, with few resources at his disposal. He loved us as much as he was able, I know that. At some point he gave up, I know that too. Perhaps there was a series of giving ups.

And look: his final obsession in life was to give us everything he had, which in the end, wasn't much.

A year before he died, I took my daughters to see him for the first time in a few years. This was a bit of a worry, given the way he treated me, and we all prepared ourselves for the worst. Would he say something painful, racist, insulting?

But he fawned over them. 'Isn't she beautiful?' he said. 'Like a supermodel.' He was delighted, and delightful with them. He was the best version of himself he could be that day, even offering his queer granddaughter his bed so that she could come and visit with her partner. 'I'm not prejudiced!' he declared.

Dad was always perplexing like this. I think anyone close enough to him must've thought he was terrible at one time or another, but then he could be so very loving, so very human, so very clever, it was clear he was more than he ever allowed himself to be. I bought him the book *Sapiens: A Brief History of Humankind* by Yuval Noah Harari for Christmas once, and he made a project of reading a bit every day. 'It's pretty hard-going,' he told me over the phone. 'I don't understand most of it.' But then he told me he thought he might be Buddhist. After his death, I found *Sapiens* with a piece of blue notepaper carefully folded and stapled on a particular page, 'BUDDHISM' scrawled in his blocky capital letters. In another part of my life I had been talking to a PhD student about Māori philosophies and metaphysics, and I couldn't help but see Dad through that prism: he had lived with an intense illusion of separateness all his life, and enforced it on others. He was a product of his culture and even though it was so painful to him, he couldn't see things differently. He could not see himself as part of a whole, as connected in any way to the rest of humanity, even to the rest of his family, yet he yearned for it endlessly. He was an extreme version of most of us: the most human thing in the world is to think ourselves separate when in fact we are always part of the whole.

I feel, even now, a strong sense that writing this may be a betrayal. But this book has given me back my father, given me back a higher sense of him, at least, and what he could have been. Who he was in his best moments. Who we were to each other. In writing this book, I have found beauty in my father's life. That's all this is. It's not beautiful, not at all, when it's there in front of you, but writing transforms.

The only other person in the world who knows what it was like to live with Dad is my big sister, a visual artist, who I think lost more in the experience than I did. She protected me. Completing this book has become more difficult than I anticipated, but this is my sister's book too, so I publish it for her. We didn't get to have a lot of the things parents bestow, in childhood or adulthood. We both had to find other ways to survive, then thrive. What we get instead, what our children get, is this: our art.

This book is about so many other things, things that my father would have rejected. I have lived my life mainly in opposition to him. And yet my life would not exist as it is—the writing, the beauty, the love of culture, the politics—without him. There was never going to be a way to exist in the world without his legacy. This is the kind of paradox, complexity, contradiction, that sits at the heart of the writing.

Somehow, in writing these essays, I moved past indifference and learned how to connect with my father again. And it's better for us if we can love all the people inside us, all the ones who make up who we are, even if they are difficult, or ridiculous or just plain mean and shameful. But sometimes that's not possible, and none of us should be judged if we have to estrange ourselves from those who have hurt us. Dad hurt me most days, but still there are some boundaries he did not cross, and I'm grateful for that. He wasn't a bad person, not in a conscious way. On a lot of his days on this planet, he tried. I think he wanted other things. He was damaged. He was ill. It could have been worse. It could have been better.

Notes

Meeting the Ancestor on the Road

1   Toni Morrison, 'Toni Morrison interview | American Author | Award winning | Mavis on Four | 1988', YouTube, 22:15, 7 August 2019, https://www.youtube.com/watch?v=UAqB1SgVaC4.

2   Carl Mika, *Indigenous Education and the Metaphysics of Presence: A Worlded Philosophy* (Routledge, 2018); 41.

3   Mika, 41.

4   Mika, 41.

5   'History', *Taranaki Mounga—He Kawa Ora—Back to Life*, 27 May 2021, https://taranakimounga.nz/nga-mounga/history/.

6   Jeremy Wilkinson (quoting Tim Stern), 'Geologists Inch Closer to Understanding Mt Taranaki's Mysteries', *Stuff*, 17 February 2017, https://www.stuff.co.nz/environment/89510777/geologists-inch-closer-to-understanding-mt-taranakis-mysteries.

7   Jane McRae, *Māori Oral Tradition: He Kōrero nō te Ao Tawhito* (Auckland University Press, 2017), 34.

8   Mika, 45.

9   Mika, 45.

An Englishman, an Irishman and a Welshman Walk into a Pā

1   Shekhar Kapur, 'We Are the Stories We Tell Ourselves', filmed November 2009 in Mysore, India, TED video, 20:57, https://www.ted.com/talks/shekhar_kapur_we_are_the_stories_we_tell_ourselves.

2   Chimamanda Adichie, 'The Danger of a Single Story', filmed July 2009 in Oxford, United Kingdom, TED video, 18:32, https://www.ted.com/talks/chimamanda_ngozi_adichie_the_danger_of_a_single_story.

3 Trevor Bentley, *Pakeha Maori: The Extraordinary Story of the Europeans Who Lived as Maori in Early New Zealand* (Penguin, 1999), 85.

4 It would be reasonable to assume this, given that Taranaki was tapu to Māori. Local Māori who accompanied Dieffenbach and Heberley stopped where the snow-line began.

5 Roger Neich, 'Jacob William Heberley of Wellington: A Maori Carver in a Changed World', *Records of the Auckland Institute and Museum* 28 (1991): 71.

6 Neich, 71.

7 'The Oldest of Old Settlers', *Otago Daily Times* (11 October 1899): 3. http://paperspast.natlib.govt.nz/cgi-bin/paperspast?a=d&d=ODT18991011.2.8.

8 James Heberley, *Reminiscences, Jan 1809–Jun 1843*, Ref: MS-0971, Alexander Turnbull Library, Wellington, New Zealand.

9 Heberley.

10 Heberley.

11 Heberley.

12 Neich, 74.

13 Heberley.

14 Bentley, 193.

15 Bentley, 195.

16 Bentley, 201.

17 Subsequent research has shown Jackson is known in the whakapapa and perhaps to other families as John.

18 'History and Traditions of the Taranaki Coast, Chapter XVIII, The Defence of Otaka or Nga-Motu', *Journal of the Polynesian Society* 19, no. 1 (1910), https://www.jstor.org/stable/20700898.

19 Morris Love, 'Te Āti Awa of Wellington—The Migration of 1832', *Te Ara—The Encyclopedia of New Zealand*, http://www.teara.govt.nz/en/te-ati-awa-of-wellington/3.

20 'History and Traditions of the Taranaki Coast'.

21 'Local and General News', *Marlborough Press* (1 October 1880): 2. https://paperspast.natlib.govt.nz/newspapers/MPRESS18801001.2.7.

22 Mike Taylor (Picton Museum), personal communication.

23 Also empathy, compassion.

24 'Our History', Otaki-Māori Racing, https://otakimaoriracing. co.nz/our-history.

25 F.S. Simcox, *Otaki: The Town and District* (A.H. and A.W. Reed, 1952), 188–119.

26 A.J. Dreaver, *Horowhenua County and Its People: A Centennial History* (Dunmore Press, 1984), 125–6.

27 *Cyclopaedia of New Zealand Vol. 1: Wellington Provincial District* (Cyclopedia Co. Ltd, 1897), 1090, New Zealand Electronic Text Centre, http://www.nzetc.org/tm/scholarly/tei-Cyc01Cycl-t1-body-d4-d121-d1.html.

28 Shekhar Kapur.

Twitch

1 Brian May, Patrick Moore, Chris Lintott, *Bang! The Complete History of the Universe* (Carlton Books, 2006), 28.

2 Bill Bryson, *A Short History of Nearly Everything* (Broadway, 2003), 10.

3 Michael P. Shirres, *Te Tangata: The Human Person* (Accent, 1997), 114. The author profoundly regrets that this essay was written a decade before Shirres' abuse of children became public knowledge. His name has been removed from the body of the essay for this reason. His text was originally used because the versions of creation whakapapa he refers to are already in the public domain. Popular and published texts are chosen in order to avoid using esoteric or protected knowledge. However, for those who would like to know more without referring to his text, a reliable source of information about the creation whakapapa can be found at *Te Ara—The Encyclopedia of New Zealand*.

4 H.W. Williams, *Dictionary of the Maori Language*, 7th ed. (1992), 78.

5 Quoted in Shirres, 114.

6 Shirres, 114.

7 Bryson, 10.

8   Shirres, 116.

9   May et al., 44.

10 A.W. Reed and Ross Calman, *The Reed Book of Māori Mythology* (Reed, 2004), 4.

11 May et al., 44.

12 Te Ahukaramū Charles Royal, 'Te Ao Mārama—Te Ao te Pō', *Te Ara—the Encyclopedia of New Zealand*, http://www.TeAra.govt.nz/mi/whakapapa/7960/whakapapa-o-te-ao.

13 Bryson, 38–39.

14 May et al., 93.

15 Nicolas Cheetham, *Universe: A Journey from Earth to the Edge of the Cosmos* (Quercus, 2008), 171.

16 Bryson, 294.

How to be a Māori Woman

1   Ngahuia Te Awekotuku, *Mana Wahine Maori: Selected Writings on Maori Women's Art, Culture and Politics* (New Women's Press, 1991), 9.

Poutokomanawa—the Heartpost

1   This is an edited, condensed transcript of the University of Auckland Public Lecture given at Auckland Writers Festival on 17 May 2017. It began with a mihi to the tangata whenua of Tāmakimakaurau and Maualaivao Albert Wendt, who introduced the author.

2   Patricia Grace, *Potiki* (Penguin, 1986), 104.

3   Patricia Grace, 'Love Story', *Small Holes in the Silence* (Penguin, 2006).

4   Albert Wendt, 'Towards a New Oceania', *Mana Review* 1, no. 1 (1976): 49.

5   See: Tina Makereti, 'Stories Are the Centre: The Place of Fiction in Contemporary Understandings and Expressions of Indigeneity. Part 1, Critical Component' (doctoral thesis, Te Herenga Waka—Victoria University of Wellington, 2013), 18–19, https://doi.org/10.26686/wgtn.20387607.

6 Tina Makereti, 'The Story that Matters', *The Fuse Box: Essays on Writing from Victoria University's International Institute of Modern Letters*, ed. Emily Perkins and Chris Price (Victoria University Press, 2017), 96. The full version of this essay can be read on page 123 of this book.

On All Our Different Islands

1 Kei Miller, 'Place Name: Oracabessa', *In Nearby Bushes* (Carcanet, 2019), 34.

Māori Writing: Speaking with Two Mouths

1 Raymond Williams, 'The Future of English Literature', in *What I Came to Say* (Hutchinson Radius, 1989), 153.
2 As this book goes to print, there are at least three New Zealand university courses that focus on Māori literature in English literature departments. At the time of writing, there were none.
3 Morgan Davies, '*Where the Rēkohu Bone Sings*: A Few Thoughts', *From the Morgue* (blog), 12 March 2014, http://morgue. isprettyawesome.com/?p=6548.
4 Tina Makereti, 'An Amazing Year, An Important Review', *Tina Makereti*, 23 March 2015, archived at http://web.archive.org/ web/20160329234231/http://www.tinamakereti.com/k332rerorero/ an-amazing-year-an-important-review.
5 Adam Dudding, 'Patricia Grace: The Interview', *Academy of New Zealand Literature / Te Whare Mātāhui o Aotearoa*, n.d., http://www. anzliterature.com/interview/patricia-grace-in-conversation-with-adam-dudding.
6 Raymond Williams, 'Culture is Ordinary', in *Conviction*, ed. Norman MacKenzie (MacGibbon and Kee, 1958), 75.
7 Williams, 'Culture is Ordinary', 75.

This Compulsion in Us

1 In this essay, 'Wanganui' refers to the town of my childhood, while 'Whanganui' refers to the contemporary place. 'Whanganui' is

the correct spelling, but the previous colonial spelling, and all it represents, seems more apt here.

2   Paul Tapsell, 'The Art of Taonga', Gordon H. Brown Lecture 09, Victoria University of Wellington, 2011, https://www.researchgate.net/publication/279195274_The_Art_of_Taonga.

3   Brian Gill, *The Owl that Fell from the Sky: Stories of a Museum Curator* (Awa Press, 2012), 9.

4   Gill, 7–8.

5   'Sadiah Qureshi, 'Displaying Sara Baartman: The "Hottentot Venus", *History of Science* 42, 233, https://articles.adsabs.harvard.edu/full/2004HisSc..42..233Q.

Tea

1   The Anthropocene Project, https://theanthropocene.org/.

2   Karlo Mila, 'Inside Us the Dead (The NZ-born Version)', *A Well Written Body* (Huia Publishers, 2008), 10–11.

3   Claire Wilcox, 'In Conversation: Perspectives on Frida Kahlo', V&A, 2018, https://www.vam.ac.uk/articles/in-conversation-perspectives-on-frida-kahlo.

This Broken Jaw of Our Lost Kingdoms

1   The title and the stanzas at the beginning and end of this essay are borrowed from T.S. Eliot's 'The Hollow Men'.

Lumpectomy

1   Gabor Maté, *When the Body Says No: The Cost of Hidden Stress* (Scribe, 2019), 73.

2   Maté, 76.

3   Maté, 75.

4   Arline T. Geronimus, Margaret Hicken, Danya Keene and John Bound, '"Weathering" and Age Patterns of Allostatic Load Scores Among Blacks and Whites in the United States', *American Journal of Public Health* 96, no. 5 (May 2006): 826, doi.org/10.2105/AJPH.2004.060749.

5   Geronimus et al.

6   'Kiri Allan reveals grim cancer prognosis', *New Zealand Herald*, 4 May 2021, https://www.nzherald.co.nz/kahu/kiri-allan-reveals-grim-cancer-prognosis/4Y5PTU7COFCIJVA2OGQULNWLQA/.

7   'Cancer', Manatū Hauora—Ministry of Health, 2 August 2018, https://www.health.govt.nz/our-work/populations/maori-health/tatau-kahukura-maori-health-statistics/nga-mana-hauora-tutohu-health-status-indicators/cancer.

8   Donna Cormack, personal communication, 23 September 2024.

9   Geronimus et al., 830.

10 Geronimus et al., 830.

11 Geronimus, 831.

12 Nancy Krieger, 'Measures of Racism, Sexism, Heterosexism, and Gender Binarism for Health Equity Research: From Structural Injustice to Embodied Harm—An Ecosocial Analysis', *Annual Review of Public Health* 41 (2020): 37–62, doi.org/10.1146/annurev-publhealth-040119-094017.

13 'Pathways of embodiment especially relevant to exposure to unjust isms involve adverse exposures to (95–99) social and economic deprivation; exogenous hazards (e.g., toxic substances, pathogens, and hazardous conditions); social trauma (e.g., discrimination and other forms of mental, physical, and sexual trauma); targeted marketing of harmful commodities (e.g., tobacco, alcohol, other licit and illicit drugs); inadequate or degrading medical care; and degradation of ecosystems, including degradation linked to the alienation of Indigenous populations from their lands. These pathways, and multiple isms, occur—and are embodied—concurrently and interactively.' Krieger, 47.

14 Krieger, 45.

15 Krieger, 50.

16 Krieger, 50.

17 Leonie Pihama and Linda Tuhiwai Smith, *Ora: Healing Ourselves—Indigenous Knowledge, Healing and Wellbeing* (Huia Publishers, 2023), 16–17.

18 Geraldine Moane, *Gender and Colonialism: A Psychological Analysis of Oppression and Liberation*, rev. edition (Palgrave Macmillan, 2011).

PAO PAO PAO

1   I remember hearing this from the artist herself, but this memory is more than 15 years old, so my apologies if I have any details wrong.
2   'Ngahina Hohaia, 26 September 2009–1 September 2010', City Gallery Wellington, http://citygallery.org.nz/exhibitions/ngaahina-hohaia/.
3   Malcolm X (1964). See Mateo Askaripour, 'Falling in Love with Malcolm X—and his Mastery of Metaphor', *Lit Hub*, 10 April 2019, https://lithub.com/falling-in-love-with-malcolm-x-and-his-mastery-of-metaphor/.

Bibliography

Adichie, Chimamanda. 'The Danger of a Single Story'. TED video, 18:32, filmed July 2009 in Oxford, United Kingdom. https://www.ted.com/talks/chimamanda_ngozi_adichie_the_danger_of_a_single_story.

Askaripour, Mateo. 'Falling in Love with Malcolm X—and his Mastery of Metaphor'. *Lit Hub*, 10 April 2019. https://lithub.com/falling-in-love-with-malcolm-x-and-his-mastery-of-metaphor/.

Baker, Joanne. *50 Physics Ideas You Really Need to Know*. Quercus, 2007.

Bentley, Trevor. *Pakeha Maori: The Extraordinary Story of the Europeans Who Lived as Maori in Early New Zealand*. Penguin, 1999.

Bryson, Bill. *A Short History of Nearly Everything*. Broadway Books, 2003.

'Cancer'. Manatū Hauora—Ministry of Health, 2 August 2018. https://www.health.govt.nz/our-work/populations/maori-health/tatau-kahukura-maori-health-statistics/nga-mana-hauora-tutohu-health-status-indicators/cancer.

Cheetham, Nicolas. *Universe: A Journey from Earth to the Edge of the Cosmos*. Quercus, 2008.

Cyclopaedia of New Zealand Vol. 1: Wellington Provincial District. New Zealand Electronic Text Centre. http://www.nzetc.org/tm/scholarly/tei-Cyc01Cycl-t1-body-d4-d121-d1.html.

Davies, Morgan. 'Where the Rēkohu Bone Sings: A Few Thoughts'. *From the Morgue* (blog), 12 March 2014. http://morgue.isprettyawesome.com/?p=6548.

Dreaver, A.J. *Horowhenua County and Its People: A Centennial History*. Dunmore Press, 1984.

Dudding, Adam. 'Patricia Grace: The Interview'. *Academy of New Zealand Literature / Te Whare Mātāhui o Aotearoa*, n.d. http://www.anzliterature.com/interview/patricia-grace-in-conversation-with-adam-dudding.

Eliot, T.S. 'The Hollow Men'. This poem is in the public domain. Published by the Academy of American Poets, https://poets.org/poem/hollow-men.

Geronimus, Arline T., Margaret Hicken, Danya Keene, and John Bound. '"Weathering" and Age Patterns of Allostatic Load Scores Among Blacks and Whites in the United States'. *American Journal of Public Health* 96, no. 5 (May 2006): 826–833. doi.org/10.2105/AJPH.2004.060749.

Grace, Patricia. *Potiki*. Penguin, 1986.

Grace, Patricia. *Small Holes in the Silence*. Penguin, 2006.

Heberley, James. *Reminiscences, Jan 1809–Jun 1843*. Ref: MS-0971, Alexander Turnbull Library, Wellington, New Zealand.

'History'. *Taranaki Mounga—He Kawa Ora—Back to Life*, 27 May 2021. https://taranakimounga.nz/nga-mounga/history/.

'History and Traditions of the Taranaki Coast, Chapter XVIII, The Defence of Otaka or Nga-Motu'. *Journal of the Polynesian Society* 19, no. 1 (1910). https://www.jstor.org/stable/20700898.

Kapur, Shekhar. 'We Are the Stories We Tell Ourselves'. TED video, 20:57, filmed November 2009 in Mysore, India. https://www.ted.com/talks/shekhar_kapur_we_are_the_stories_we_tell_ourselves.

'Kiri Allan reveals grim cancer prognosis'. *New Zealand Herald*, 4 May 2021. https://www.nzherald.co.nz/kahu/kiri-allan-reveals-grim-cancer-prognosis/4Y5PTU7COFCIJVA2OGQULNWLQA/.

Krieger, Nancy. 'Measures of Racism, Sexism, Heterosexism, and Gender Binarism for Health Equity Research: From Structural Injustice to Embodied Harm—An Ecosocial Analysis'. *Annual*

Review Public Health 41 (2020): 37–62. doi.org/10.1146/annurev-publhealth-040119-094017.

'Local and General News'. *Marlborough Press*, 1 October 1880. https://paperspast.natlib.govt.nz/newspapers/MPRESS18801001.2.7.

Love, Morris. 'Te Āti Awa of Wellington—The Migration of 1832'. *Te Ara—The Encyclopedia of New Zealand*. http://www.teara.govt.nz/en/te-ati-awa-of-wellington/3.

Makereti, Tina. '14 Saint Mary Street'. In *Room to Write: 20 Years of Randell Cottage Writers*, edited by Linda Burgess and Maggie Rainey-Smith. The Cuba Press, 2022.

—. 'Address to the Tauihu in the *Face to Face* Exhibition'. *Five Dials* 32 (2014): 11.

—. 'An Amazing Year, An Important Review'. *Tina Makereti*, 23 March 2015. Archived at http://web.archive.org/web/20160329234231/https://www.tinamakereti.com/k332rerorero/an-amazing-year-an-important-review.

—. 'An Englishman, an Irishman and a Welshman Walk into a Pā'. *Sport* 40 (2012): 5–20.

—. 'Bleeding on the Page: On Writing, Community and Reviews'. *Kete Books*, 19 September 2020.

—. 'By Your Place in the World, I Will Know Who You Are'. In *Extraordinary Anywhere: Essays on Place from Aotearoa New Zealand* edited by Ingrid Horrocks and Cherie Lacey. Victoria University Press, 2016.

—. 'Funny Little Ugly Baby'. *Flash Frontier: An Adventure in Short Fiction*. Phantom Billstickers, 2023.

—. 'Gods and Ghosts'. *Hue & Cry* 4 (2010).

—. 'Lumpectomy'. *Landfall* 244 (2022): 8–17.

—. 'Māori Writing: Speaking with Two Mouths'. *The Journal of New Zealand Studies* NS26 (2018): 57–65. https://doi.org/10.26686/jnzs.v0iNS26.4842.

—. 'Meeting the Ancestor on the Road'. In *Bending Genre: Essays on Creative Nonfiction*, edited by Margot Singer and Nicole Walker. Bloomsbury Academic, 2023.

—. 'On All Our Different Islands'. In *Home: New Writing*, edited by Thom Conroy. Massey University Press, 2017.

—. 'PAO PAO PAO'. In *Women Now: The Legacy of Female Suffrage*, edited by Bronwyn Labrum. Te Papa Press, 2018.

—. 'Stories Are the Centre: The Place of Fiction in Contemporary Understandings and Expressions of Indigeneity. Part 1, Critical Component'. Doctoral thesis, Te Herenga Waka—Victoria University of Wellington, 2013. https://doi.org/10.26686/wgtn.20387607.

— 'Poutokomanawa—The Heartpost'. *Academy of New Zealand Literature*, n.d. https://www.anzliterature.com/feature/poutokomanawa-the-heartpost/

—. 'The Story that Matters'. In *The Fuse Box: Essays on Writing from Victoria University's International Institute of Modern Letters*, edited by Emily Perkins and Chris Price. Victoria University Press, 2017.

—. 'This Compulsion In Us'. *Landfall* 229 (2015): 33–45.

Maté, Gabor. *When the Body Says No: The Cost of Hidden Stress*. Scribe, 2019.

May, Brian, Patrick Moore, and Chris Lintott. *Bang! The Complete History of the Universe*. Carlton Books, 2006.

McRae, Jane. *Māori Oral Tradition: He Kōrero nō te Ao Tawhito*. Auckland University Press, 2017.

Menakem, Resmaa. *My Grandmother's Hands: Racialized Trauma and the Pathway to Mending Our Hearts and Bodies*. Penguin, 2021.

Mika, Carl. *Indigenous Education and the Metaphysics of Presence: A Worlded Philosophy*. Routledge, 2018.

Miller, Kei. *In Nearby Bushes*. Carcanet, 2019.

Moane, Geraldine. *Gender and Colonialism: A Psychological Analysis of Oppression and Liberation*, rev. edition. Palgrave Macmillan, 2011.

Morrison, Toni. 'Toni Morrison interview | American Author | Award winning | Mavis on Four | 1988'. YouTube, 22:15, 7 August 2019. https://www.youtube.com/watch?v=UAqB1SgVaC4.

'Ngahina Hohaia, 26 September 2009–1 September 2010'. City Gallery Wellington. https://citygallery.org.nz/exhibitions/ngaahina-hohaia/.

Neich, Roger. 'Jacob William Heberley of Wellington: A Maori Carver in a Changed World'. *Records of the Auckland Institute and Museum* 28 (1991): 69–146.

'Our History'. *Ōtaki-Māori Racing*. https://otakimaoriracing.co.nz/our-history.

Pihama, Leonie, and Linda Tuhiwai Smith. *Ora: Healing Ourselves— Indigenous Knowledge, Healing and Wellbeing*. Huia Publishers, 2023.

Qureshi, Sadiah. 'Displaying Sara Baartman, the "Hottentot Venus". *History of Science* 42 (2004): 233–257, https://articles.adsabs.harvard.edu/full/2004HisSc..42..233Q.

Reed, A.W., and Ross Calman. *The Reed Book of Māori Mythology*. Reed, 2004.

Shirres, Michael P. *Te Tangata: The Human Person*. Accent, 1997.

Simcox, F.S. *Otaki: The Town and District*. A.H. and A.W. Reed, 1952.

Te Awekotuku, Ngahuia. *Mana Wahine Maori: Selected Writings on Maori Women's Art, Culture and Politics*. New Women's Press, 1991.

'The Oldest of Old Settlers'. *Otago Daily Times* (11 October 1899), 3. http://paperspast.natlib.govt.nz/cgi-bin/paperspast?a=d&d=ODT18991011.2.8.

Wendt, Albert. 'Towards a New Oceania'. *Mana Review* 1, no. 1 (1976): 49–60. Reprinted in *The Arnold Anthology of Post-colonial Literatures in English*, edited by John Thieme. Edward Arnold, 1996.

Wilkinson, Jeremy. 'Geologists Inch Closer to Understanding Mt Taranaki's Mysteries'. *Stuff*, 17 February 2017. https://www.stuff.co.nz/environment/89510777/geologists-inch-closer-to-understanding-mt-taranakis-mysteries.

Williams, H.W. *Dictionary of the Māori Language*, 7th ed. Government Printer, 1992.

Williams, Raymond. 'Culture is Ordinary'. In *Conviction*, edited by Norman MacKenzie. MacGibbon and Kee, 1958.

Williams, Raymond. *What I Came to Say*. Hutchinson, 1989.

List of Illustrations

pp. 11, 72, 169 and 185: Illustrations copyright © Kōtuku Titihuia Nuttall.

p. 104: Tāne-nui-Rangi, Waipapa Marae, University of Auckland. Photograph: Kahuroa, Wikimedia Commons, 21 May 2006.

p. 106: Interior of Te Whai-a-te-Motu meeting house, Mataatua. Blue album. Ref: PA1-o-042-15-2. Alexander Turnbull Library, Wellington, New Zealand. https://natlib.govt.nz/records/22699547

p. 153: Carved bone pendant by Gareth McGhie. Photograph copyright © Tina Makereti.

p. 207: Tauihu, *Face to Face / Kanohi ki te Kanohi / Faʻafesagaʻi*, Weltkulturen Museum, 2012. Photograph copyright © Lisa Gardiner.

p. 209: Tauihu, *Face to Face / Kanohi ki te Kanohi / Faʻafesagaʻi*, Weltkulturen Museum, 2012. Photograph copyright © Tina Makereti.

p. 273: Illustration copyright © Tina Makereti, based on *He poi manu* (2012) by Ngahina Hohaia.

p. 283: Waikawa and the Sounds. Photograph copyright © Lawrence Patchett.

Ngā Mihi Nui ~ Acknowledgements

While I'm oversharing, I may as well admit that acknowledgements are almost always the first thing I look at when I buy a book, sometimes before I buy a book. I started doing this long before I published anything of my own. I think I was always fascinated by the mechanics of the thing: how a book comes to exist and the people who might be involved in the process. Sometimes secrets and connections and surprises can be found in the acknowledgements section, sometimes gossip. It's either nosiness or a lifelong desire for those connections, and for whakapapa, that drives my interest. But I've been worried about this acknowledgements page—how can I possibly get a lifetime of connections right? The acknowledgements page I wrote five years ago is quite different from the one I'm writing today, so I have finally realised: acknowledgements are only a snapshot of a moment in time.

In thinking about these essays, I wanted to acknowledge first of all my teachers, but then I realised a large number of these have also been friends and family, so this is simply a list of all those who have influenced these essays through their own work, their presence, and their generosity: Tusiata Avia, Sarah Jane Barnett, Marie Cocker, Thom Conroy, Donna Cormack, John Currin, Deidre Dahlberg, Kate Duignan, Mason Durie, Bonnie Etherington, Laurence Fearnley, Alison Glenny, Patricia Grace, Katarina (Ani) Gray-Sharp, Ngahina Hohaia, Ingrid Horrocks, Suzi Hume, Witi Ihimaera, Moana Jackson, Ravelle and Warren Jaggard, Robert Jahnke, Tina Jamieson, Lynn Jenner, Dame Fiona Kidman, Joanna Kidman, Stacey Kōkaua, Paul Kos, Vana Manasiadis, Marcia MacDonald, Bill Manhire, Selina Tusitala Marsh, Laura Jean McKay, Dougal McNeill, Bill Nelson, Heather Diane Noisy, Kōtuku Titihuia Nuttall, Olive Shell Nuttall,

Rachel O'Neill, Lawrence Patchett, Patchett whānau, Sakina Reijners (especially for helping us come home, so many years ago), Charlotte Seymour, Jimmy Skipper, Olivia Simpson, Skipper whānau whānui, Ruby Hinepunui Solly, Maui Solomon, Alice Te Punga Somerville, John Summers, Susan Thorpe, Ngāhuia Te Awekōtuku, Aquila Merewitikau Underwood, te whānau o Waikawa marae, Damien Wilkins, Robyn and Greg Wrightson and family. Special thanks to all of my students, many of whom have become friends (if I start naming you, I'm sure to miss someone) and to my English and Art History teachers at high school—ki mua ki muri. Thank you Witi Ihimaera, Kirsten McDougall and Brannavan Gnanalingam, for Toronto times. We were a TEAM. Thank you Witi, Paula Morris, Karlo Mila, David Eggleton and Eleanor Congreve for London. What an extraordinary privilege to be by your side. When I read this list I cannot quite believe my good fortune in knowing all of you. I also want to thank all the other writers and artists I have learnt from (too numerous to list!).

Fifteen-plus years of nonfiction writing has only been possible due to a range of funders, including: Creative New Zealand, Te Herenga Waka—Victoria University of Wellington, Massey University, Canterbury University/the Ursula Bethell Residency, Otago University Press/the Landfall Essay Competition, the Commonwealth Foundation, the Beatson Fellowship, Randell Cottage Writers Trust, Auckland Writers Festival, Weltkulturen Museum, Wellington Museum, the Royal Society of New Zealand/Manhire Creative Science Writing Prize, and numerous other New Zealand publishers/publications and festivals. I am incredibly grateful—without your support this book would not exist.

Thank you Fergus, Ashleigh and all at THWUP, for making this into a book, and being exceedingly patient for *years*. Thank you Ebony Lamb and Chloe Reweti for your exceptional work and care with the images and design.

Thank you, Dad. I only wish peace for you. Thank you, Dee, for being the only other person who was there, and for looking after me. Thank you Piki and Nala, for joy. Thank you, most of all, Lorry and Kōtuku and Aquila. My heart, each of you.

Publishing a collection of essays is something I've always wanted to do, and now that I'm doing it, I'm not so sure. It's a bit of a mess, life, isn't it? Thank you, reader, for spending some time with these pages.